IMAGES OF AFTERLIFE

The soul ascending at death through a dark tunnel into the Empyrean of Light.

From a panel by Hieronymus Bosch (c. 1450–1516), in the Ducal Palace in Venice and reproduced by the kind permission of the Director, who also provided the photographs. The soul is guided along the way by angels, in accord with the ancient prayer for a departing soul: "May Christ receive thee, who hath called thee, and may angels bear thee into Abraham's bosom."

Note the remarkable similarity between what is portrayed here, some five hundred years ago, and what is described in the reports of those who today describe their "near-death" experiences.

IMAGES OF AFTERLIFE

Beliefs from Antiquity to Modern Times

GEDDES MacGREGOR

PARAGON HOUSE

First edition, 1992
Published in the United States by
Paragon House
90 Fifth Avenue
New York, N.Y. 10011

Library of Congress Cataloging-in-Publication Data

MacGregor, Geddes.
    Images of afterlife : beliefs from antiquity to modern times /
Geddes MacGregor. — 1st ed.
        p.   cm.   .
    Includes bibliographical references and index.
    ISBN 1-55778-396-9
        1. Future life—Comparative studies.   I. Title.
BL535.M23   1992
291.2'3—dc20   91-870
                                                    CIP

Manufactured in the United States of America
10 9 8 7 6 5 4 3 2 1

Contents

Contents

PART TWO

Contents

Contents

Contents

Acknowledgments

I wish to acknowledge assistance so generously given by librarians, notably Dr. Ross Scimeca of the Hoose Library of Philosophy and Mrs. Marion Schulman of Special Collections, both in the University of Southern California. Their help has been always gracious and their interest unremitting. I am grateful also to Mrs. Alice Buse, Librarian, the Philosophical Research Society, Los Angeles, for her help in tracking down some elusive illustrative material.

To the various scholars and other friends with whom I have conferred on certain points I wish to express my appreciation for the personal insights they have provided. I owe special gratitude to Professor Samson Levey for his help on a rabbinical topic. My gratitude to those who have specifically helped with the illustrations is recorded elsewhere in the book.

PART ONE

way or the other. Why should we take our cue from them? If we look at the history of afterlife beliefs and detach it from its anchorage in beliefs about divine Being—monistic or monotheistic, Hindu or Muslim, Christian or Buddhist—what reason, if any, can we have for hope of afterlife? Why indeed should we consider afterlife worth hoping for? As a means of redressing the injustices of the present life? "Human society," wrote Charles William Eliot (1834–1926), president of Harvard University, "may most wisely seek justice and right in this world without depending on any other world to redress the wrongs of this."

The mood is of great antiquity among thoughtful men. Lucius Annaeus Seneca, the Roman Stoic philosopher who lived through the first half of the first century C.E. and was therefore a contemporary of Jesus, wrote "After death, nothing; and death itself is nothing": *post mortem nihil est ipsaque mors nihil.* His outlook on the subject is typical of that of many thoughtful people in antiquity and has been expressed in a variety of ways in modern times. Shaw expressed his view on the idea of immortality in typically Shavian terms: "What man is capable of the insane self-conceit of believing that an eternity of himself would be tolerable even to himself?"

In the everyday parlance of many, hope of afterlife is called hope for "pie in the sky." Belief in afterlife, however, can be fear of retribution as much as hope for the redress of wrongs or the desire for a fuller and better kind of life than the present one. The belief can function as hope or fear and be rejected in the one case as a pipe dream, in the other as cowardice, and in both as failure to face the realities of life that include its final episode: death.

This attitude toward afterlife beliefs is by no means confined to Western thought. If we look to Asia we find that while Indian thought, for all its diversity, has shown on the whole a strong preoccupation with the concept of afterlife, Confucian thought has been strikingly geared to the this-worldly. Historically the most potent influence in Chinese thought, culture, and civilization, it has been the main influence in making the Chinese people noteworthy for their family loyalty and their practical turn of mind. Confucian ideas have also deeply influenced Korea and other societies affected by Chinese thought and culture.

The Chinese philosophy of Taoism in its classic form, although more generally open to speculative ideas, including personal immortality, was on the whole almost as much directed toward the this-worldly as has been its historical rival, the philosophy of Confucius. True, as Taoism grew into a popular religion that accommodated all sorts of emotional influences, it became capable of hospitality to almost any sort of practice, including

4

magical techniques for the attainment of immortality, but such developments have tended to be peripheral to the mainstream of the Chinese outlook, the this-worldly cast of which has been long widely recognized.

The main influence against such a this-worldly focus, and one coming extraneously into China, has been that of Buddhism, which, in its Mahayana form, first entered China during the Han dynasty (206 B.C.E.–220 C.E.) but did not spread widely till after the fall of that dynasty and did not reach the peak of its influence till the T'ang dynasty (618–907 C.E.). No other powerful extraneous influence on China has deeply affected that great civilization till Marxism in the twentieth century. We may confidently conclude, therefore, that disinterest in, if not hostility to, the concept of afterlife has been historically as well as in our own time very widespread both in the Orient and in the Occident.

Materialism

In the West, *materialism* has been popularly used as a generic term to designate a variety of outlooks and attitudes of mind that are in one way or another inhospitable, if not hostile, to concepts of afterlife. Such "materialistic" modes of thought in modern times have included, for instance, behaviorism, Marxism, the kind of Darwinism developed by Herbert Spencer, the important twentieth-century philosophical school known as logical positivism, and much else.

How does such an outlook emerge and what makes it plausible? It is a very natural place for the human mind to begin philosophical reflection, indeed the process of thinking. One may start by distinguishing what one sees and hears and tastes and smells and touches from what one can imagine. I shut my eyes and imagine a horse. I open them and find out whether the horse is there, independent of my mind as informed by my senses, or exists only in my imagination. There is nothing wrong, of course, with my imagining things that are not there in front of me. Imagination is an indispensable instrument in even the most rudimentary kinds of human thought. If you want to tell me about a horse on your brother's farm, I instantly imagine an animal such as I have often seen. This is part of the process of conceptualization. I have to do it with great rapidity even simply to follow and to make sense of your conversation.

So may well begin my understanding of the crucially important distinction between what is "out there" independent of my mind and what I have put in my mind for the purpose of thinking about external realities. To lack a

5

vivid imagination is to be condemned to a very boring existence, for 90 percent or more of the joy of human life depends on our use of imagination, which distinguishes human life from that of even the highest of the simians, to say nothing of cats and dogs. Lack of imagination would bring me nearer to the life of a chimpanzee than that of a cultivated human being. Yet to be unable to distinguish clearly between what I see and what I imagine would border on autism or another form of mental disorganization.

A large part of human development has consisted in the clarifying of the distinction. Eventually the process gives rise to questions about the nature of reality. Indeed, the most elementary of philosophical questions are such questions as "Is seeing believing?" and "Are rainbows 'real'?" To the latter question we may say yes, inasmuch as I can see when and where there is one to be seen and when and where there is not; yet I might plausibly contend that they are not real in quite the same sense as are houses or doors. I cannot, except in fairy tales, catch the rainbow's end, for it is that sort of phenomenon that is visible but not tangible. In making this distinction, however, I am led (if I have incipient tendencies to philosophical reflection) to asking precisely by what criterion or criteria I am to judge what is "real" and what is a construct of my mind. I soon discover that I bring to what I call real at least a considerable element of my own mental construct. Thus my life of philosophical reflection and analysis may begin in earnest.

Modern physics has accustomed us to think in terms of dimensions of existence that are invisible and intangible in the sense in which such adjectives as *visible* and *tangible* are ordinarily understood. Physicists today know and work with not only the vast world of outer space but with a world unobservable in the way in which "observation" has been traditionally understood. One does not "see" electrons in the way one sees Venus or the moon or the table I am writing on. The wavelengths to which the human eye is sensitive are larger than a virus and so even with an ordinary microscope one cannot resolve an object as small as a virus. With a videoscreen or other transduction device, however, one can convert the image of even a virus so that the human eye can perceive it. A good example is a piece of X-ray film, by means of which one can see a virus or even molecules.

Modern Attitudes Toward Matter

What does this tell us about the difference between the modern scientific attitude to matter and that of the outmoded physics of Newton's time, when it was possible to think of the universe in mechanistic terms? It changes the way in which we must think about *matter*, which after all is merely a convenient name for "that which scientists are trying to understand." We certainly can no longer think of the universe as an engine with God as the chief engineer or as a vast edifice with God as the great architect. If we are to believe in God and the afterlife that is the corollary of such a belief, concepts of the God in whom we are to believe must be beyond concepts of that kind and afterlife must be beyond the concepts that might have been designed to fit such eighteenth-century molds. It is fair to say that what has been discovered of that dimension of being beyond what our forefathers could possibly have conceived about the nature of the universe does make talk of notions of God and afterlife more open—that is, less circumscribed by the presuppositions of those outmoded Newtonian concepts. But are we therefore entitled to dispense with traditional scientific methods altogether as irrelevant to our new situation, in which we know of another dimension of existence and the possibility of other dimensions beyond even what modern physics has discovered?

By no means. The fact that modern physics employs methods beyond the range of the old ones, making the old positivistic view one that artificially limits the concept of reality, does not make the old findings wrong; it makes them only limited and inadequate. The classical physicists took energy, for instance, to be a property of matter that might appear in two forms: kinetic and potential. Modern physicists still do, but with important modifications. Energy was then, as now, a precise operational concept. Modern physics, however, has introduced the need for a radical revision of our understanding of the nature of energy and mass, entailing more and more precision. Nobody ever sees energy and mass in the way in which one sees a body that *has* mass and energy. So we must recognize that by "observation" must be understood something very much more complex than any strictly positivistic procedure would or could connote. Nevertheless, scientists today still have to rely, as did the classical ones, on measurability and precise quantitative relationships that make possible the exact calculations necessary for authentic scientific discovery. Any advances made today depend no less than those made two thousand years ago for their success on the use they make of mathematical calculations.

The difference lies in the range and scope of what there now is to be calculated. Physicists have always had to rely on instruments and other equipment to assist their observation—for example, telescopes. The invention of the compound microscope about the end of the sixteenth century opened up enormously the range of human observation, making possible the resolution of objects previously undetectable by the unaided human eye such as a bacterium. When attempting, however, to resolve objects so small as to be beyond the range of the human eye even with such devices, one can do so only by some form of transductive device, the use of which enables one to transcend the limitations of the range of wavelengths of which the human eye is capable even with mechanical aid such as the telescope or ordinary microscope. Ultraviolet, for instance, being a shorter wavelength than visible light, can resolve objects smaller than the range of capability of the human eye. This makes it possible to "see," by transduction, what we cannot see directly, as seeing is commonly understood.

What are traditionally called the natural sciences (*Naturwissenschaften*) as contrasted with the "mind" or "mental" sciences (*Geisteswissenschaften*) encompass more, of course, than does physics. Biology must surely be included among them, although it adapts the methods to fit its special subject matter. Experimental psychology likewise uses the observation-and-calculation methods common to the "hard" sciences. Indeed, the humanities, while transcending the aims of the natural sciences, make more copious use of these methods than may be commonly understood. Historians and literary critics (not least biblical critics) worth their salt could not pursue their work respectably without abundant use of the methods habitually employed by the hard sciences. So we must not by any means seek to bypass these methods, which never lose their basic relevance to even such questions as afterlife. We may nevertheless maintain that so far as we can ascertain at the present stage of human knowledge, nothing can be shown to put belief in afterlife entirely out of court. Indeed, one might even plausibly argue that the customary scientific objections raised against such belief are insufficient to warrant one's doubting that there is such a prospect ahead of us. Openness, however, is as far as scientific knowledge can at present take us on the prospect of afterlife.

Scientific Advances in Antiquity

Moreover, the greater scientific openness to beliefs such as afterlife must not be attributed to any steady development or improvement in either the methods that have been developed or the findings that have been made over the course of the centuries. There has been no such steady development but, rather, dramatic discoveries with long periods of stagnation in between. In astronomy, for instance, the oldest of the sciences, the Babylonians and the

8

Egyptians had been observing the heavens for thousands of years before the Greeks and had learned through mathematical calculations how to predict lunar eclipses and (although much less accurately) solar ones. The Pythagoreans, however, through astonishingly felicitous hypotheses discovered as early as the end of the fifth century B.C.E. that the earth is approximately spherical. About a century later Eratosthenes succeeded in calculating its diameter within about fifty miles of what is known today. Also in the fourth century B.C.E., Heraclides of Pontus discovered that the earth rotates once a day and that the planets Venus and Mercury orbit around the sun. So remarkable were the advances among the Greeks at this stage of history that Aristarchus of Samos (who flourished about 270 B.C.E.) worked out what were virtually the systems developed about eighteen hundred years later by Copernicus. When one considers that during the intervening centuries between Aristarchus and Copernicus the notion that the earth is flat was widespread and persistent and that the sun moves round the earth was a view held by learned churchmen and others, one can hardly think in terms of steady scientific progress. What made the work of astronomers in the golden age of Greek astronomy so successful was its careful use of observation and its attention to precise mathematical measurement and quantitative relationships. Today even greater precision is needed.

Scientific objections to belief in *individual* afterlife remain by any reckoning relevant to all questions about afterlife. They are intrinsically important in the sense that the foundations of a building are important to all the upper floors of the structure. They are important too because, however strong one's conviction that such an afterlife lies ahead of one, one's faith must, like that of the eleventh-century Christian thinker Anselm, be a *fides quaerens intellectum*: a faith seeking understanding.

The Mind/Body Problem

The primary objections scientists and philosophers are likely to raise against concepts of individual afterlife focus on the mind/body problem. Some element in me is supposed to survive the event of death. What can it be?

Before attempting to lay bare the type of objection as expressed in modern philosophical terms, let us glance at the traditional candidate for that part of me that has been supposed to survive my body at death. It was called my "soul." The notion that I have a soul that is, so to speak, detachable from my body and is so detached at my death is a primitivistic one that cannot be

9

sustained in anything like any of its traditional forms. Whatever we are to think of the relationship between mind or soul and body, it is not of that kind.[1] We shall see why as we proceed.

But let us first look at a popular notion that has its roots in the religious literature of India: the notion of a "backup" or "astral body," conceived as an energy field serving as an embodiment much finer than can be seen by the human eye as can be our arms and legs. It is said to be perceived by clairvoyants who have developed techniques for seeing it. In 1939, in Krasnodar in the south of Russia, Semyon Davidovitch Kirlian discovered a means of photographically reproducing an image of the astral body or aura by placing an object on top of the film or plate and shooting a low-voltage electrical current from the back of the plate through to the object. By such means living objects were reproduced showing an oval-shaped aura around them that exhibits what energies are at play at the moment the photograph is taken. If one has the necessary skill or equipment or whatever is required, one learns to distinguish, for instance, anger, devotion, patience, love, irritation, sexual energy, and so forth. The story behind this discovery is recounted in a fascinating book by Sheila Ostrander and Lynn Schroeder, *Psychic Discoveries Behind the Iron Curtain* (Bantam Books, 1971).[2]

The notion of such an astral body has a respectable ancestry in Hindu and Buddhist thought and merits serious consideration, to say the least. It is not at all absurd, as many have instinctively supposed. Most sensitive observers of human behavior, while not claiming any supranormal powers of clairvoyance, can usually detect feelings, emotions, and energies reflecting what is going on behind the mask that any of us under observation may don to disguise such emotional states as we may wish to hide from public view. Many of us are highly skilled in donning such a mask. In popular discourse we speak of ways in which as observers we uncover the disguise when there are no frowns or smiles or other visible signals to guide us. We talk of "vibes": vibrations that emanate from another person in spite of his or her poker-face skill.

Where sexual emotions are involved such experiences are almost commonplace, so it may be that we should not too readily dismiss the notion of an astral body. Even if we accept it, however, it could not function in the way it would have to function for permanent individual survival after death, for it is as ephemeral as the emotions and passions it is supposed to display. It is as ephemeral as the music the pianist has just played before he fell dead. In any case, the Hindu doctrine of the self is much more complex. The notion of the astral body, much popularized in the West, does not help here except to exhibit one important aspect of the problems objectors to afterlife beliefs readily see.

If we are to try to make sense of the *concept* of individual afterlife, we must first identify who or what precisely is supposed to be promised that afterlife. It is "I" who expects or does not expect an afterlife, but who or what is this "I"?

Consider me first as a living organism, putting aside for the moment what I call my mind. Even to be merely alive I need some sort of infrastructure of organized matter. Compared with the body of a fish or a bird, mine is more complexly organized. Compared with such simple forms of life as an amoeba, the complexity of my body is immensely greater. Nevertheless, for any life to exist at all it needs some infrastructure, some organization of inorganic matter to embody it. There can be no disembodied life. For mind, whatever it is, to exist there must be not only matter but life; that is, as we cannot have life without embodiment we cannot have mind without life.

What is it that I call *mind*? Let us ask a question to help us understand the nature of the problem. When I see a light or hear a sound, what exactly is going on? First, there is a series of physical events occurring in my brain. Then, second, there is a mental event: a visual or auditory sensation takes place in what I call my mind. I am aware of the sensation. It is a state of my consciousness. All this, of course, happens so fast that I am unlikely to be aware of any time having passed at all. More important, I do not normally give any thought to distinguishing the physical events, which could be seen taking place in space (for example, by a neurosurgeon equipped with the appropriate instruments). The sensation, however, is not spatially extended; it has occurred in my mind—a mental event stimulated by the physical events. The sensation or state of consciousness is not detectable in space because it never was nor ever can be in space.

So also with memories of places or events. The brain events that might be said to jog my mind into having the memory could be inspected, for they are physical and open to public view. A neurosurgeon who had me under anesthesia might point to the occurrence of such physical events in my brain, but he could not have the memory sensation I was having, for example, the memory of the Taj Mahal that I had visited the year before. I can vividly call to my remembrance a field of poppies I saw in extremely early childhood and you might conceivably be able to look into my brain and see excitement among the ganglia therein, but you could not see the poppies that I saw and can now see in my memory, for they are literally invisible, not being located anywhere in space. I cannot measure for you the area of the field and it would

11

be meaningless to ask me to try to ascertain the acreage, for the image is "in my mind," not located in space as was the original poppy field from which the long-standing memory is derived.

Likewise, the pleasure or pain I feel, however intense, is necessarily private to me. Its privacy is guaranteed to me by the fact that it is not extended in space and therefore not inspectable as are, say, archeological finds. You may envy me when you see me jump ecstatically at the memory of the pleasure or perhaps weep with me, being the sympathetic friend that you are, at the thought of my pain; but you cannot be said to *feel* my pleasure or my pain. From my behavior you can infer what it is likely to have been, but you cannot ever feel it and your kindly attempts to understand it and empathize with me may be far off the mark.

I talk habitually of having something in my mind or even "somewhere" in my mind or "at the back of my mind" as though my mind were a box or drawer. I even talk occasionally of something "weighing on my mind" as though the thoughts or feelings to which I allude had weight like a jar of marmalade. Such language is of course figurative. To your question "Where, then, is your mind?" I might say in reply, "Oh, excuse me, it was wandering as you spoke; it was wandering to that Hindu temple I visited in Mahabalipuram in 1977." You would know quite well, of course, that I was not in India while you were questioning me, for at that time you were a witness to our talking together in San Francisco.

Yet I do talk of my mind as if I owned it. Then must not it exist, if only as that "other dimension" in which mental events (sensations, memories, and other states of consciousness) exist? May not we then conclude that minds do have a certain special kind of existence, albeit in a nonempirical dimension of being?

Whatever I may choose to say in response to such a proposal, I inevitably add to the puzzlement, if only because I keep talking about *me* as *having* a mind. True, I did have a tutor long ago who, in writing recommendations, would affirm that "he is a good mind" or even "he is not a very quick mind." It is a perfectly legitimate way of expressing the facts; but it does nothing to help us here. For I sometimes, no less legitimately, use *I* in a purely physical sense ("I am brown-eyed" or "I am heavier than you") and I certainly do not mean, in so talking, that *I* = *my body*. So if I used *I* as identified with *my mind*, as did my tutor long ago, it would not mean that I was insisting that *I* = *my mind*; it would mean only that for the purpose in hand I chose to identify myself with the mental aspect of whatever *I* means.

What *is* this elusive entity I call *I*? It is neither my body nor my mind.

Otherwise I could not talk of "my" body or "my" mind as I talk of "my" house or "my" shoes. In the long history of philosophical discussion of the mind/body problem many views of the relation between body and mind have been proposed and upheld. We need not discuss them all in detail and what is to be said for and against each of them, but we should at least examine what the principal options are.

Epiphenomenalism and Other Theories

One of the most ancient formulations, considered and attacked by Socrates in Plato's account of the latter's forensic triumphs, is nowadays called *epiphenomenalism* and is still widely debated. It may be stated crudely thus: the body secretes thought as the liver secretes bile and the testes sperm. Such a view lies behind the celebrated pun of Ludwig Feuerbach (Marx's teacher) that *der Mensch ist was er isst*: man is what he eats. Pierre Teilhard de Chardin, in conceding that man must indeed eat in order to be able to think, adds discerningly: "But what a variety of thoughts we get out of one slice of bread!" Epiphenomenalist presuppositions probably lay behind the primitive concepts of afterlife expressed in ancient Greek notions of Hades and ancient Hebrew ideas of Sheol: an underworld in which shadows of deceased men and women survive in an attenuated form, at least for a while. The physical element in man, in this view, is the cause of the epiphenomenon, the product secreted and exuded. The mental or spiritual element in man cannot cause anything in his body.

Against that view is the one called *interactionism*, according to which the relationship is a two-way one: When you hit me I feel pain (physical event causes mental event), but likewise, feeling afraid of you (mental event), my heart pounds in fear (physical event).

The view called *parallelism* seeks to avoid the difficulties entailed in the causation implicates of the other views just considered by denying any causal relationship between body and mind: they are simply two aspects or (to use Spinoza's language) "attributes" of one universal "substance": God or Nature. Parallelism evokes criticism from various quarters. For our purpose here suffice it to note that it rules out the possibility of any survival in any sort of individual afterlife.

The view called *identity theory* is that physical and mental states are not correlated; mental states are identical with certain physical states or brain processes. For example, if on a very busy day I have not had time to grab more than a coffee and half a slice of toast for breakfast and then miss lunch altogether, I am likely by dinnertime to hear my stomach rumbling; I may well be telling you that I am famished or that I feel I could eat a horse; I may also feel faint or lightheaded; I may even feel so desperate that I sneak a goodie from the table when I think nobody is looking. Can one distinguish among such events some that are physical, others that are mental? On the identity theory, no; they are all ways of reporting the same thing: that I am very hungry.

Can Personal Identity Persist into Afterlife?

Although all these views have been subjected to much philosophical criticism, none is entirely implausible and none is hospitable, to say the least, to any theory of individual afterlife. To entertain any such theory we must have some entity that can be said to persist through the present life and beyond physical death. We have seen that "mind" will not qualify any more than can "soul." In order to recognize its failure to qualify we need not deny its reality and importance. What disqualifies it is that whatever view we take of it, it cannot subsist on its own. The most compelling reason against this is that it cannot be identified with the *I* who "has" or "owns" it as I have or own my body. How then can I entertain the notion of a personal identity that could persist through this life and beyond into an afterlife?

David Hume (1711–1776), one of the most important philosophers in the history of Western thought, denied the existence of the self except as a bundle of the sensations and ideas that constitute what is commonly called the self and to which each one of us purports to allude when using the first-person pronoun *I*. There is, he contended, no such entity. The bundle of experiences that constitute that to which I allude when I say "I" is constantly changing as is the content of a great river such as the Mississippi as it pursues its long course from its source to its outlet. If I say "I" have lived in this house since my earliest childhood, I must recognize how vastly that which I keep calling "I" has changed. Not only has my body changed in size; I have gone through the dramatic physical, emotional, and mental changes consequent on puberty; I have matured intellectually and emotionally and I have aged so that not only is my once-brown hair now white; I view myself and the world around me very differently from the way I did when I was three. Am I the same person? Hume would say not only are you not the same person you were at the age of three; you are not the same person you were a few minutes ago

14

when you were having experiences you are not having now and were lacking others that now you have, even so short a time later. Hume was right, of course, in recognizing all this. Moreover, he was not really denying the existence of a self but, rather, denying what is commonly assumed about its nature.

Even so Hume, while recognizing the perpetual state of flux in which I live and the changes my personality undergoes in the process, fails to account for the fact that the "I" who remembers, talks about, and can in some measure relive many past experiences from early childhood onward is aware of the flux yet is no less aware of connecting all of them as the owner of a collection of videotapes is aware of the entire range of his or her reactions to all of them and can distinguish those reactions experienced ten years ago from those experienced last night. Who is this "I" who commands and controls such a range of experiences throughout life?

Note that the ability I have for such command and control is peculiar to human beings, who besides so commanding the range of all that they have experienced in life can also acquire, by training, a historical perspective enabling them to relate historical events such as the fall of Constantinople in 1453 and the sailing of Columbus in 1492. Not even the most intelligent dog, cat, or monkey could be trained to see even its own life in historical perspective and many human beings are incapable of attaining the historical sense that a historian must have. If a human being can have such capacities, might not at least some human beings have the capability of extending their awareness of personal identity from one embodiment to another, whether by resurrection or reincarnation?

It might be argued (although not without expectation of objection from several quarters) that there is no reason why, if I can be assured of a persistent self-identity, I should not survive and function in another body, even a very different kind of body than the one that is now mine. One might well object that I could not be in fact the same person. Of course not. Even if I had a very similar embodiment except for being, say, Chinese, I should not be exactly like any of the manifestations of myself that you have ever seen in my present life. Nevertheless, since I am in any case, whatever my embodiment, always in process of flux, would even being Chinese make me so *totally*, so *radically* different from what I now call myself? Even my way of thinking would no doubt be different from what it is now, but would it be different enough to destroy all continuity with whatever it is that warrants my claim of personal identity in the life I am now living?

One could well contend that it would not, since even without any Chinese parentage or other ancestry I might conceivably have been adopted by a Chinese family in infancy and educated like a little Chinese boy, learning to speak and eventually to write in Mandarin, to think in a Chinese way, and to enjoy Chinese music, even Chinese opera, which few Europeans or Americans ever learn to appreciate. Yes, of course I should be different from what I am now, but to some extent, lesser though it would be, I should have been different even because of some comparatively minor circumstance in my present life, such as my never having heard of plainsong or never having visited London. If I had been born female I should certainly have been not only in many respects but through and through, physically, emotionally, and otherwise different without, however, necessarily surrendering the identity I now have.

The fundamental difficulty in carrying over my present identity into an afterlife lies elsewhere. In the absence of some special claim I might make, I must face the crucial objection: my brain, including every one of its millions of cells, will have been totally atrophied at my death and the three pounds of matter in which it functioned will be either cremated with the rest of my body or else left to rot in a grave. Even supposing that there is another embodiment awaiting me, how is that which I presently recognize as myself when I say "I" to be transferred from my present embodiment to the one that awaits me? The difficulty applies to any sort of future embodiment, to both resurrection and reincarnation.

Objections to the concept of afterlife are indeed serious. Having considered the standard ones, let us now look at parapsychological phenomena as they have been reported and examined since the middle of the nineteenth century.

Notes

1 A medical man in Düsseldorf nevertheless claimed to have measured the weight of the human psyche. He placed the beds of his terminal patients on ultrasensitive scales and claimed that as they died he found that the needle dropped 21 grams. (See Dr. Nils-Olof Jacobson, "Life After Death," in the Boston *Globe*, 19 December 1972.)
2 See particularly Chapter 16, "Kirlian Photography—Pictures of the Aura?" (pp. 200ff).

CHAPTER II

-------------------◆-------------------

Raising Ghosts: Frauds and Facts

All argument is against it, but all belief is for it.

—Samuel Johnson, alluding to the idea of
spirits returning from beyond the veil of death.

The history of what are now called parapsychological phenomena goes back to
the earliest stages of social and religious development. The shaman (or his or
her counterpart) is a familiar figure in primitive societies. We read of seers in
the days of Samuel and David (e.g., I Samuel 9). The latter apparently had
seers at his court and consulted them. In Greece the oracle at Delphi had
similar functions.

Modern Spiritualism

What is now known as spiritualism[1] is, however, a modern phenomenon with
mid-nineteenth-century origins that seem to have been, from a scientific
standpoint, unpromising, not to say inauspicious, although, as we shall see,
the spiritualist movement led to very rigorous scientific inquiry into the
nature of the phenomena.

But let us look first at the unpromising beginnings, which may be said to

-------------------◆-------------------

date from 1848, when two American girls, the Fox sisters, then aged fifteen and twelve, began to hear in their family home in Hydesville near Rochester, New York, rappings that resolved into alphabetical messages that presaged the development of what was to become, in effect, a new way of looking at life, even a new religious movement. Tables moved, invisible musical instruments played, flowers and other objects "materialized," poltergeists rattled dishes and sometimes played mischievous tricks that were taken to be frolicsome communications from the spirit world. The chief focus, however, was on the use of mediums who by their "gifts" or "powers" acted as go-betweens from the spirit world to the material or empirical world that was taken for granted by society in general to be the only one.

Without prejudging the claims of the practitioners of this new movement, there is no doubt that it quickly achieved a considerable vogue. Although in both America and England it was widely disparaged as a craze or a fad and treated by many with derision, it excited considerable curiosity. Yet it was often more than mere curiosity. The Church had failed (many felt) to foster awareness of the spiritual dimension that ought to have been and ought always to be its primary focus and concern. Many of the faithful, tired of the

Fig. 1. The home of the Fox sisters in Hydesville, a hamlet twenty miles from Rochester, New York, which may be regarded as the birthplace of modern spiritualism. It was in this house that the Fox sisters first claimed to have heard, about 1848, rappings and other mysterious phenomena that they interpreted as issuing from the spirit world. An international congress at Rochester in December 1927 resolved to erect a twenty-five-foot shaft to commemorate the beginnings of modern spiritualism at Hydesville. Reproduced with permission of the Library of Congress.

18

preoccupation of their religious leaders with what they felt were materialistic concerns, were not disposed to dismiss out of hand a movement, however fanciful its claims might seem, that set its sights where church people ought to have been setting theirs. They had heard conventional sermons about the hope of immortality, but here was a movement against which preachers often fulminated from fashionable pulpits yet which offered actual communication with those on the other side of death in attestation of the reality of afterlife.

The Role of Women In both England and America women played a crucial role in the new spiritualist movement. That women are more sensitive than are men to beauty and other "spiritual" influences was virtually dogma in mid-Victorian society. Deeply ingrained in the minds of men and accepted by most women of the time was the notion that women, being by nature physically recipients, not to say receptacles, are mentally designed to be more receptive than men to influences, good and bad, that chance to come their way. It was thought that their strength and weakness alike lay in this quality, making them much at the mercy of the vicissitudes of chance and circumstance. This sort of outlook in society made mediumship seem natural for women. As it became indeed a burgeoning professional opening for some women and an accessible avocation for many others, it gave some women a niche and a role in a male-dominated society that provided very few comparable outlets for educated women.

The Power of the Medium Consider the séance over which a medium presided as a sort of priestess of what many liked to think of as a new religion or perhaps, more precisely, "religion come of age." She wielded a unique kind of power hitherto virtually unattainable to a woman in her social milieu. Men and women consulted her. She consoled them with feminine kindliness and sympathy or pitilessly exercised over them whatever lust for domination her whim dictated. She had in her hands the keys of heaven and earth. Her power, if she was unscrupulous and her fraud not yet uncovered, could be awesome. But fraudulent or sincere, she possessed a mysterious skill that she could use to fascinate and to awe her audience. With lights lowered or extinguished she could "materialize" as an imperious princess or, with a subordinate male associate, bring forth a man who in the dimmed light looked the very image of Uncle Bob or his father Harry.

Some mediums specialized in a sort of Victorian pornography, emerging out of total darkness and suddenly appearing under a momentary bright light in a sexually provocative half-nude pose, inciting the resentment of the women participants and tantalizing the men. Moreover, she could disclaim all responsibility for the character of the show; all could be laid at the door of the visiting spirit whose behavior, coy or saucy, brassy or genteel, obscene or demure, she could not be expected to control. She could enjoy the privileges of an actress who commits murder on the stage or appears in the role of angel today and bitch tomorrow, always immune from reproach. Indeed, the medium was even less accountable than the actress who, at least theoretically, had some say in the choice of her role, while the medium was but the mouthpiece of the malignant or benign spook she raised. Many mediums used their position, consciously or unconsciously, to give rein to their most outrageous impulses. A great-aunt of mine told me when I was a little boy that around 1880 she knew a fraudulent medium who, before being found out, had gratified her most sadistic instincts in the exercise of her professional activities.

Frauds notwithstanding, the movement did call attention to a spiritual dimension of existence widely unsuspected and generally derided. For all the jibes about sex-starved women impelled to release their energies in bizarre ways, the spiritualist movement brought to the notice of even the dullest and most prosaic of people the fact that there are "more things in heaven and earth" than were dreamt of in their philosophy. The movement, which no doubt had always included many sincere practitioners, seemed both unscientific and untheological. Gradually, however, it began to attract the attention of serious scientific and scholarly investigators.

Societies for Psychical Research

The Society for Psychical Research was founded in England in 1882 for the scientific study of what would later be called parapsychological phenomena. Philosophers and scientists of the highest eminence and repute participated in the quest. The American Society for Psychical Research was first organized in 1885, with the astronomer Simon Newcomb as president. It functioned in Boston under the guidance of Richard Hodgson, formerly of the University of Cambridge, till his death in 1905. Soon thereafter a newly organized and independent American Society for Psychical Research was founded in New York, with James H. Hyslop, formerly professor of logic and ethics at Columbia University, as its secretary. Hyslop greatly enhanced the scope of the society's work between 1906 and his death in 1920. In 1907 the first of the society's *Journal* and its *Proceedings* appeared; they have been published continuously ever since. Both the British and the American societies have accumulated a vast amount of important scientific data and recorded them in the course of the years.

Some areas of the societies' early inquiries (particularly into telepathy and hypnosis) have become so universally recognized that they have largely ceased to be in need of the kind of investigation to which they were formerly subjected.

Telepathy is almost commonplace. It is most generally manifested in strongly emotional situations. Typical is that of a mother in, say, London, who wakes in the middle of the night with a strange sense of sudden distress that is at the time inexplicable but later turns out to have occurred at precisely the instant at which her son was killed in, say, Melbourne, Australia. Much rarer (if at all) would be such telepathic communication between, say, a geophysicist in Oxford and another at Yale on some technical aspect of their common scientific field. It would seem that whatever the telepathic channel of communication, it flows in the dimension of the unconscious, where emotions meander in more uninhibited ways. Telepathy seems to prosper especially well, for instance, in relationships involving intense, overpowering sexual passion, demonstrating the capacity of love, erotic or otherwise, to overcome geographic distance as well as other obstacles, expressed in the ancient maxim "Love conquers all"; *Omnia vincit Amor.*

Hypnotism in modern times may be said to go back to Franz Anton Mesmer (1734–1815), who studied medicine at Vienna, where eventually he began to hold séances and was thereupon ordered to leave the city. After going to Paris in 1788 he quickly attained such renown in fashionable circles that the medical establishment, regarding him as a charlatan, appointed a commission to investigate the psychic powers he claimed. This commission condemned as unscientific and even "dangerous" his theory that all beings, animate and inanimate, are under the influence of a universal magnetic fluid through the control of which a skilled practitioner can learn to control everything by the trained use of that mysterious fluid and the skillful manipulation of its agency.

No doubt Mesmer's teachings and the categories he chose to use in advancing them were unfortunate, not to say grossly inadequate. They nevertheless contained the roots from which modern hypnotism, with its notable clinical successes, has developed. Mesmer's name, by the way, was immortalized (perhaps through the popularity he had achieved under Louis XVI when his teachings and performances had become the rage in Parisian society) in the French language in standard words such as *mesmérisme* and

Fig. 2. Friedrich Mesmer (1734–1815), who studied medicine at Vienna, may be regarded as a forerunner of modern spiritualism, at least in the sense that he claimed to have (and to be able to teach others how to attain) psychic powers. Reproduced with permission from the Manly P. Hall Collection of the Philosophical Research Society.

mesmérien. In English too the verb "to mesmerize" has become widely used by many who have never even heard of the man from whose name it was originally derived.

The history of the development of modern hypnotism is recounted by F. W. H. Myers (1843–1901) in a chapter of his classic *Human Personality and Its Survival of Bodily Death*. We need not repeat it here, although we must note that such has been already its clinical success as a parapsychological procedure that it is used effectively in childbirth and in some surgical operations as an alternative to traditional, more conventional forms of anesthesia.

Public displays of hypnotic procedures, partly for entertaining the public, partly for their education, have long been widely available. I remember being much impressed by one that I saw in London many, many years ago, when I was seventeen.

The hypnotist called for volunteers from a very large audience. Before putting them under hypnosis he told them what they were to do in response to certain cues he would give them. For instance, he would tell a group of eight, four ladies and four gentlemen, that they would read in turn passages from a book during which exercise the others would attentively listen. The word *tapioca* would occur once only, and at its mention the entire group would jump to their feet, the ladies discarding their shoes and the gentlemen their jackets.

Another group was set up to provide even greater merriment among the audience. They were required to withdraw briefly out of hearing, while the audience was told that the trays of drinks with which the group was to be plied would appear to carry glasses each generously filled with whisky and soda, but the amber fluid in them would be in fact mere colored water, entirely nonalcoholic. The group, having returned, were then informed that they were all to be treated to whiskies in unlimited quantities in order to discover who would succumb first and who last to the inevitable inebriation. After only the first glass one of the women was already showing slight manifestations of the first effect expected of alcohol: a barely detectable unsteadiness and a vague thickening of speech as she strode forth for her refill. After several glasses the group had burst forth into song; some were stumbling on the floor; some were weeping, others emitting whoops of glee. One couple was locked in each other's arms in passionate embrace, while the audience, knowing that no alcohol at all had been consumed by anybody on the stage, was convulsed with merriment, which was renewed when the victims, taken out of their hypnotic trance, became instantly their sober selves, puzzled by the ludicrous positions in which they found themselves.

In view of such striking success in these and some other areas of parapsychology, we might expect no less in that of communication with the departed. Predictably, interest in this possibility has been superabundant, not least in the years after World War I and other times of unusually widespread bereavement. If we assume that there is an afterlife, then theoretically one might suppose that, since erotic love can overcome geographic barriers, those even deeper and nobler forms of love that we so often feel for those from whom death has parted us should be able to penetrate even the veil of death itself. Innumerable stories are told of such encounters, many of them accompanied by detailed reports of the feeling tone of the experiences, the nature of the manifestations, and the content of the conversations. So frequently is fraud proved (a peculiarly cruel form of fraud) that even the most sympathetic and open-minded develop a very skeptical view of all such stories. Where there is no question of fraud the phenomena can often be explained in other readily convincing terms. This is not least the case with claims of having crossed beyond death to the threshold of the life beyond only to step back again into our present form of life.

Nevertheless, the idea of *revenants*, the ghosts of the departed returning to greet friends on this side of the veil is both ancient and persistent. Beliefs of this kind are deeply entrenched in the fabric of primitive societies and emerge in full bloom, along with immense interest in other parapsychological phenomena, in the culturally most advanced circles of the most developed civilizations in the world. Not only have they long been immensely strong in America, in Britain, and in continental Western Europe; they were exerting a very powerful influence in Russia and her Soviet satellites in the middle of the twentieth century at a time when most people in the West thought of Soviet society as too "materialistic" to dabble in, much less to take seriously, parapsychological experiments and enterprises.

Parapsychology in the Soviet Union

Whatever conclusions one may draw from *Psychic Discoveries Behind the Iron Curtain* by Sheila Ostrander and Lynn Schroeder, one cannot doubt the extraordinary interest revealed and by then well established in that part of the world in all aspects of parapsychology, extending even to experiments by cosmonauts in outer space. There seems to be an ingredient in the Slavic as in the Celtic temper that is irresistibly fascinated by extrasensory perception (ESP).

Be that as it may, what was perhaps from the first most distinctive in the work of the Soviets in this field was an insistence on treating it as simply an aspect of what we might call regular scientific inquiry. In the Czech manifesto presented in 1968 at the Moscow Parapsychology Conference was noted the fact that a group of theoretical and practical workers in this field had coined a new term, *psychotronics*, to replace the traditional *parapsychology*, which, they held, seemed "improper and inadequate" for a scientific discipline. Psychotronics, these researchers argued, is essentially "the bionics of man." At any rate, the aim was to make the study of such phenomena continuous with the studies in which physicists and other scientists ordinarily engage.

The relevance of this digression on the work in psychic research that was going on in official laboratories from Prague to Moscow by the middle of the twentieth century is that while it included topics as "far out" as astrological birth control, artificial reincarnation, pyramid power, Kirlian photography of the aura, dowsing, and UFOs, the lengthy report by Ostrander and Schroeder is virtually silent on the question of communication with the departed, which from the earliest days of the societies for psychical research in the West has been such an important focus of investigation. This forces upon our attention the following questions.

Suppose we do take seriously the possibility of the return of the dead in some form or other. Among the various concepts of afterlife that we shall have to consider in this book, which of them, if any, might provide at least intelligibility to the idea of such "returning from the dead"? In which form could the dead return? How could we expect, at least on rare and special occasions, to communicate with them? From what kind of afterlife is such a return conceivable?

Death as Barrier

It certainly could not be from anyone already in heaven, hell, or limbo as represented in Christian thought, for they entail an unbridgeable gulf. In the parable Luke relates about the rich man in torment in hell and the poor man, Lazarus, in the bosom of Abraham (Luke 16:19–31), the rich man calls out to Abraham begging him to send Lazarus with just a drop of water to cool his tongue. Abraham, having reminded the rich man that on earth he had enjoyed good things while Lazarus had suffered misery, goes on: "But that is not all: between us and you a great gulf has been fixed, to stop anyone, if he wanted to, crossing from our side to yours, and to stop any crossing from your side to ours" (Luke 16:26). According to this picturesque parable, presented in the Judeo-Christian thought pattern of the time, there is no communication between heaven and hell. This is as we might expect. The parable goes on, however, to say that the rich man then begs Father Abraham to send Lazarus to earth to warn the rich man's five brothers so to live that they do not also end up in the place of torment. He argues that if only someone would come to his brothers from the dead, they would listen. Abraham replies (Luke 16:31) that if they will not listen to Moses and the prophets, they would not be convinced even if somebody were to rise from the dead. The implication is clear: there is no communication between those on earth and those who have gone beyond. The road to heaven and to hell has one-way traffic only. No one can return from either. There is no way back.

Return in a reincarnated state on planet earth would not qualify as what we understand by return from the dead, and since resurrection to a new embodiment is generally understood (although Christian eschatology is very confused on this and other subjects) as occurring at the end of all things, at the great Day of Judgment, such a return would likewise be out of the question. The only scenario that seems to fit the hypothetical return from the dead would be the ancient one according to which a vestigial residue of the human being is left to wander in Sheol or Hades, being something less than the formerly living man or woman. This "something less" could be the astral body, which could be supposed to survive the death of the body at least for a while. That such survival of the "ghost" or "spirit" is temporary accords with a widely held interpretation of what happens after death. "Temporary" need not be as temporary as the smoke that lingers after the fire has gone out; it could conceivably be many years, even centuries, but it would be nonetheless a transitional state in which no *new* embodiment of any kind had been attained but only a vestige, a shadow, or—as we sometimes say—a ghost of the old one. That would make possible the recognizability of the apparition, which would have retained some characteristics of the man or woman who had died.

Moreover, the aura need not be described in such dreary imagery as has been used for it in some of the literature about ghosts. It could be as colorful as auras are commonly depicted in occult literature. It could even be, in some highly favored cases, a "body of light" such as is often reported in accounts of out-of-the-body and end-of-the-tunnel experiences just after death in cases in which the person has allegedly returned to the land of the living. The halo or nimbus or aureole traditionally accorded in iconography to saintly persons could also be part of the picture.

Frederic Myers provided in his classic study a salutary warning about the nature of entities that might be called phantoms or ghosts. He warned that "we have no warrant for the assumption that the phantom seen, even though it be somehow *caused* by a deceased person, *is* that deceased person in any ordinary sense of the word." He goes on to offer a valuable proposal on how to define a ghost: "*a manifestation of persistent personal energy*, or as an indication that some kind of force is being exercised after death which is in some way connected with a person previously known on earth."[2] This definition not only eliminates, as he claims, a great mass of popular assumptions; it is supportive of the view that I have been suggesting as the most plausible interpretation of the meaning of *spirit* or *ghost* or *phantom*. It is not, in this view, the person we have known who has now been transformed in afterlife; it is the residual *effect* of the person we have known. Myers goes on to consider how a communication, if there be one, from a person who has departed this life could take place. It is, ex hypothesi, a communication from a mind in one state of existence to another in a very different one. It passes, moreover, through a channel other than the ordinary channels of communication.

Myers suggests that a ghost is "probably one of the most complex phenomena in nature. It is a function of two unknown variables—the incarnate spirit's sensitivity and the discarnate spirit's capacity of self-manifestation."[3] Again, this would be consistent with the concept of the ghost as the astral body of the formerly living person. The view, if true, would assure us of the reality of a "spirit world" such as millions of people have believed in from antiquity to the present, both in primitive societies and, in our own time, in spiritistic circles that not infrequently contain men and women of the highest order of intelligence and critical acumen.

For those who may not be familiar with the character and caliber of Myers, a few words here may be useful. After a good classical education at Trinity College, Cambridge, of which he became a Fellow, he formed a lifelong friendship with Henry Sidgwick (1838–1900), Knightsbridge Professor of Moral Philosophy in the University of Cambridge, who had been his tutor. From 1869 they were both ardently devoted to the scientific study of parapsychological phenomena that eventually led to the founding of the Society for Psychical Research. Myers originated the terms *telepathy*, *subliminal consciousness*, and many others that became part of the standard vocabulary of parapsychology. Both Henry Sidgwick and Frederic Myers not only had

Fig. 3. Frederic William Henry Myers (1843–1901), author of probably the most highly esteemed classic in modern psychical research, Human Personality and Its Survival of Bodily Death, *originally published in 1903. As an undergraduate at Cambridge, where he prepared for a career in classical Greek and Latin studies, he conducted conversations with his favorite teacher, Henry Sidgwick, out of which an informal association was formed that eventually led to the foundation of the Society for Psychical Research. Reproduced with permission from the Manly P. Hall Collection of the Philosophical Research Society.*

rigorously trained minds but were men of considerable courage, for they had to put their professional reputations in jeopardy as their work exposed them to the ridicule of their colleagues and other professional scientific associates. Their investigations led them to strong belief in the reality of some of the phenomena they investigated.

There is no doubt that certain people have very strong personalities and, during their lives, exude very distinctive psychic energies. As certain voices are unmistakable on the telephone even after long absence, so such people seem to leap out at you in a crowd. Even the clothes that they wear seem to carry traces of their individuality. John Masefield, who succeeded Robert Bridges in 1930 as British Poet Laureate and who believed in reincarnation, as did his close friend the Irish poet W. B. Yeats, no doubt had something of that concept in mind when he wrote:

> Wherever beauty has been quick in clay
> Some effluence of it lives, a spirit dwells.[4]

Two Twentieth-Century Pioneers

Before concluding this chapter we ought to take note of two pioneers in the recording of voices claimed to be from the dead: Friedrich Jürgenson and Constantine Raudive. The story of their experiences is recounted by François Brune in his book *Les Morts nous parlent*.[5]

In 1959, the Odessa-born Jürgenson, who had lived in Stockholm since 1943, being then forty, had begun to receive recognition for his work in the production of art films. (The Vatican later gave him exclusive rights to do a film on St. Peter's, Rome, in the course of which Pope Paul VI appeared in person.) On June 12, 1959, near Stockholm, Jürgenson had undertaken to record some birdcalls. When he heard his tape he was astonished to hear a trumpet solo ending in a sort of fanfare, followed by a man speaking in Norwegian about the night cries of birds. At first, supposing that there was something wrong with his apparatus, he tried to discover what the fault might be. No conclusive result. A month later, while he was doing work on a radio program about Anastasia, he heard a voice speaking to him in German but emanating from Russia, addressing him by his given name. Sometimes he would hear himself being addressed in Italian: Federico. For a time he wondered whether he might be receiving messages from extraterrestrial entities. Then, having tired of his experiments, he was about to end one of them and in fact had his finger on the off button when he heard a voice say "Please, wait, wait, listen to us." From then on, as he persevered with his experiments and his ear became more sensitive to the sounds he was hearing, he began hearing more clearly. Soon he was able to hear the voice of his mother, who had died several years earlier. This and other messages convinced him that he was now in direct communication with "the other side." The voices, as if knowing his polyglottal abilities, not only continued to speak but to repeat messages in one language after another, talking of intimate details in the life of his family. They presented themselves as deceased relatives, friends, and acquaintances. He became convinced that he was being charged with the task of bridging the gulf between the here and the hereafter.

Raudive, born in Latvia in 1909, studied in Paris, Salamanca, and London; then, after a long stay in Spain, he settled in Uppsala, Sweden. According to a report by Jean Prieur,[6] Raudive happened one day toward the end of 1964 to have to leave his home in a hurry and left his recording machine going. Desiring to hear the beginning of the tape, he found to his astonishment that he was listening to the voice of his deceased mother, who was calling him by the affectionate pet name she had used in his childhood: "Kosti, Kosti!" Raudive, having heard of Jürgenson's experiments, invited him to Uppsala, where they might look together at the results. From then till his death in September 1974, he went on recording until, by the time of his death, he had collected, according to Jean Prieur, more than seventy thousand voices. Seeking to improve on his methods, he enlisted the help of technical experts. Franz Seidl of Vienna, for example, a distinguished engineer, constructed various instruments to facilitate Raudive's work. A Roman Catholic parish priest from Oeschgen, Switzerland, was among several who, impressed by the results of Raudive's recordings, made them known widely in circles interested in such claims of communication with the dead.

One dare not ignore such impressive testimony. True, one may ask why spirits beyond the veil of death would use such technical means of talking across that veil. In the computerized age in which we live one tends to be more than ordinarily skeptical of such reports and the methods so employed. We all recognize the ingenuity with which computer buffs can introduce "bugs" into a system in such a way as not merely to distort but to play havoc with the most highly sophisticated system. Clever but comparatively inexperienced young people have wrought mischief of this kind without any unusual knowledge or out-of-the-ordinary expertise. Any technical device is susceptible to such abuse if only because, having been invented by a human agency, it can be by a human agency perverted. Why, then, use methods so susceptible to such abuse? Why not rely on the clairvoyance and clairaudience that many people enjoy? Is the testimony more convincing because more "objective" when recorded on a machine? Once again, "If they hear not Moses and the prophets, neither will they be persuaded. . . ."

Yet if we take seriously the concept of the survival of the aura or astral body of the deceased, either pending further development and eventual reincarnation or otherwise, then some form of magnification of the voice from beyond might be just what is needed to effect the desired communication. Who can tell? The work of men such as Jürgenson and Raudive is certainly worthy of the most respectful attention.

If we take seriously Frederic Myers' admonition, then I suggest that we take the phenomenon we call ghost very seriously indeed, perhaps as an aspect or temporary deposit of the energy of the deceased person that could function as a "field" providing the necessary link between one embodiment and the next. It could be a diminishment of the person, although a temporary one (whether hours, years, or centuries), for ex hypothesi it would be itself an embodiment of sorts and therefore capable of consciousness. What that would mean and how it might work is something that must be deferred to a later chapter. First, however, we must consider out-of-the-body experiences and other phenomena attending the process of dying, such as reports of passage through a dark tunnel to a world of light beyond.

Notes

1 The term *spiritism* is to be preferred, since *spiritualism* is used to designate other and very different standpoints and schools in the history of Western philosophy. *Spiritualism*, however, has become so widely used for the movement considered here that the use of *spiritism* might seem pedantic.

2 Frederic H. Myers, *Human Personality and Its Survival of Bodily Death* (New York: University Books, 1961), pp. 208f.

3 Ibid., p. 210.

4 John Masefield, *Collected Poems* (London: W. Heinemann, 1923), p. 436.

5 François Brune, *Les Morts nous parlent* (Paris: Editions du Félin, 1988), pp. 16ff.

6 Jean Prieur, *L'Aura et le corps immortel* (Lanore et Sorlot, 1983), p. 164, as cited by Brune, p. 19.

CHAPTER III

Near-Death and other Experiences of "Crossing Over"

The spiritual life is a grand experiment which ends in an experience; but it is not merely a leap in the dark.

—William Ralph Inge, Dean of St. Paul's, London,
1911–1934

Current parapsychological literature abounds in accounts of alleged pre-death, dying, and postdeath experiences. Being or feeling "out of the body" and looking down on one's own physical body in bed or on an operating table is frequently reported by those who have been on the verge of death. Very persistent among such reports is that of passing through a dark, spiral tunnel at the end of which is a radiant light. Among those who have claimed to have crossed through the veil of death but returned we often have reports of their having encountered, on "the other side," a "Being of light" whom they variously identify as the Risen Christ, an angel, or a beloved parent or other relative.

Such concepts, although they have had a special vogue in recent times because of the writings of Elizabeth Kübler-Ross, Raymond Moody, Kenneth Ring, Michael Sabom, and others, are by no means novel in the history of religious ideas or religious art. In the traditional prayers for a departing soul in the Roman Ritual are the words "May Christ receive thee, who has called thee, and may the angels bear thee into Abraham's bosom." In Catholic mystical literature are to be found even more specific allusions. The great Flemish mystic Jan van Ruysbroeck (1293–1381), in his *Adornment of the Spiritual Marriage*, alludes to the notion of being drawn at death by way of an abyss toward a vast effusion of light that attracts and envelops the person passing across the veil of death. To the Flemish painter Hieronymus Bosch (Jerom van Aeken, *c.* 1450–1516), who may well have been influenced by that or some similar reference in Ruysbroeck's mystical writings, is attributed a painting on a panel, entitled *The Ascent into the Empyrean*, in the Ducal Palace in Venice, showing the souls of the dead floating upward through the darkness into a spiral tunnel at the end of which is an orb or circle of light and what appears to be a human-shaped being therein (see the frontispiece). This work of art is profoundly significant. The universality of the concept that it represents is, however, subject to more than one interpretation. Are such phenomena really adumbrations of afterlife or are they biochemical phenomena accompanying brain death?[1] They could very well, of course, be both, but they might be merely the latter. The fact that they are so frequently reported in such similar terms and the history of the idea behind such representations and reports (the floating in air, the seeing of one's body below, the plunging into a dark tunnel or spiral, the emerging into bright light, and the encounter with a Being of Light) suggests a biochemical episode in the brain, but it *can* also be interpreted as something more. It is the "something more" that most interests those engaged in spiritual quests.

After all, the experience of dying is unique in the sense that, unlike all others of which we ordinarily have any recollection, most of us have nothing to say about it and even those who claim to have can have nothing with which to compare it. We can all remember what a toothache feels like, or the comfort of a hot bath at the end of a trying day, or the joy of first seeing a rainbow in the sky, or a severe blow on the head, or the calm of sailing gently down a shaded river; but among all the experiences of life we have none to compare with that of dying unless it be the experience of birth, of which few if any can have any conscious recollection.

The first person in recent times to have become famed for his studies in near-death experiences was Raymond Moody, who after studies at the University of Virginia where he took his B.A. in 1966 and his Ph.D. in 1969, later earned an M.D. and went into medicine. His book *Life After Life*, published in 1975, quickly became an international best-seller, so much so as to embarrass him because the popularity of its reception only aggravated the predictable initial skepticism of his medical colleagues. What precisely is the nature of the significance of the reports that have since been pouring forth from many sources, all describing in similar terms the kind of experiences that Moody's subjects reported?

What I find especially noteworthy in this literature is the variety of interpretations of an experience that seems to be virtually universal. Such is that variety that the reports, whatever medical, psychological, and other clinical interest and importance they may have, really do not tell us anything at all about afterlife. Nor is there any conceivable way of scientifically improving the experiments to achieve that end. Dr. Melvin Morse of the University of Washington made a study of children very unlikely to have heard of, much less read about, the much-publicized reports of near-death experiences—children largely uninfluenced, moreover, by religious indoctrination. One girl, for instance, reported seeing her body below her with two doctors nearby. A boy of six whose heart had stopped during his tonsillectomy recalled floating above the operating table with the tube still in his mouth. He remembered a long tunnel lined with lights such as he had seen in airplane landings. This boy had no religious upbringing and probably had never heard of heaven or any other image of afterlife. A sixteen-year-old boy of Mormon parentage, however, told his parents that he had been climbing a dark staircase "halfway to heaven." How do such attempts to improve the scientific quality of the experiments advance our knowledge or understanding of the afterlife or establish that there is or is not any such life?[2]

Discussions have been provoked by the suggestion that drugs that are often administered to dying patients may act as hallucinogens. The answer to such a question may be of medical or psychiatric interest, but it is not and could not be relevant to the existence or nonexistence of a state such as we call afterlife or the like. If the reports were multiplied a hundredfold and the experiments conducted with greater and greater scientific precision, they would still tell us nothing decisive about afterlife. In that respect they would neither add to nor subtract from what we already believe or disbelieve about it.

The death event, whatever it be, is unique and, if for that reason alone, many fear it. Yet it would seem, from the reports of the experience of near-death and dying, that it can be pleasant, even blissful. It is, after all, as natural as birth. Many can look toward it with resignation, some even with curiosity. Everyone who gives any serious thought to its inevitability hopes for what is commonly called a "happy" death. Societies exist, such as the

Bona Mors, whose members pray for a happy death both for themselves and for others. But what precisely is a happy death? Presumably one would wish that death, since it is inevitable, might be nonviolent, not caused, for instance, by a horrible automobile accident or an attack by another human being. Many hope to die in their own beds, yet not of a long and painful illness. Then what would be the ideal? Most people, in response to such a question, imagine dying in one's sleep to be the happiest way to die. Yet thoughtful people ask for more: to die at peace with oneself, which some will regard at an entailment of dying at peace with God.

Deathbed conversions, however, are widely and rightly suspect. Generally speaking, people die as they live; that is to say, their attitude at death is in effect a summing-up of their attitudes during life. If one has lived much at peace with God and aware of His overwhelming love and also of the support of loving agents of God whoever they may be (angels, counselors, teachers, friends), then death, despite the wrench, will be happy, since there is nothing to fear in it save evil that one has put there oneself and not deleted by acceptance of the boundless forgiveness of an all-loving Creator.

To attend the bedsides of dying friends when this is possible is not only a sacred duty; it is surely the best preparation for understanding death and eventually facing it with equanimity and acceptance. In witnessing that inevitably crucial episode one has a unique opportunity of seeing a special manifestation of the nature of the spiritual dimension of being. If one is at all sensitive to that dimension in which any help one gives to others returns in superabundance to one's own development and strengthening, then the reward of assisting at the passing over of a friend, or indeed of anyone, is even more incalculable.

I can never forget being summoned, as a young clergyman, to the bedside of a dying lady whom I not only did not know but knew nothing about. It was quite late when I received an anonymous telephone request from a friend or relative of hers, who reported that before the now-dying lady had lost the power of speech she had been incessantly demanding to see a clergyman. By the time I saw her she was unable to speak, but as I entered the room she struggled to clasp my hand, which she held in a death-grip as she looked intently into my eyes. There was no one else in the house but an elderly servant. The lady herself was probably in her late fifties. There was no sign of any connection with any form of organized religion and no means of ascertaining anything about that or anything else about her, for the telephone caller had left no information and no telephone number. Verbal communication on her side was impossible. She was obviously a person of good breeding

35

and culture. I prayed by her side for some time and she seemed to relax, yet would not yield for an instant from the intensity of her grip of my hand. She seemed to be understanding at least some of what I was saying but could only look earnestly into my face. Young and inexperienced, I could not be sure how much she understood or what more I could usefully say. It was getting very late indeed, past eleven o'clock. Although she was dying, she seemed to be full of a supernormal strength far beyond her somewhat fragile face and emaciated body. I happen myself to have always had a strong handgrip, but as I tried gently to loosen her hand she intensified her grip on mine. Then, becoming very agitated, she made a Herculean effort to speak and said very firmly in a voice that seemed to emanate from above her body: "Stay, stay, stay." Then very slowly: "I am going on a long, long, dark journey. Stay, stay, stay." I stayed of course, praying softly over the sound of her now chain-stroke breathing. Finally, a look of infinite peace came over her as her hand dropped. I rose to leave, then, glancing back, I saw a dim bluish-green light hover above her body and the now-peaceful half-smile upon her face.

"She's gone, has she?" murmured the elderly housekeeper.

"Yes," I said. And the old woman picked up the telephone. Then suddenly it dawned upon me that this was the first time I had ever actually seen anyone die. I was still in my twenties. I had seen many people nearing that final episode and many more already dead. I had heard from early childhood of people actually seen dying, but this was the first time I had personally witnessed the process. Needless to say, I had never heard at that time of work such as that of Raymond Moody. It all happened, indeed, in 1939, several years before he was born.

I am far from denigrating the value and interest of reports of near-death and other experiences related to the process of dying. I ask, however, with what interpretations are they compatible? I find that they are compatible both with their interpretation as a biochemical event, explicable totally in such terms, and with their interpretation as pointing to some kind of afterlife. But this is the point at which I would suggest that we paraphrase Hamlet: "Aye, there's the rub!" For what does this latter interpretation really tell us (based solely on the evidence provided by such reports) of the *nature* of that afterlife? That some wisp of us may survive brain death may be interesting in its way and perhaps, even, it may be on the verge of being established as scientifically explicable in the way that electrons are. But that would tell us no more about the nature of the hypothetical afterlife than do electrons about the love of God.

It would not tell us even anything about the quality of the afterlife and

36

certainly nothing at all about any hope of immortality. For in dealing with the spiritual dimension of being that interests those of us who have long become attuned to it we need a different approach. We can no more provide by the methods of the natural sciences the kind of answers we need than can the methods of the mechanistic physics of Newton's time provide the kind of answers that modern scientists need in dealing with, say, the submicroscopic world. Biologists may show that prayer or yoga is good for the digestive process or even that it improves the health of our skin, but that is far from telling us what prayer or yogic exercises are, why they should have such effects, and above all why such effects are to be regarded as incidental.

We have seen in these introductory chapters something of the force of scientific and philosophical objections to the concept of any form of afterlife and we have also seen, I hope, that these objections are not fatal. That is to say, not only do modern concepts such as transduction make it possible to construct arguments in favor of survival of some aspect of what I call "my self"; the careful examination of and research into parapsychological phenomena strongly suggest the plausibility of the contention that in some cases at least (to use all due caution) some kind of survival takes place after bodily death.

That is not by any means a negligible result. It is far, however, from justifying any of the classic beliefs that have been held through the ages concerning the nature of afterlife. It does not even in any way corroborate or support, much less demonstrate beliefs about afterlife such as resurrection, immortality, or reincarnation, to say nothing of images of afterlife such as heaven or purgatory or hell.

One of the most cherished beliefs about afterlife, especially among those held in the West, is that we may meet again our loved ones and be joined with them in new and fuller life with God. For many of us any belief in afterlife that would exclude the realization of such a hope would make the concept of afterlife seem at best an empty expectation and at worst a selfish enterprise. To have learned through these special relationships here and now something of the character and value of sacrificial love and then to be separated forever from those in, with, and through whom we have learned it would deprive life of the richest part of whatever meaning it has for us. Christians, who believe that Jesus Christ, through his death on the Cross and his resurrection (however interpreted) did something for us that in some way "opens to us the gates of everlasting life," could not be satisfied with an afterlife bereft of the society of those with whom they have "walked in Christ." Indeed, no thoughtful person, whatever his or her formal religious attachment or affiliation, who has any appreciation of what the great religions of humankind have to say about divine love and our relation to it as that which, in the words of the concluding line of Dante's great epic, "moves the sun and the other stars," could be content with some form of mere personal survival, which is all that, even at most, can be established by the techniques of modern psychical research and the observations and reports of experiences such as we have been considering in these first few chapters.

What is needed is a historical review of images of afterlife and an attempt to sort out of the confusion a system of eschatology such as can provide an intelligible presentation of the meaning of afterlife to those who by their knowledge of God's nature have already seen, if only "through a glass darkly," that this life is but a stage in the growth of our relationship to God and the fulfillment of our individuality.

Notes

1 J. E. Owens, E. W. Cook and I. Stevenson, "Features of near-death experience in relation to whether or not patients were near death," *The Lancet*, 336, 8724 (10 November 1990), pp. 1175–1177.
2 Melvin Morse, Doug Conner, and Donald Tyler, "Near Death Experiences in a Pediatric Population," *American Journal of Diseases of Children* (June 1985), pp. 595–600.

PART
TWO

CHAPTER IV

Afterlife as Corollary to Belief or Disbelief in God

The undiscovered country, from whose bourn
No traveler returns. . . .

—William Shakespeare, *Hamlet*,
Act III, scene 1

Before turning to the history of human thought on afterlife we should consider some basic questions of meaning. What exactly do we mean by belief or disbelief in afterlife? What precisely are we affirming or denying? First let us look at four basic categories under which ideas about afterlife have been conceived.

Survival, Immortality, Resurrection, and Reincarnation

The earliest forms of belief about afterlife are vague. They antedate recorded history and are known to us, so far as they are known at all, through archeological evidence. They seem to be instinctive convictions that something in a person survives death. They may be conceived in various ways, but there is no doctrinaire theory about the nature of afterlife or why it should be this or that. There is no developed view that the afterlife should entail any particular quality, although generally the image is of an attenuated form of this present life. The ghost of a man is somewhat shadowlike; indeed, the Greek word *skia* is used alike for the shadow of a man and for whatever it is of him that survives his death. What remains is to the living man as smoke is to the fire. It may persist briefly or for long. There is no reason to suppose that it persists forever.

In sharp contrast is the doctrine of immortality as classically understood. Here what persists is the essence of the man, which is imperishable. The concept of the immortality of the soul as expounded and argued for by Plato, for instance, is built upon the view that the body, being merely the instrument used by the soul, is no more than an instrument. The man as we know him is composed of soul and body. The body, however, is to the soul as the violin to the violinist. Moreover, because the soul comes in one way or another from divine Being (e.g., as a spark of the divine Fire), it is by its nature immortal; it *cannot* die.

Another view is that of resurrection. At death the man as we know him, body and soul, does indeed die, but thanks to God he will be raised to life again at some point in the future. This is the mainstream view in the monotheistic religions, of which the best known are Judaism, Christianity, and Islam.

Resurrection is the view that since the human being is a composite of body and soul and that is how God has created human beings, then afterlife must, at least in the last resort, consist of a raising of the human being to a state in which this union of body and soul is in some way more fully achieved than it is in our present state. This is the view of afterlife upheld in orthodox Christianity and orthodox Islam. In Judaism, although it does not speak with a single voice on the subject, this is a well-represented view, to say the least. It was the view upheld by the Pharisees, for instance, although the Sadducees did not accept it. All monotheistic religions are hospitable to this understanding of afterlife hope. It is the view that seems to be most generally expressed in the biblical tradition in which all of these religions have roots.

Reincarnation (also known as transmigration or metempsychosis) takes many forms, from primitivistic notions to highly developed and deeply ethical ones. It is widely, if not universally, held in Hinduism, Jainism, and Buddhism. Although it is presented in a large variety of interpretations, the basic presupposition that typically underlies it is that this present life is but a slice of a much larger evolutionary process of spiritual development toward higher forms of life. The present life is part of an enormously long educational process in which the individual self is disciplined and encouraged, rather than punished and rewarded, for his or her actions in this or in other lives in the incalculably long series. The concept of reincarnation, while it fits very well into the ways of thought most characteristic of India, is not at all incompatible with Western thought. Plato, in this following his master Socrates, expressly takes it for granted when he does not explicitly teach it. It fits his teaching on the immortality of the soul. The Christian Way has a long, partly underground tradition of reincarnationist teaching, although resurrection has been the one most generally favored by the Church in all its branches: Eastern Orthodox, Roman Catholic, Anglican, and Reformed. Some traditions within Judaism have also been very hospitable to reincarnationist concepts of afterlife, which also are to be found even under the Islamic banner, very notably among the Druze. [1]

We should note that a doctrine of immortality of the soul need not presuppose, as it does in Plato and elsewhere, that the human soul is by its nature indestructible. Some forms of immortality doctrine expound the view that immortality is something that must be won; it is by no means a quality of the human soul. This view is sometimes called conditional immortality. Paul seems to imply this in his letter to the Romans (Romans 6:21–23). Neither form of immortality doctrine need be seen as incompatible with either resurrection or reincarnation.

Ambiguities in Afterlife-Talk

What is vital to intelligible discussion on the subject of afterlife is that participants in such discussion understand their own and their adversaries' meaning. The language used in popular discussion of belief or disbelief in "afterlife" is notably ambiguous. We read of polls that purport to tell us that, say, 55 percent of Presbyterian physicists "believe in immortality," while only 11 percent of Baptist attorneys disbelieve in it. Terms such as *immortality*, *resurrection*, and *reembodiment* may be understood, however, in many different ways. To ask "Do you believe or disbelieve in immortality?" is like asking "Do you believe or disbelieve in God?" Such questions should evoke a response such as "It depends what you mean by 'immortality' and what you mean by 'God'."

Central, indeed, to this book is the premise that this or that kind of belief or disbelief in afterlife is a corollary to this or that kind of belief or disbelief in

God. So intimate is the connection that if one knows what kind of belief or unbelief in afterlife a person is entertaining, one should be able to reconstruct from that information, at least broadly, what is the person's belief or disbelief in God. One can do so because one's attitude to afterlife is to one's attitude to God as is a corollary to the mathematical theorem from which the corollary is derived.

History and Interpretation

To understand the issues involved in the task that lies ahead of us we must clear the ground in three distinct ways.

First, we must recognize that nothing can be fully understood apart from its history. Therefore we must inspect, however cursorily, the history of belief in afterlife from earliest times (from prehistoric archeological evidence) to the ways in which it has come to be conceptualized both in the various major religions of mankind and in literature generally down to the present time.

Second, we must explore how the metaphors used to express such beliefs about "life after death" are to be understood. For instance, to what extent, if any, are assertions about "life everlasting" or "eternal life" or "immortality" to be taken literally? What would taking them literally actually mean? Much of the language used on this subject is poetic. Poetry is a great (perhaps the greatest) vehicle for the communication of the most important truths. Nothing could be more foolish than writing off a statement as "mere" poetry or "mere" metaphor. Nor are the truths so conveyed psychological truths only. As truths about the nature of human existence they are ontological truths: truths about the realities that we encounter in the universe itself, not only truths about what we spin out of our own minds.

Third, whether we are inclined or disinclined toward any sort of belief in afterlife, we must recognize that the terms often used, whether understood metaphorically or literally, are often extremely ambiguous. For instance, what is popularly called "immortality" may mean one of several notions. Does the user mean that although at death I (what I call my self) am extinguished, some effluence of me somehow persists, as a perfume lingers after its wearer has left the room or as smoke may persist for hours or even days after the fire is extinguished? Or does one mean, as well one might, that I "live on" in the memories of my friends and my children, or in my writings or other works? So famous in American history are names such as George Washington and Thomas Jefferson that we may call their bearers immortal in the sense that so long as culture and civilization continue in anything like their present state such men cannot be said to die as does a stray fly under the swatter. As the writer of Ecclesiasticus (44:4) says of the great ones of old, "Their bodies are buried in peace; but their name liveth for evermore." Very different is the affirmation that I (whatever it is that I identify as my self) shall "live on" in such a way that I can claim to have the assurance of everlasting life as my inheritance as an individual being. The difference might be likened to the difference between a picture of your mother in the family album and your mother herself.

Immense philosophical and scientific puzzles attend the concept of a self that persists beyond brain death. Even the concept of the self within this present, mortal life provides a plentiful supply of such problems without going beyond that span. I am not even the same "person" that I was last year, and the difference between the "self" of which I felt aware at the age of three and the one of which I am aware now is so great that I may well wonder how I can identify the one with the other at all as when I say "I remember how I felt when I was three." Who is this "I," this "self" that claims continuity beyond the immense changes, mental and physical, that have occurred in "me"? If one can say, as almost everyone does at one time or another, "I feel a different person when I stand before a class of students" or "when I speak French" or "when I put on my uniform," who is the "I" of whom one talks as if it transcended all such different forms of one's awareness of it?

Pantheism versus Monotheism

I have affirmed the view that belief in afterlife is directly related to belief in God and so is disbelief in afterlife related to disbelief in God. Of course the situation is much more interesting and complex than can be adequately expressed in such a bald way. What is loosely called "belief in God" can take innumerable forms: forms as innumerable as are the concepts of God that philosophers throughout the ages have proposed and that theologians have claimed to have been revealed. One very broad distinction, however, may be perceived between an outlook that has generally prevailed in the thought of people in the great subcontinent of India, on the one hand, and in the monotheistic religions of the West (Judaism, Christianity, and Islam), on the other. John Toland (1670–1722) called the former outlook pantheism, to signify that those who hold it see God in everything (Greek *pan*: everything). This terminology is somewhat misleading however, because the monotheistic religions (proponents of which are traditionally called theists) would claim to see God in everything, in the sense that they see the *works* of God in everything. The difference is better expressed by saying that what has come to be called, in the West, pantheism differs from the central teaching of the monotheistic religions by the insistence of the latter on the Otherness of God who, in these religions, is seen as totally different from everything else because he is the Creator and all else his creatures. They differ from God in a radical way, since they owe their existence ultimately to God their Creator. Let us see how two such disparate understandings of the nature of God are reflected in their proponents' respective views of afterlife.

What is loosely called pantheism has been argued by some Western thinkers too and has become from time to time fashionable in some circles, including "New Age" groups and others disaffected from traditional expressions of the Judeo-Christian tradition but deeply interested in religious ideas.

The thought of one of the greatest philosophical minds in human history, Baruch Spinoza (1632–1677) looks at first sight pantheistic, for he talks of God and Nature as two aspects of one ultimate reality. Spinoza, however, is by no means so simplistic. His famous phrase *Deus sive Natura* ("God or Nature") sounds pure pantheism, but Nature, according to Spinoza, is to be understood in two ways. He calls the one *Natura naturata* (literally "Nature natured")—the reality that follows by necessity from the nature of God understood as the whole of reality. The other he calls *Natura naturans* ("Nature naturing")—God as free cause, as the eternal infinite essence. So for Spinoza God and Nature are by no means just two synonyms. God is the *cause* of all else, so one cannot simply identify oneself with God as in a thoroughgoing pantheism.

A proponent of a thoroughgoing pantheism, whether in Oriental or Occidental dress, might well say in response to the question "Do you believe in afterlife?" something like this: "Yes, of course I do, for everything is God and I am a part of this universal, immortal reality the totality of which is God. I submerge myself in it, rejoice at being a part of it, and try to enhance my awareness of the whole of which I am a part."

Very different would be the response of a thoughtful Jew or Christian or Muslim, which would be on lines such as these: "There is no reason why I should be immortal or have any afterlife at all except for the overriding circumstance that I am created by God, who I believe has created me for a specific purpose that is motivated by His love for His creatures. Since in the life of faith I have found from childhood onward that I have grown in the service of my Maker (my waywardness and my follies notwithstanding) and have developed my individuality in a unique way through serving Him 'whom to serve is perfect freedom' (as the ancient Christian prayer puts the paradox), I am assured that He who has so shown me His grace and His care for me even in this life shall most certainly not abandon me when I die. Such is the earnest that I have already received of His love and care for me that I know He will *never* desert me. Not only shall I survive death; I shall be, through His grace a fuller and better *me*, for I shall be closer than ever to Him and better able to attain freedom through service to Him. In the words of the Second Isaiah (Isaiah 40:31), I shall 'put out wings like eagles,' and 'run and . . . not grow weary, walk and never tire.' Yes, of course I must have an afterlife in order to fulfill the loving plan that I have discerned for me in this present life through all its tribulations and its joys."

There is a reason for the comparatively long-winded answer that I have attributed to the hypothetical monotheist: The monotheist has a more complex *as well as* a more paradoxical understanding of afterlife to expound in his response. The question has been the same question, but because it has been understood so differently by the two persons to whom it was addressed and because the difference has been due to a radically different understanding of the nature of God, we can see better what it means to affirm, as I do, that the kind of belief in afterlife one may be willing to entertain is a corollary of the kind of one's belief in God. Moreover, what is the case with belief is also the case with disbelief: A person who starts from a pantheistic background and rejects its presuppositions will be a different *kind* of unbeliever from the one who, having started from a monotheistic basis, renounces it. His renunciation of belief in afterlife will be no less radically a different renunciation.

Community versus Individuality

Of course the hypothetical characters answering the question are singularly well-informed exponents of their respective outlooks. Not very many adherents of any of the religions of mankind have thought through their beliefs or unbeliefs so carefully. Many, confronted with the question, would waffle, because they have already internally waffled about such belief in God as they feel to be somehow expected of them. By no means do all Christians, for example, see so extraordinary a value in their own individuality as is implied in the monotheistic answer as presented here. Yet that sort of understanding of the uniqueness of the individual is inherent in the stance of all the monotheistic religions. They do not *begin* with a fully developed form of it.

The Hebrew people began with the image of God as covenanting with his people; Christians began with the notion of the Christian way as belonging to the community that is the Church; Muslims began with the sense of belonging to the Islamic community. The Church remains an important element in the development of the Christian life; yet what is developed is a vivacious sense of the uniqueness of the individual.

Why? Because God is perceived as individual par excellence (in Kierkegaard's term, "pure subjectivity") individuality is seen as reflecting the individuality of God. Until one sees something of the extraordinary value of one's own individuality, such as calls for interpreting it as depending in the last resort on a benevolent and intelligent Creator beyond humanity and all the rest of his creation, one will not readily see any warrant for believing in any form of immortality, re-embodiment, or resurrection as any such vision of the afterlife may be presented within a monotheistic framework. If all that I see of value in my life is what can be fully accounted for by the generative act of my parents that resulted in my conception, then not only is God an unnecessary hypothesis; belief in any kind of individual afterlife must seem at best pointless and at worst selfish, not to say arrogant. In such circumstances, the honest and sensible thing to do is humbly to recognize oneself as a fortuitous occurrence in the purposeless maze of what may be called "the way things are." Indeed, to believe oneself worthy of an afterlife extension of one's existence, beyond one's natural biological span, would suggest a pathological sense of one's own importance. When, however, an individual has a positive, lively sense of the action of God in his or her life, the notion that it is to end in death is absurd, as much so as would be a carefully worked out geometrical theorem the last line of which has nothing to do with the mathematical argument leading up to it.

Belief in Individual Immortality

The last line of the Christian creed known as the Nicene is about "the life of the world to come." It comes properly at the end because it is really QED: which was to be demonstrated. Many churchgoers, however, after having vigorously said or sung the Nicene Creed, will tell you that they do not believe the part about everlasting life. The reason for their disbelief is that they do not believe the antecedent affirmations about God. They would not like to be set down as atheists; that would seem to them too specific, too peremptory. Nevertheless, they do not find that they can attach any clear meaning to the concept *God* beyond a vague sense of security that the concept seems to engender in their hearts or minds. Naturally so, since they have discovered no purpose in life that could properly be attributed to the action of a Being such as the creeds of the Church portray. Until one has discerned some such purpose in this life, however opaquely, one can hardly expect to be able to warrant belief in an afterlife. Any belief that I may entertain about life everlasting depends upon my belief in an everlasting God.

When people water down such belief in God as they may have hitherto entertained, of course their belief in afterlife will be correspondingly impoverished. If my concept of God deteriorates to the point at which it represents no more than a function of the human mind that somehow holds society together, the consequences for belief in an afterlife are very predictable. The most to be expected is belief in the continuation, in one form or another, of that species of mammalian life that we call human. I shall die, but perhaps my great-grandchildren, when they gather round the fire on a winter evening for chats about the days of long ago, will recall what they have heard of me or read about me and in such ways I may achieve a sort of "immortality" in and through their minds. If I have no such descendants to commemorate me on such nostalgic occasions, perhaps readers of my books (if people then still go on reading books) may remember me through them. So the best that friends who eulogize me at my funeral can do to make their aspirations for me sound in the least convincing is to say that I shall somehow "live on" in the memories of future generations. Such a hope, if warranted at all, is surely insubstantial. It goes little beyond a promise that if I should die before finishing my breakfast, the uneaten part will not be wasted, since it may nourish the birds or otherwise contribute to the life-sustaining elements in our planet.

By contrast, suppose my belief in God to be belief in an ontological reality to whom all creatures owe their existence and who, while letting his creatures freely evolve and grow, cares for each one of them and guides each one of them as thoughtful and loving parents care for the welfare of their children while respecting and encouraging their children's independence. Then I shall find it impossible to suppose that such a God, having so lovingly guarded and guided me through the earthly pilgrimage that we call human life, will end by extinguishing the object of his incomparable solicitude and love. A painter would not so treat even a canvas on which he had worked for a few months; nor would a composer so treat a musical score. Self-centered indeed would be the mother who, having conceived and eventually given birth to her child and seen her offspring through the hazards of infancy and the trials of

49

adolescence, let that offspring die when she could have prevented it. It would mean that, having fulfilled her experience of motherhood, she could contentedly conclude that episode in her life as one concludes the experience of eating breakfast and perhaps washing the dishes afterwards. Of course she could not. Nor could any lively believer in God, Jew or Muslim, Zoroastrian or Christian, believe that God would bring him or her into being and then discard his creation like a plaything, not to say toss it into the trash like a dead rat.

Disbelief in Individual Immortality

Quite different is the prospect proper to those who have no such belief in God as Creator. The concept of "life everlasting" is likely to seem to them at best wildly speculative, at worst sheer madness, and in any case unbearably tedious. If, as some physiologists seem inclined to expect, the span of human life will eventually be so extended by medical advances that one might foresee for oneself a life in good health extending to several hundred, perhaps even a thousand, years, the prospect might well intimidate rather than gratify even the most stouthearted. One questions, at least, whether such a prospect would be desirable. Suppose that Milton, born in 1608, had gone on living not only through the Wars of Religion but into the Age of Enlightenment, through the French and American revolutions, the battles of Trafalgar and Waterloo, the Diamond Jubilee of Queen Victoria, the horrors of two world wars in the twentieth century, and that he was even now being felicitated by his friends on the prospect of celebrating his four-hundredth birthday in the near future, in fairly good health except for the total blindness from which he had suffered since 1652. Could we expect even a Milton not to cry out "Enough!"? Precious as life is even to a person of ninety in good mental and physical health, the burden of so many memories begins to be troublesome. One would suppose that in four hundred years it would have become intolerable to even the most zestful man or woman. Without a very strong belief in a benevolent and purposive God, one would surely tire of life sooner or later. One has no inbuilt capacity for living on and on at a godless level of existence.

At such a level, indeed, one could hardly expect to avoid thoughts of suicide. Hamlet, in his great soliloquy, toyed with the notion of making his quietus "with a bare bodkin," and there are easier ways of attaining such a goal. Hamlet was deterred only by the fear of what may lie beyond in "the undiscovered country, from whose bourn no traveler returns," even on the assumption that there is any such "country" to be discovered. True, the societies for psychical research adduce evidence of some sort of personal survival, questionable though the evidence be to many. No such evidence, however, could compel the assent of an unbeliever in God as Creator in such a way as to cause him or her to thirst after the "life everlasting" that Christian faith holds out as the most glorious of the promises of God.

For those, however, who believe in God as Creator, it is not life itself that is so prized; it is, rather, the kind of life that such believers call "life with God." For them, the only question about afterlife must be What is its nature? There could be no thought of one's energy flagging or of one's becoming bored, for as God has provided so far the impetus, the will to live, so He will continue to do so forever.

Belief in some sort of afterlife is, however, by no means confined to those who derive it from a trust in the loving purpose of God as Creator. On the contrary, a preoccupation with the mystery of death is perhaps the oldest manifestation of religious concern. In various forms it appears at all stages of religious development. It cannot be dismissed as wishful thinking, for some of its forms (such as the horrific imagery of hell) cannot be the content of any pipe dream; they might be said to spring from fear, an ignoble emotion. But then if one professes belief in afterlife one is exposed to the charge of being on the one hand full of idle, romantic hope and, on the other, paralyzed by ignoble fear. Surely there must be more to the persistence of belief in some sort of afterlife than such a paradoxical combination of hope and fear can provide. At any rate, our next task will be to inspect the principal ways in which the concept of afterlife has developed from the mists of prehistory down to the present. That exercise will clarify the issues we are talking about.

Note

1 For a highly reliable account of this movement, its tenets, and the social fabric of those upholding them, see Robert Brenton Betts, *The Druze* (New Haven, Conn.: Yale University Press, 1988), which contains among much else an important and up-to-date bibliography. The Druze, although the smallest of the three Arab communities living in Israel, are the one most favored by the Israeli government. The Druze are also found in Syria, Lebanon, and elsewhere and are emphatically monotheistic wherever they are. *Tanasukh* (the Arab term for reincarnation or transmigration of souls) is a distinctive teaching of the Druze.

CHAPTER V

Early Development of Concepts of Afterlife

To be ignorant of what happened before one was born is to be forever a child. What is a human life unless the memory of past events is woven with those of earlier ones?

—Cicero, *Orator* [120].

Prehistoric Beginnings

In trying to think ourselves back into the early development of religious ideas in which afterlife concepts emerge, we must not hope to be able to present any neat sequence of events such as we might expect in, say, an economic history of New York or a historical account of French painting. Not only do religious ideas first emerge in a prehistoric mist, they appear in one society or region at a vastly different epoch in human history from that in which they appear elsewhere. Moreover, when we do reach a point at which we might hope to detect the influence of one society's practice over that of another, the question of who has influenced whom or indeed whether the developments have not been independent of one another is often highly controversial. It is easy enough to say with certainty that Plato influenced Aristotle and that

Plotinus affected Christian thought from a certain period in history; it is virtually impossible to explain with even mild confidence precisely when and, more important, why the practice of cremation instead of burial was introduced. It *would seem likely* that cremation was first developed in India. One might then go on to say that the hot climate of India would make it a practical idea. People, however, do not always or even usually act from motives of practicality or common sense and certainly not where religious considerations enter into their decisions.

Of course one may very plausibly argue that the Hindu outlook, from very early times, has tended to separate body and soul in such a way that the body is to the soul somewhat as is a dress or other clothing to the body, so that it is convenient to discard it as expeditiously as possible. It has really no importance. One may then go on to recall the sacredness of fire in Indian religious thought and to see some religious significance in the choice of cremation over burial. Here, however, we are on much shakier ground, for we may be arguing in an after-the-fact way, somewhat as one might speculate (as has indeed been done) that the use of candles in Christian churches arose from complicated theories about the symbolism of the candle's construction out of beeswax from the virgin bee representing the body of Mary enclosing the wick representing the human body of Christ and the light his divinity, and so forth, when in fact the candle was at first used simply to give light for the priest to see the book from which he had to read. Yet what I have just proposed is too simplistic if allowed to stand all by itself. Who can plot a precise moment in time at which the utilitarian motive suddenly becomes a religious one? Is there (indeed, could there be) such a point in time? The first time the candle was lighted to perform its obvious function, it might well have sparked in the mind of at least someone present the germ of some symbolism out of which very gradually would have been developed the spiritual significance of lights on the altar and in Christian procession. But who can tell when the transition took place even in the mind of such a hypothetical worshiper? It would be difficult, to say the least, to plot any such date or period within the historical framework of even the Christian Church and to say when the now-complex symbolism of lighted candles and sanctuary lamps had its first beginnings, let alone when it reached the mature form it had taken by, say, the time of Michelangelo (1475–1564).

How then can we hope to provide any reliable and dependable account of how and in what form religious ideas emerged in prehistoric times? Besides, it is not as though we could set the Bronze Age or any other period at the same time bracket all over the world. [1] Some societies were far more advanced than were others. Moreover, some were more advanced in certain ways, more backward in others. That is so even in the contemporary world. Much more important, even within any society at any particular period in its history, certain groups and (more important still) certain individuals are far more advanced, not least in religious but also in literary, artistic, and other sensibilities, than are their contemporaries within the same society.

The Meaning of Monotheism

Take, for example, the account of the development of monotheism in the Bible. There is plenty of evidence, both from extrabiblical sources and in the Bible itself, that the Hebrews were originally, like their neighbors, polytheistic; that they thought in terms of an innumerable series, a panorama, a pantheon, of deities, among whom, as in other societies, some would be fertility gods and goddesses, others gods of home and hearth, others national gods or tribal totems. Yahweh was their distinctive tribal or national deity. All that is plain enough. But at what point precisely can we say that they became monotheistic? The change is of incalculable importance. It is by no means merely that from having a thousand gods they came to have only one. It is a radical shift in the entire mind-set, which might have taken a different turning. It affects the way one looks at *everything*, including afterlife.

No one would be so simplistic as to pretend to set a year to the occurrence of the change; the fact is that we cannot put even a century or even several centuries to its occurrence. Of course, we can point to certain prophets and what they proclaim. We can show how and even why they inveighed against "false gods" and decried attention to them as idolatry. When they warned the people as they did against "whoring after" such false gods, what were they saying? In large part they were bemoaning the loss of the tribal or national identity that meant so much to their survival, somewhat as, say, the Bretons and the Flemings in modern times have resisted being engulfed by and into the great French culture and civilization around them along with the French language, and as immigrants to America from Greece and other countries long kept themselves apart from a cultural mainstream as they had been forced to do for their cultural survival under the Ottoman Empire and the hated Turkish rule. In doing so, however, the Hebrew prophets made a much more far-reaching discovery: not only was the "whoring after" false gods bad for their national and cultural identity; it was morally, intrinsically wrong. Why? Because, as they were now perceiving, their god, Yahweh, was in fact no mere national deity or tribal emblem but the One Supreme God, the Creator and Source of all being.

Had Amos or Hosea or Isaiah grasped the full implications of what they were preaching? Who can tell? Who can say more than that they were leaders in the ideological revolution that was leading toward the monotheistic stance? Many of us in the Judeo-Christian heritage have not fully grasped it yet, otherwise so many would not have been so easily seduced into other ways of thinking; nor would superstitions that imply a nonmonotheistic world view so widely prevail, with mere lip service to the central monotheistic claim that God, even if He enters into and suffers with His creation, remains eternally the Other, the Creator, the Source of all being.

Archeological Clues

Notoriously, even with good textual evidence, we cannot get fully into the mind-set of even our great-grandparents, much less of the men and women of the Middle Ages, however much we study history and whatever the quality of our historical sense. When we go beyond recorded history into the dim and stupendously long period before its dawn, we can expect to fare even less well. Nevertheless, from archeological evidence we can discover how the Neanderthals buried their dead a hundred thousand years ago. Although what we have found can do no more than help us to guess from that hard evidence at the magicoreligious outlook of these remote ancestors of ours, at least we get some notion of their belief in some sort of afterlife and, following the general principle set forth in the preceding chapter, we are not entirely ignorant, therefore, of their religious outlook.

In the graves of their deceased, along with broken bones that point to their burying their dead with food offerings, have been found flint implements such as awls and scrapers. Our remote ancestors seem to have continued such practices over tens of thousands of years, surrounding their dead with food, tools, weapons, and ornaments, even covering the bones of their dead, either at interment or later, with some sort of red paint, suggesting the idea of blood: a universal symbol of life.

In the Neolithic Age, which varied from place to place but may be set very roughly from, say, 7000 to 3000 B.C.E., burials were conducted with more elaborate ceremony. In some regions, heavy stone tombs were constructed. The megalithic monuments we know as menhirs, dolmens, and cromlechs (single upright stones, double uprights with a capstone, and circular arrangements as at Stonehenge) belong to this period. Archeologists debate the precise function of such monuments. From practices in underdeveloped countries today we may find hints that point us in the right direction. The practice of piling a heap of stones on a grave and, in some African tribes, a pile of thorns, provides a clue. It reflects a certain fear that the dead may come back to haunt the living. Such monuments may be construed as impeding them.

Fear in Primitive Afterlife Beliefs

That the origin of religious awe may lie in fear is not only plausible but likely. *Primus in orbe deos fecit timor*, wrote Petronius (*c.* 26–66 C.E.): It was fear that first made gods in the world. *Plurima versat pessimus in dubiis augur timor*, writes Statius (*c.* 40–96 C.E.): Fear, the very worst of prophets in misfortune, anticipates many ills. Fear of ghosts is an emotion of great antiquity and is by no means unknown today; tales of haunted houses still enthrall us with a fear that, delicious though it be, is not entirely such a laughing matter as we may like to pretend. What if a dead enemy might come back to haunt us and do us harm? Monotheism should safeguard us from such antiquated superstition, but then, as we have seen, most of us are by no means fully beyond the antecedent stages in religious development: some of them more primitive than polytheism, preceding which are stages historians of religion call animism and dynamism, which entail respectively fear of spirits and fear of energies or powers that are believed to inhere in certain areas as we, with our more scientifically oriented minds, might perceive areas to be affected by radiation. Such forces or spirits may be seen as beneficent or maleficent, depending on how they are handled. In many regions of the world today such scenarios are commonplace.

Perhaps it may not be entirely idle to see in them the ideological ancestors of the Christian doctrine of the Communion of Saints celebrated especially on the Church's Feast of All Saints (November 1) together with the primary Catholic prayer for the dead—*Requiescant in pace*: May they rest in peace. The latter hardly fits the official teaching of the Church that the departed are either undergoing spiritual discipline in purgatory or enjoying the bliss of spiritual activity in heaven, neither of which can well be described as rest. The idea of repose, however, probably echoes the sense among the early Christians that the departed were asleep, awaiting the imminent return of Christ. This in turn might have a much more distant archetype in the outlook of our far remoter ancestors. The most noble and lofty religious ideas may have simplistic beginnings—as do the greatest architectural triumphs such as Chartres, Reims, Durham, Ravenna, and Santa Maria Maggiore.

Where Dwell the Spirits of the Dead?

When we go back to the beginnings of recorded history, we find that concepts of the afterlife tend to be indistinct and vague; yet that does not by any means diminish the certainty with which they are held. The Dieri of Southeast Australia (aborigines whose beliefs and practices reflect those of tribespeople of the remote past, even perhaps antedating the Neolithic Age) see in the Milky Way, which they call the River of the Sky, the place where the spirits of the dead dwell. It is regarded as a happy place. Nevertheless, the spirits sometimes leave it to visit people, often in their sleep.[2]

In other cultures, however, the abode of the dead was underground and a shadowy place. Both in ancient Greek culture and in classical Hebrew times, for instance, the future life is depicted in somewhat dreary terms, as a shadowy realm of ghosts. Its location varied with geographic and astronomical concepts. In the *Iliad* it is situated in the Far West, beyond the river Oceanus that was believed to encircle the earth. Later it was taken to be underground in a place where the departed spirits live an attenuated existence, colorless, noiseless, insubstantial. No wonder that Homer suggests that one would rather be a beggar in the land of the living than a king in the land of the "shades."

In Greek mythology, however, a few—those favored by the gods or (in later versions of this concept) heroes or patriots—enjoy a pleasant and richer life in Elysium, the Islands of the Blest (*makarōn nēsoi*), while others who have incurred the anger of the gods or in one way or another merit punishment for their wrongdoings in life go to Tartarus, conceived as a sort of region of Hades set aside for this purpose.

The concept of an underworld of darkness and dust was widespread in the Middle East. *Sheol* in the Bible is the designation given to this underworld in classical Hebrew usage. In many respects it is very much the same concept as that of Hades, but it also acquires various secondary meanings; for example, it can be a synonym for death itself. There is no praise or remembrance of Yahweh in Sheol (Psalm 6:6), although his power extends even to that depth. In later Hebrew thought (the intertestamental period, *c.* 165 B.C.E.–50 C.E.) Sheol becomes a place for the wicked; but as thought on the afterlife develops, confusions arise (the righteous go to Paradise and the wicked to Gehenna, a development of the concept of Sheol), yet the concept of Sheol as a place of punishment survives in intertestamental literature. Then in the New Testament and other early Christian literature, although the term *Sheol* or *Hades* becomes less frequent, it survives to some extent. As in later Judaism, however, it is generally conceived as relating to a temporary arrangement, pending the final judgment—when it is to become a place of permanent torment. Meanwhile Hades is an enemy, as is death itself, yet its power is limited: Jesus promises that even the gates of Hades shall not prevail over the Church (Matthew 16:18).

A word of caution may be warranted here for those who tend to assume that peoples whose socioeconomic life-styles are simple and by our standards "underdeveloped" must be similarly "primitive" in their cosmological and religious ideas. The notion that the earth is flat and is covered with a sort of inverted bowl (the sky or "heaven") with a saucer beneath it containing Hades or Sheol certainly sounds very primitivistic. From one point of view of course it is, but from that obvious conclusion we must not go on to deduce that it is easy for us to understand. Anthropological studies of the religious beliefs and practices of South American Indians, for instance, may make them seem at first sight notably primitivistic, not to say barbaric.

Afterlife Beliefs in Pre-Columbian America

In Venezuela and southward in Pre-Columbian America, for example, the whipping dance was a widespread feature of religious ritual. The participants, often masked, in the course of complex mimetic dances severely whipped one another on the legs and buttocks. Initiation ceremonies at puberty were also painful and complex. But behind such ritual, easily dismissed as sadomasochistic, could lie a highly complex network of cosmological ideas.

Afterlife Beliefs in Egypt

Perhaps nowhere in antiquity was the concept of afterlife developed with such complexity as in Egypt. The Egyptians enjoyed life as we know it and did all that they could to extend it, yet more than any other society in human history they lavished their attention upon the disposal of their dead. At first this attention was more or less accorded only to kings and other grandees, but after the power of the pharaohs began to diminish (2200–2000 B.C.E.), the notion of immortality for all spread, developing into a highly complex theory and issuing in some of the most interesting practices relating to belief in afterlife. The theory, although apparently based upon deep conviction, was not by any means unmarred by the confusions to be found generally in afterlife beliefs.

From very early times the Egyptians had conceived the view that in the human torso (the belly or the heart) is a soul depicted as a human-headed bird that flees from the person at death; they called it the *ba.* The *ba* retains a hunger for food and drink and other physical needs and desires. It tends therefore to return to haunt the body in search of satisfaction. It has a nostalgic longing for the body that it has departed, somewhat as an exile feels homesickness for the land he has left. Therefore arrangements, often elaborate, were made for the provision of food, drink, and other comforts in the tomb, and passageways were constructed to make possible the ingress and egress of the *ba*. There is, however, in this system, another soul: the *ka,* which represents the more intellectual and spiritual aspects of the person. The *ka* is depicted by two arms outstretched, also by a replica of the person placed in the tomb, in which the *ka* could take up its abode and contemplate and enjoy pictures and other representations of the life of the deceased. The *ka* itself has two aspects: a higher one, the *ikhu* (spirit or intelligence), which at death soars directly to heaven, and the *khaibit*, a sort of shadow or *Doppelgänger* (double).

The Egyptians emphatically held that the preservation of the body is essential for a happy afterlife, so they devised processes of mummification on an extraordinarily complex scale. Herodotus gives an account of the embalming process. The belly was opened up and filled with pure myrrh mixed with various spices such as cassia. Then the body was sewn up. Wine, cakes, dates, dehydrated beef, and other provisions were made for the needs of the *ba*, while the *ka* was accorded even more elaborate arrangements such as house furnishings, chariots, various games, and sometimes even works of art and other treasures, including models of servants and others to minister to the needs of the *ka*.

Ancient Egyptian expectations of afterlife, however, went far beyond what is reflected in such funeral customs. Many highly imaginative and picturesque theories were expounded about the pilgrimage of the soul after death. Typical was the notion that the soul, after a long journey, attended by arduous exercises, would reach the blissful Kingdom of Osiris. Before admission to it,

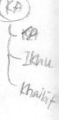

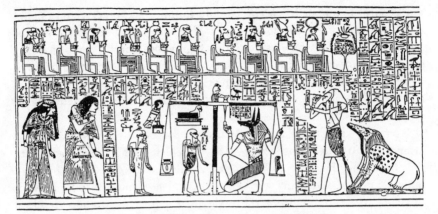

Fig. 4. The heart of the ancient Egyptian scribe Ani is being weighed in the gods' presence. *From E. A. Wallis Budge,* Egyptian Ideas of the Future Life *(London, 1899). Ancient Egyptian religious ideas are notoriously complex, but the concept of judgment is pervasive. The heart of the deceased is weighed in a balance in the Hall of Maāt and is expected to balance exactly the feather, her symbol of what is right and true.*

the soul had to be examined in the presence of Osiris himself. The court that judges the supplicant is on a very grand scale. After the latter sets forth his case his heart is weighed in scales against an ostrich feather. A good heart will be so light that it will not tip the scales against the feather and its owner will then be admitted to the realm of bliss. A heavy heart will fail the test and the soul it represents will either be devoured by a fierce monster or, according to other versions (there is little coherence in the expectations of afterlife except that the good are rewarded and the wicked punished), punished in a fiery furnace. Unlike the hell of Christian tradition, however, the punishment is of limited duration and so functions more as does the Christian concept of purgatory than as the horrific doctrine of eternal torture in hell.

Death, Judgment, and Resurrection in Zoroastrianism

A somewhat similar examination system is to be found in Zoroastrian accounts of judgment, although there the result is achieved automatically, without the ceremony of a court. On the fourth day after death the deceased is required to cross a bridge called Chinvat that connects this world with the unseen one beyond. The good find the crossing easy and arrive without

Fig. 5. Ancient Egyptian portrayal of the Elysian fields, from the Papyrus of the Priestess Anhai, who lived c. 1000 B.C.E. *From E. A. Wallis Budge,* Egyptian Ideas of the Future Life *(London, 1899). The Sekhert-Aaru (Field of Reeds) was a sort of paradise conceived as a fertile region where agriculture could be conducted with ease and pleasure. There dwelt the spirits of the dead who were deemed worthy of such bliss. This portrayal of these Elysian fields dates from the XXIInd dynasty. It would seem that the ancient Egyptians, at least at some point in their history, expected to meet members of their families in the afterlife.*

difficulty on the other side, in the House of Song, where they await the Last Day. The wicked, by contrast, somehow find the bridge like the edge of a razor and fall off it into the place of punishment which, like the Egyptian counterpart and unlike the traditional Christian concept of hell, is temporary and therefore also corresponds more to a purgatorial discipline than to the everlasting torment of hell.

According to classic Zoroastrian teaching, just before the Last Day Zoroaster will return as a prophet conceived of a virgin by his own seed, stored in a mountain lake. On the Last Day, Ahura Mazda, the Supreme Being in Zoroastrianism, will finally defeat the forces of evil and reign over the whole world. There will be a general resurrection and everyone, whether from the House of Song or from the place of punishment, will enter new life in a renovated world.

The extent of Zoroastrian influence on Judeo-Christian concepts is debatable. It does seem likely, however, that Judaism and Christianity did in one way or another owe something to Zoroastrianism: the concept of resurrection. The Pharisees, we know, accepted the concept of resurrection. The Sadducees, according to Acts 23:6–8, did not. The resurrection of Christ became, for those of the Christian Way, central to the apostolic proclamation. In the early Church it continued to be central doctrine and was generally understood and expounded in terms of rising from the dead with the same body, but vivified and transformed. Because Christ has so risen from the dead, those who link themselves to him can so rise also. This resurrection concept, although representing a form of re-embodiment, is, as we shall see, to be distinguished from the transmigrational or reincarnational forms of rebirth that play so great a part in the history of concepts of afterlife.

Transmigration or Reincarnation

The alternative concept of reincarnation or transmigration (also called metempsychosis) is one that has arisen in innumerable forms, from the most primitive to the most advanced. In undeveloped societies it is often found in forms that are scarcely distinguishable from arbitrary metamorphosis. That is to say, there is little if any ethical content. One may be re-embodied, at the whim of a god or goddess acting in a fit of temper, into a pig or frog or into a handsome prince or a beautiful young girl. For at this stage of religious development we mortals are no better than the playthings of the gods who "kill us for their sport," as in King Lear the Earl of Gloucester aptly echoes the ancient notion. At a far more advanced stage, however, the doctrine of rebirth, now married to the highly ethical concept that one reaps what one sows, assumes a very different form indeed and one that expresses a concept that lies at the heart of all the great religions of the world, not least Christianity. "Don't delude yourself," writes Paul to the Galatians (6:7, Jerusalem Bible), "into thinking God can be cheated: where a man sows, there he reaps: if he sows in the field of self-indulgence he will get a harvest of corruption out of it; if he sows in the field of the Spirit he will get from it a harvest of eternal life."

The concept of re-embodiment, decorously governed by this type of ethical outlook, is found in abundance in the most cultivated thought of the Greeks of antiquity. The Pythagorean brotherhood, following their founder Pythagoras, who was born at Samos about 580 B.C.E., not only taught reincarnation but also accepted it as a matter of course. Their founder himself had claimed to remember his earlier embodiments. The idea of transmigration of souls appears also in the Eleusinian "mystery religion." Plato, who was by no means inclined to teach the ancient Homeric myths indiscriminately to the young on the ground that they were unable at their age to understand the difference between the allegorical and the literal, was deeply influenced by all these sources: Pythagoras, the Eleusinian mysteries, Orphism, and the entire climate of thought in which the transmigrational concept was taken seriously. He represents his own master Socrates as taking reincarnation as a matter of course. In contrast to the popular religion of the time, used by the poets as a literary convention but not taken seriously by thoughtful people in Greece or Rome, transmigration was accepted by many philosophers, including Plato, because it appealed to both reason and moral sense.

As we turn to the great subcontinent of India, however, we find, in the vast clearinghouse of religious ideas and practices that we call Hinduism, a culture so saturated with the concept of transmigration, from its most primitive to its most developed form, that it is there that many people look for a history of the notion. It is a convenient place to look—so long as we bear in mind that the history of the concept extends far beyond the shores of India and comes in many forms, from the most primitive to the most highly developed. So mixed is the population of India, both ethnically and linguistically, that disentangling the various elements and giving time frames to their appearance is extremely difficult.

The name Dravidian, for instance, is applied both to a group of languages and to the indigenous peoples of India south of the Vindhyas and in the northern part of Sri Lanka. These peoples vary very much in development and quality of civilization, but those representing the earliest element are typ-ically short, dark, with broad noses, long heads, wavy hair, and possibly some negroid affinities. Forms of reincarnational ideas may have existed among such groups from prehistoric times and the notion would inevitably, at such a cultural level, take vague forms. On the Indus River, however, before 2500 B.C.E., an ethnically mixed people combined to form a Bronze Age type of civilization with a high quality of artistic and architectural attainment and a religion that exhibited (at least embryonically) the ad-vanced ideas on the karmic principle and its reincarnational implicate that were to be systematically expounded in the philosophy of the Upanishads, which were eventually composed orally during a period from about 600 to 300 B.C.E. The upanishadic tradition represents an intellectual movement away from both priestly ritualism and the political and legalistic develop-ment of the caste system that had already begun to take shape by the end of the seventh century B.C.E. and that served to support socioeconomically the concepts of karma and reincarnation.

The Aryan occupation of the Ganges Valley about this time had brought into existence various states, some ruled monarchically, others more in a republican fashion. Eventually four distinct social groups came into exis-tence: (1) the Kshatriyas (nobles or warriors), (2) the Brahmins (priests), (3) the Vaisyas (artisans and farming people), and (4) the Shudras (servants). By about 500 B.C.E. the Brahmins were taking first place, with the Kshatriyas second. Beyond this caste system were the pariahs or outcastes (untouch-ables), the dregs of society. (In this form the Indian caste system has remark-able affinities with the tripartite structure of the ideal society proposed by Plato in his *Republic*. Nor is that surprising when we reflect that, about 2000 B.C.E., Greek-speaking Indo-Europeans were coming into the Greek peninsula while their Aryan kinsmen were beginning to move into India.

Reincarnational ideas and the karmic principle behind them not only could be but certainly were fitted into the institution of caste in India. Brahmins, for instance, could claim a kind of innate superiority on the ground that their status was due to good karma accumulated in previous lives, while the lowlier condition of the poorer and less educated castes could be explained by bad karma, likewise inherited from the past.

Both Mahavira, the founder of the Jains, and Gautama Buddha, who were contemporaries, detached the karmic principle from caste in such a way as to spiritualize it. One might be born into a high caste because of a good karmic inheritance, but again, an advanced soul might need the experience of a low-caste birth to advance spiritually in a special way. In these two great religions reincarnation, dissociated from the structures of a caste-divided society, became axiomatic as a religious tenet. The karmic principle invested it with profound ethical meaning.

The Law of Karma is only one expression of a principle that is universal in the history of religion: that sooner or later, in one way or another, virtue is rewarded and vice punished. *Karma* means literally "action" and the karmic principle is a principle of balance. The "law" operates in the realm of the spirit, as do the so-called "laws of nature" (such as the law of gravity) in the empirical world. Standing by itself the karmic principle may sound cold, even tyrannical, but espoused to the concept of reincarnation it is transmogrified. For through the *samsara* or chain of embodiments one develops and grows. It is a means of self-education. Not only is the process liberating, the liberation can be in some cases breathtaking. For as in biological evolution there are "leaps" from a lower to a higher and finer form of life, so in the spiritual realm one may achieve dramatic developments even in one lifetime, rising from spiritual rags to spiritual riches with meteoric speed. One may spend a series of embodiments trying to unravel the knots in the tangled web of one's own making and then at last the tangle falls apart and one feels the joy of a new stage in freedom.

The entire process of re-embodiment is about emancipation. One is given a set of circumstances, a "prison," and challenged with the task of freeing oneself from it. The karmic principle is very conspicuously a free-will principle. I have some good karma from a previous embodiment and some bad. The bad impedes my progress and hinders my growth, but by use of the good karma I can melt away the power of the bad to impede me. There is plenty of time. If I do not succeed in one environment I shall be accorded another.

What, then, is the *goal* of this immensely long spiritual travail? In Hinduism and the religions that have their roots in the Hindu heritage (for example Buddhism and Jainism) the end tends to be conceived in terms of a relinquishment of one's self and an absorption into the divine or a self-realization of one's own divinity—one's being an aspect of or an element in the divine that is the only reality.

The models used in expressing such a general outlook vary. The Jains put the stress on conduct and regard matter as the great impediment to spiritual advancement. The Buddhists tend, rather, to see the mischief to lie in desires, whether of the flesh or of the spirit, so that the remedy lies in extirpating all desires, even those that seem right and noble. As to be expected, however, from what we have seen in the first chapter, the goal is seen in terms of how God is conceived. The end of the process that involves the *samsara* or chain of embodiments that provide the purgatorial discipline through which spiritual triumph is attained is conceptually determined by the model of God that this family of religions has, generally speaking, in common. The Upanishads, the classic Hindu literature in which Indian forms of reincarnational belief are developed, do certainly allow for an almost infinite variety of ways of looking at the realm of the spirit, but certain presuppositions tend to override all else and a paramount presupposition is that focus on the individual self (self-centeredness) is an impediment to self-realization as part of the "Great Self." My task is by no means (as it is in the great monotheistic religions to which we are about to return our attention) to tend my soul so that it is developed as a unique flower in the garden of the Creator. It is, rather, to divert my preoccupation with the "little" self that stifles my spirituality and to focus on the "great" self of which I am a part. I must lose my "little" self to gain awareness of my being part of the "great" self.

Resistance to the Monotheistic Solution

As we saw in the preceding chapter, the great biblical tradition that lies behind the three monotheistic religions, Judaism, Christianity, and Islam, does not represent a unified philosophical and theological stance but a miscellany of literature. True, we do find among the Hebrew prophets proclamations that enunciate in one way or another the monotheistic direction in which they wish to lead their people, but not till a few centuries B.C.E. is there any clear indication that the people at large have taken seriously the message that their prophets had been preaching to them centuries before. Even then, there are still remnants of older ways of thinking.

How the prophets themselves came to their monotheistic stance and their vision of the Otherness of God that is in such contrast to the aim of the great Oriental religions that look to the attainment of awareness of one's unity with the "Great Self" is impossible to determine with certainty. There are of course special circumstances to which scholars have pointed as contributing to the process of such development; for instance, the isolation of the Hebrew people from their powerful neighbors and their inevitable preoccupation with their own survival could have assisted in the process, as could have their discovery, during their exile in Babylonia, that their God was not merely the God of their land but could go with them in their minds wherever they went.

66

Homesick by the rivers of Babylon, they had wept when they remembered Zion (Psalm 137), but then their captors asked them to sing some of their own songs. At first they had wondered how they could sing the songs of Yahweh in a foreign land, but they found that Yahweh had accompanied them and that they could sing his songs with greater zest than ever.

That hardly accounts, however, for the gradual transformation of the people to a monotheistic stance. Moses, when he gave the commandments, had enjoined the people that they must have no other gods before Yahweh; but that was far from the monotheistic stance that became so central to Judaism and the religions rooted in it. For the commandment implies that there *are* other gods; the gods of other peoples, for instance, were surely real and only too powerful. Some scholars have given a name to this stage: *henotheism*, the worship of one God while not denying the existence of other gods. Although perhaps a useful distinction for some purposes, it tends to blind us to the immensity of the gulf between authentic monotheism and all its ideological antecedents. For one of the principal proclamations of authentic monotheism is that these other "gods" are *false* gods; that is, in the last resort they have no real power, so we have nothing to fear from them. Moreover, the consequences of the monotheistic stance for concepts of the afterlife are stupendous, for it warrants the belief that to be with God hereafter no less than here and now is assured by the nature of God as the Source of all being. No less assured is the uniqueness of the quality of such afterlife. Not only is the fundamental difference between Creator and creature maintained, so also is the reality of both.

In the Bible, however, are many vestiges of the persistence of older, more primitive beliefs about the soul and the spirit world to which it belonged, beliefs of a type common in primitive forms of religion: the Hebrews had inherited many such notions, among them the idea that inside everyone is a tiny replica of the man or woman, the soul or *nefesh* that at death slips out through the nose or mouth, invisible and intangible because of a finer substance than the body, and goes wandering. In the case of a violent death it might slip off the point of the sword that slew the man. (The Arabs inherited a similar view of the *nefs* or soul.) In the Old Testament there is even an echo of a belief in a class of wicked witches who hunted for the souls of unwary people. They caught them in handkerchiefs or the like, stuffed them in elbow pockets, then sold them to families who, having a sick person at home, believed that a replacement soul would help the victim. In Ezekiel 13:17f. we find an echo of this primitive outlook in a denunciation of those false prophetesses. The Lord says: "Trouble is coming to the women who sew frills around their wrists, who make veils for people of all sizes, the better to ensnare lives! You ensnare the lives of the men of my people while looking after your own." The allusion is clear. There could be nothing so evil about a frilly adornment of a female wrist that could merit so vehement a denunciation were it not for an underlying, more sinister significance. The significance lay in the association of such frills with the nefarious intent of those witches who used them as an instrument for stuffing souls into elbow pockets, stealing them from unsuspecting families for selling to equally unsuspecting customers. Against such primitive notions of the soul and the afterlife the Hebrew prophets inveighed, but as Moses had found with the people who so easily reverted to the worship of the Golden Calf, the transition from primitive concepts and practices to more advanced ones is not easily accomplished, and even when it seems to have been completed people readily revert to the old habits, which demand less ethical reflection and fewer challenges to the mind.

"Undeveloped" and "Developed" Religious Thought

Before leaving the earlier development of afterlife concepts, to go on to the later stage of the developmental process, let us take a moment to reflect upon what distinguishes the one from the other. First, there is nothing to disparage in primitive religious beliefs. As well might one disdain a child for being a child and not an adult. Adults have much to learn too, but if they have matured and undergone thought-provoking education, something will have happened to their minds that precludes them from ever having the simplicity of heart and mind that is so endearing in children. In some ways this is to be regretted, for, as Jesus reminded his hearers, one needs to have something of the child's sense of wonder, something of the open-eyed simplicity of the child, in order to penetrate the mysteries of the spiritual realm of being. What distinguishes the religious outlook of people at less developed stages is that, while their capacity for imagination and for intuiting great truths and speculating about them can be startling, their analytical capacities have not yet been comparably developed. We are likely, indeed, to be so foolish as to put into their mouths questions that they could not possibly have been able to ask. That can be almost like speculating what sort of computer system Plato would have chosen or whether Solomon would have preferred Palladian over Early English architecture. The greatest difficulty in trying to understand the outlook of the people of antiquity is in divesting our own minds both of their sophistications and of their prejudices. Our sophistications may prevent us from perceiving the penetrating vigor of their thought while our prejudices blind us to the fact that those cultural ancestors of ours were not infrequently in their own way subtler in the use of their concepts than are we in the use of ours.

What strikes us above all in primitive concepts of afterlife is their vagueness. They are vague because they are the consequences or concomitants of a belief in God that is vague. There is no danger of intolerant dogmatism in the way in which primitive peoples think of God and afterlife, because their outlook is the result of a groping to express both the wonder and the perplexity of minds not yet equipped to formulate an intelligible position on such questions. We cannot view what they say as right or wrong, because they really have not thought out what they are groping toward or its consequences for their destiny. When we find a person packing food and tools alongside a corpse in a tomb (perhaps even also a little money), we ask Why? We are likely to get an answer such as:

"We love him so we want him to have a pleasant journey. We always do that with our friends when they are going on a journey."

"What journey?" we may well ask. "He is *dead*."

"Of course he is dead. We don't know exactly where he is going. But wherever he is going we want to provide him with whatever it takes to make his journey as easy as possible."

"A very thoughtful and considerate gesture," we rejoin. "But what makes you think he is going anywhere?"

"He must be going *somewhere*," says the bereaved friend.

"Why?" A slight pause ensues. Then a spokesman from the others standing by makes a suggestion:

"His *spirit* is going somewhere. We know that because that's what spirits do."

If we saw any point in pursuing such a conversation we might ask how they can be sure that a spirit could handle the money that has been stuffed in the corpse's mouth and, even if he could, how do they know that the kind of currency they have given him will be accepted in the spirit world or wherever the deceased is bound for. It is perhaps possible, although not very likely, that a clever person among the untrained minds of those standing by might interpolate a suggestion:

"Our money will be exchanged for whatever they use over there."

Whatever turn the conversation takes, however, it cannot issue in anything that we could recognize as this or that kind of model of belief in God or disbelief in God or of the consequent corollary of this or that type of belief or disbelief in an afterlife. To reach that stage in human development much cerebral activity must take place. Historically, such activity is always initiated by a few very special people such as prophets, sages, or seers. It is often centuries before the teachings of such thinkers issue in the development of a popular outlook that reflects them.

We must soon consider examples of how, in a variety of societies and cultures, this transition has in fact occurred, resulting in both clarification and limitation in the ways in which concepts of God have been developed—and more especially, of course, the corresponding visions of the nature of afterlife. Before doing so, however, we shall find advantage in examining in more detail a concept of afterlife that we have mentioned in passing already: that of Hades. This has special importance not only because it was a view common to ancient Greek and Hebrew thought but because of the pervasive influence of the notion in many other cultures.

Notes

1   The term *Bronze Age* signifies that stage in any human society in which copper alloyed with tin came to be widely used as a substitute for or supplement to stone in making weapons or tools. Copper had been known and used from the remote past in the Middle East and thence to the Mediterranean lands and beyond. Bronze probably did not come into use till around 2000 B.C.E., speading rapidly throughout much of Europe. The Bronze Age was followed, very generally speaking, by the Iron Age, which in Egypt, for example, began sometime around 800 B.C.E. We must recognize, however, that bronze was used here and there before the date assigned to the Bronze Age in any particular locality, as was iron before the Iron Age. In a more recent scenario we talk of a Machine Age, but when precisely does a primitive tool become a machine? We say we are now in the Computer Age, but was not the abacus an early form of computer? Above all, such evolutionary developments certainly do not proceed at the same pace throughout the world. Moreover, some societies have gone directly from candlelight to electric light without any intervening stages.

2   See the important paper by Johannes Wilbert on the destinies of the soul among the Warao Indians of Venezuela, in Elizabeth P. Benson (ed.), *Death and the Afterlife in Pre-Columbian America*. (Wash., D.C.: Dumbarton Oaks, 1975).

Hades and the Transition to Orphism

Although the Greek concept of Hades is by no means monolithic, it does have
some fairly constant features. Homer provides both the earliest and the most
comprehensive portrait of the life of those who, having passed through death,
go to the "abode" of the dead. He sees them as dreamlike figures, lacking
menos (strength) and therefore generally speaking unable to exercise anything
such as we today would call political or social influence. The dead are for the
most part witless. They are pale shadows of their former selves.

The name *Haidēs* was applied both to the god of this nether world and to
his realm. The god was also known as *Plutōn* (literally, "the Rich"), which the
Romans translated into Latin as *Dis*. Hades, with his consort Persephone, a
daughter of Zeus and Demeter, both carried off the spirits of the dead and
ruled over them in his realm.

As time went on the geographic location of Hades changed. In Homer's
Iliad the river Oceanus was popularly supposed to encircle the earth and
Hades was located in the far west beyond it, but later it was conceived as
somewhere underground, accessible by various valleys and other geographic
features. Generally it was believed to be separated from the realm of the
living by one of the rivers of Hades such as the Styx. The entrance to Hades is
guarded by Kerberos (Latin *Cerberus*), a many-headed monstrous watchdog.
The Homeric description of Hades suggests a dark, dreary, murky place. This
remains the general, if vague, image of Hades throughout the centuries after
Homer. In *The Frogs*, a comedy produced by Aristophanes in 405 B.C.E., we
have the first literary post-Homeric description of Hades. It is approached by
a boat across the river Styx and the ferryman, Charon, demands an obol, a
small coin; hence the practice common in many primitive societies of burial
with a coin in the deceased's mouth. (This practice continued in Greece until
comparatively recent times.) In popular mythology Hades, although remaining generally the gloomy place of Homeric tradition, comes to be associated
later with other and less dreary concepts of afterlife, such as those associated
with Eleusis and Dionysus. Such "mystery religions," as they have come to be
called, were much focused on the hereafter. Under such influence the imagery
of the ferryman Charon is sometimes embellished with picturesque elements
such as his calling out the names of places at which his boat will make stops.
So is introduced the idea that the passengers are not all destined for the same
monotonous place of gloom and idle chatter. Some are bound for other and

much pleasanter destinations. Ideas of this sort, however, were connected with the "mystery religions," esoteric cults not known to everyone.

One of the eventually most influential of these cults was Orphism, so called after the legendary pre-Homeric poet Orpheus. Before its emergence the Greeks of more primitive times and at the popular level had not yet developed any clear idea of a destiny depending on moral guilt or merit. Orphism introduced one issuing from a legend central to the basic teaching of this mystery religion, according to which Zagreus was the son of Zeus and Persephone. Hera, who was both the sister and the consort of Zeus, in a fit of jealousy instigated the Titans to destroy Zagreus and devour him. Athene, however, was able to save his heart, which she took to Zeus, who by a stroke of lightning burned the Titans, out of whose ashes grew the human race, who therefore have within them an ancestry both evil and good, including a godlike element.

So in Orphism we find a change of outlook, at least among the more thoughtful Greeks. Guilt and punishment, merit and reward become central to Orphic teaching, which recognized the importance of moral purity as a means of attaining blessedness. Hades, under such influence, came to be regarded as a place of punishment for evildoers—a sort of ideological ancestor of hell. The Orphics, who were already influential in some circles as early as the sixth century B.C.E., had affinities with the Pythagoreans and like them taught a doctrine of transmigration of souls. Both the teachings of Pythagoras and those of the Orphics were respected by Plato, who in the *Phaedo* advances the doctrine that the ordinary run of men and women, notable neither for their virtue nor for their vice, are taken to a lake or the river Acheron to live until, having been purified, they are reborn as living beings.

In Plato's *Republic* is a more developed concept of this kind. The dead, on their arrival in the underworld (still the basic theme) first come to a vast meadow, where they are judged. Some days later they are conveyed to a place where sample lives are shown to them and they make their respective choices. Eventually they pass through Lethe to the new birth that each has discerned as proper to his or her needs. Plato, although of course he does not take literally such myths as Lethe (the waters of forgetfulness that generally dim our remembrance of past lives), has a high regard for myth as an instrument for the conveyance of the most important kinds of truth, and he plainly seems to accept some form of the ancient doctrine of the transmigration of the soul.

These largely esoteric developments in the ancient Greek way of thinking of the dead did little, however, to affect the general, popular tradition in which they were commonly imagined as inhabiting the vague, shadowy underground abode ruled by Hades and eventually called after him. The gods of this underworld were themselves shadowy figures compared to the often glowingly portrayed gods whom Homer so vividly describes. Only gradually did the assistants of Hades receive anything like personal identity. Kerberos, the monstrous watchdog, is the first to be personified, appearing in art as early as the sixth century B.C.E. Hermes, a sort of general flunky to Hades and the one charged with conducting the spirits of the dead to Charon's ferryboat, is also a secondary development in what perhaps might be called the shadowy pantheon of the underworld. Subordinate to Hades, he often acts somewhat as a sort of lieutenant, a second-in-command. Thanatos (death) and Hypnos (sleep) also come to be personified, but they are not cultic figures; they receive no oblations. Indeed, Thanatos is depicted, both in literature and in art, somewhat as is Death in much later European literature. He is certainly not concerned with punishment or reward but is simply a symbol of the fact that we all die.

In Plato's *Gorgias* we do find, however, definite reference not only to the notion of retribution in the afterlife but also to the important concept that then, in contrast to now, the souls of men and women would be seen "naked"—denuded of the disguises that people succeed in using to hide their real characters. Nevertheless, the idea of judgment, even in Plato, is not prominent; there is no highly developed calculus of wrongdoing with punishments proper to each level. Hades is not a place of punishment but would be better described as an attenuated or impoverished kind of existence.

Indeed, some post-Homeric representations of it suggest, in modern terms, a dreary sort of old folks' home rather than a prison or penitentiary. The inhabitants seem to be endlessly chattering, murmuring about themselves and each other and expressing regrets that matters had not gone differently on earth. That life in Hades was aimless is evident from the reports on even its pleasanter side, which represent the inhabitants as playing games and partying. Some accounts even suggest their eating and drinking and perhaps even engaging in sexual relationships; but the essential point to bear in mind is that at the best the inhabitants of Hades did all these things, if they did them at all, only by a sort of mimicry of what the living do: more as the living do in their dreams than as in their waking hours. Besides, many people seem to have discounted the whole conception of Hades as a fairy tale.

The Biblical Image of Sheol

The Hebrew concept of Sheol, frequently mentioned in the Bible, is in many respects the counterpart of the Greek Hades. Nevertheless, some differences should be noted. The Hebrew view of the human being is that of a body animated by a spirit rather than of a spirit incarnate in a body. So when the deceased person continued in Sheol it was as a ghostly survival of the full living person. Generally speaking, however, Sheol is more usually a metaphor, not to say a euphemism, for the grave. Insofar as it is a place of any kind it is "below" and full of darkness, dust, and worms. In that respect it was very much in line with the concept of the ancient Middle East generally. We might call it a kind of nonworld. There is no activity at all. It is not merely an attenuated life; it is nonlife.

Only in later Judaism is there the beginning of a notion at which Job hints (Job 14:13) when he wishes that God would preserve him in Sheol until he be vindicated. Yahweh's power reaches even down to Sheol, for it is limitless; nevertheless it is not exercised there as in the land of the living. It is not a place of punishment except in the vague sense in which death itself may be so construed.

The Birth of the Image of Hell

Only in later Judaism (in the second century B.C.E. and later) is Sheol developed into Gehenna, a place specifically for the wicked as Paradise is a place for the righteous. Sometimes, however, the term *Sheol* continues to be used with the sense of the place whither the dead generally are sent.

In other words, the old, neutral term *Sheol* acquires some of the function that is eventually to be invested in the term *Gehenna*. In both Jewish and Christian apocalyptic, Sheol becomes, in the final destruction of all things, a place of storage for the dead, which it gives up for the final destruction of its inhabitants. When this occurs, Sheol, like Death itself, having no longer any function, is itself destroyed. In Christian thought it eventually takes on the role of Hell, the state or place in which the wicked are condemned to everlasting punishment, popularly seen most typically as fiery torture, although among the learned seen as the anguish of everlasting separation from God, the source of all life and love, and as the agony of awareness of this infinitely terrible loss.

Fig. 6. A woman, destined for damnation in hell, being carried thither by a devil. *From the* Inferno *in the Cappella di S. Brizio, Orvieto Cathedral, by Luca Signorelli, c. 1500. Photograph from Percy Dearmer,* The Legend of Hell: An Examination of the Idea of Everlasting Punishment *(London: Cassell & Company, 1929).*

Dante, in the inscription over the gates of Hell, captures a feature that is to a great extent common to both Hades (Sheol) and Hell: "Abandon hope all ye who enter here." The Hades of the ancient Greeks, in some ways a tolerable if boring existence, is—no less than the Hebrew Sheol and the Christian Hell—bereft of hope. None of them is on the way to anywhere; in none of them is any kind of growth. For all their differences all of them bear the terrible label *terminal.* An attenuated, colorless life might not be so bad if there were any way of improving it, any means of eventually transforming it into a new and better and fuller life. That, however, is precisely what is lacking in all of them. There is no evolution, no hope of growth. Even the nightmares of the living come to an end and respite comes to even the most painful of human ills and griefs, but Hades offers no hope; nor is there any escape, not even by suicide, for even that is so impossible an act as to be entirely meaningless in such miserable circumstances.

Fear of the Dead

The hopelessness of the dead as popularly conceived contributed no doubt much to the superstitious fear of them in the Greek imagination. The dead, generally speaking, were neither benevolent nor malevolent; they were annoying, troublesome, and irritating: naturally so, for they had nothing better to do, on the whole, than torment the living. The ordinary run of the dead lacked the constructive motivation either to help the living or to engage in intricate plots to harm them. There were, however, special cases. Those who had been cruelly mistreated among the living might be expected to haunt the latter and avenge wrongs by wreaking mischief upon them. The dead were more likely to be irritated at being disturbed by the living, somewhat as a sick or aged or tired person is annoyed by being roused by a youthful one full of energy and bounce. Hence the prudence of not acting in any way calculated to disturb the dead. Use such rites as are available to soothe or console them, if you will, but above all do not annoy them in any way, for since they belong to a world of negativity they are more expert than you in negative arts.

Such attitudes toward the dead are in large measure the source of the widespread fear of ghosts that expresses itself in a large variety of ways and of obedience to venerable injunctions expressed in maxims such as *de mortuis nil nisi bonum*: Of the dead (say) nothing but good. Like sleeping dogs, they are better left undisturbed. Hosts of old superstitions express such fears of the power of the dead, such as that the reason for a sudden shiver down your back is that someone is walking over the grave of your relative or friend. For although the spirits of the dead are tucked away in Hades or Sheol they still, in some circumstances, maintain a kind of negative nostalgia for places with which they have been intimately connected in life and are inclined to haunt these on even slight provocation.

Erotic Images of Paradise

Although Hades or one of its counterparts was a classic image of afterlife in the ancient Mediterranean world, there was in popular religion an alternative: the dream of a paradise of erotic fantasy, often depicted as a sort of perpetual sexual ecstasy. Plato, in the *Republic* (363 C, D), alludes to such a vulgar and simplistic concept of future bliss in which the blessed lie on couches everlastingly drunk and crowned with garlands. He ridicules the image as expressing the notion that an immortality of drunkenness should be accounted the highest reward of virtue. Whence the idea of such types of paradisal bliss came to the Mediterranean world is, to the best of my knowledge, not certain. It may have emerged independently of any extraneous influence. India, however, is a very possible source, for from the Vedas, the most ancient of the various sacred literatures of India, we have intimations of images of future bliss in which, aided by draughts of soma (a drug used in temple worship and supposed to assist in the attainment of a sensuous form of immortality), one might enjoy unremitting erotic ectasy.

Among the paradoxes of the complex culture of India is the fact that alongside a deep respect for the ascetic ideal (which includes not only fasting and other acts of self-denial but rigorous repression of the sexual appetite) is an alternative attitude in which the erotic element in human life is invested with a sort of religious status. The very explicitly erotic statuary at Khajuraho, for instance, has long been well known to travelers. Although dating from only about the eleventh century C.E., it represents a notion of far greater antiquity in India. The Chandella kings who ruled that region followed and fostered a Tantric form of Hinduism that invested sexual activity as such with a sort of divine aura. But temples saturated with erotic motifs and practices had by then been for many centuries well established, not to say commonplace, in Indian society. Ritual coitus (*maithuna*) is mentioned in the Vedas as part of the temple worship in this particular tradition. The Hindu temple could very naturally be seen, then, as a sort of stepping stone to future bliss in the afterlife; hence the promise of total sexual fulfillment in an afterlife so conceived.

Whether inspired by such models in India or emerging independently, similar images of an afterlife of unremitting sexual activity can be found in antiquity all over the Mediterranean world, where temples including erotic dances and temple prostitution were standard features of the social scene and could easily be seen by their devotees as providing foretastes of a superlatively erotic afterlife. That such images of afterlife bliss were the result of the wishful thinking of the unreflecting populace is too obvious to need any supporting argument. Sexual activity was not only the most intense but the highest form of bliss that the masses could be expected to imagine and so every form of it was celebrated in the iconography of cults of this kind, including, for instance, representations of soldiers and others separated for long periods from women resorting to copulation with animals. To men so deprived, dreams of a goddess of love (Astarte, Aphrodite, Venus) who provided in her temples fair and seductive enchantresses would seem as dreams of oases in the desert of human life. What more natural than that such a goddess of love should provide in an afterlife an infinity of such delight? If in the midst of the death-dealing desert even a mouthful of water may seem the greatest of all possible treasures, surely one's dreams of an everlasting paradise will be along the lines of an infinite and everlasting river of fresh spring water ensuring that one will never thirst again.

CHAPTER VII

Monism and Monotheism: Two Visions of Afterlife

Do not let your heart be troubled. . . . There are many rooms in my Father's house.

—John 14:2 (Jerusalem Bible)

In spite of the vast diversity of religious concepts to be found at all levels of development and issuing in variegated notions about afterlife, serious thought about the nature of ultimate reality generally moves in one or other of two general directions, each resulting in what is (or at any rate seems to be) a fundamentally different understanding of the nature of what we may expect to happen when we are said to die. The one is called Monism, the other Monotheism. Let us first distinguish them very broadly. Then we shall consider the distinction with greater precision.

Monism

Monism is the metaphysical view that all reality is fundamentally of one "substance" or character. This view is of great antiquity, although the term entered the philosophical vocabulary only in the eighteenth century, apparently coined by Christian Wolff. A monist's view of afterlife will inevitably reflect the presupposition that I am one with that one, universal reality, although I am not currently able fully to understand that great truth. Since, however, I participate in the immortality of all things, I will change and develop in one way or another after death until at last I realize myself as one with the Eternal One.

Monotheism

By contrast, monotheism is the view that stresses the immense gulf between me, as a creature of God, and God who has created me. This gulf is insuperable. I can never be God, no matter how I may advance in spirituality or love. At a certain point in the history of the Hebrew people, which we may plot at sometime about the sixth century B.C.E., this was the stance that had been taken by some of their leaders and had begun to influence the general outlook of their society. The god they had long worshipped as their national god could now be seen as the God of all nations, all peoples. This god is not only the god of Israel, ready to fight for his people as any national deity is expected to do. He is the God of all peoples, the Creator of the universe, including humankind. He will *judge* Israel as he will judge all peoples. He will do so equitably, for he is by his nature just. Likewise he will show mercy and compassion and extend forgiveness to all, for they are all his creatures. As their Creator he looks upon them as a loving father. He cares for them as a shepherd for his sheep.

The first thing to know about him, however, is that he is "the Other," the Creator of all things. Plainly, on this view I can never "become God." My goal is by no means to realize myself as God, as being in the stream of divinity. It is, on the contrary, to perceive more and more fully that God is my source, that I owe to him my entire being. Assured of my Creator's love I can confidently place myself within "the everlasting arms" of his care.

True, this awareness gives me no *immediate* sense of afterlife with him. It requires some philosophical reflection to draw forth the implications of the assurance. Nevertheless, the assurance of joyous afterlife of some kind is already implicit, for example in the loveliest of the psalms, Psalm 23: "The Lord is my Shepherd; I lack nothing." That Yahweh was the Shepherd of Israel was a common theme, but here the psalmist proclaims him to be his personal shepherd. This points to the gradual development of the importance of the individual against the traditional concept of the community as the object of God's love and care. The original Hebrew probably does not warrant allusion to the valley of death (only a dark valley such as abound in Palestine) or to dwelling in the house of the Lord forever (only to dwelling "all the days of my life"); nevertheless, such is the spirit of the psalm that the transition to such a hope would be easy for one who had taken in the implication: this Shepherd will *never* forsake his sheep. To the extent that I put my trust in this God, I have nothing to fear and everything to hope for. Eventually the hope became in popular language *Heaven* and in more learned language *the Beatific Vision*, about which we shall have more to say later. To deprive oneself of its bliss came to be called *Hell*, which will also be the subject of later consideration.

Whenever thoughtful people emerge out of the confusion of the vague gropings of primitive religious sentiment to philosophical reflection on their intellectual entailments, they express the result in one of several ways. We have noted that the two most influential ways in the history of religious thought have been monism and monotheism. Each has its own effect on the view of afterlife. Let us look first at the monistic option, which has had notable exemplars in India.

Afterlife in Hindu Thought

India is a region of immense antiquity that already contained, as noted, a much-mixed population long before even the first wave of Nordics entered it sometime between 1700 and 1500 B.C.E. (They are often called Aryans, a designation that simply means "noble" and has the same root as *Iranian*.) The so-called Vedic period in Indian literature may be said to date from about 1500 to 800 B.C.E. It was in general a period of forward-looking exuberance: an exuberance expressed in the literature of that period. While there are copious references in that literature to a large variety of gods and other agencies, we find, especially toward the end of this period, a longing for a solution to the intellectual problems that arise out of any mythopoeic, polytheistic ideology.

For long the Aryans were no doubt too much engaged in conquest to give much attention to intellectual problems of this kind. A light-skinned people of Indo-European stock, they poured from the northwest over the Hindu Kush mountain passes. Tall, energetic, and ambitious, they drove all obstacles before them as, moving east and south, they subdued the black-skinned native populations. They did not stop till they had brought the entire region of north and central India as well as the Ganges delta under their control. They transformed but were also in part transformed by the peoples they conquered.

Yet even in such times of military preoccupation are to be found hints of authentic reflection by some. Was there an eternal One, a principle, a power, a being, before the universe as we know it existed? Before even the mightiest of the gods and goddesses? Well known to scholars are lines from one of the hymns of the *Rig Veda*:

> They call it Indra, Mitra, Varuna, Agni,
>   and it is heavenly, noble-winged Garutman.
> To what is One, sages give many a title:
>   they call it Agni, Yama, Matariśvan.

More striking still are the speculations expressed in this literature that exhibit concern over problems that have occupied the attention of the greatest minds in the history of human thought. In their own way these Indian sages were raising a question that two great thinkers in the history of Western philosophy have posed, each in his own way and in very different circumstances. Leibniz in the seventeenth century C.E. and Heidegger in the twentieth have raised the question in this form: Why is there anything at all and not just nothing? This may be regarded as the most fundamental, the most radical question that can be asked. The early thinkers in India were groping for the answer to it.

In the tenth book of the Vedas, in Hymn 129, an ancient Indian writer claims that his predecessors among the sages of India had already seen a mysterious connection between *Sat* (Being) and *Asat* (Non-Being). He entertains a scenario that for those in the Judeo-Christian tradition the familiar first version of the Creation story (in fact the later of the two biblical accounts of Creation) seems to echo:

> There was neither *Sat* nor *Asat*:
> There was no air, nor firmament beyond it.
> Was there a stirring? Where? Beneath what cover?
> Was there a great abyss of unplumbed water?

83

There was no death nor anything immortal;
Nor any sign dividing day from night.
That One Thing, given no breath, was yet self-breathing;
No second thing existed whatsoever.

Yet in contrast to the first chapter of Genesis, the Indian writer offers no definite answer to the question. He provides no dogmatic assertion about it. Recognizing that the gods came later than the creation of the universe, he leaves dangling the question whether the universe created itself or was made by a power or agency other than itself. Under all his questions, however, lies the presupposition of the unity of all things, a One to which all belongs. The writer ponders again: this One, this eternal principle or whatever it may be must surely know the answer to the riddle. But then, he muses, perhaps even the One does not know the answer! What he seems never to doubt is that there is such a unity in all things. In the last resort, all things are one, be the One a "person" or a "thing."

As we enter the period of the great literature called the Upanishads, which spread over several centuries and may be said to conclude some time about 300 B.C.E., we find a change of mood. It may be regarded as in some ways a development of Vedic thought, but if so it is a very special form of development. The upanishadic literature is extremely varied, both in outlook and in form. Some of the Upanishads that are in prose—the longest (the *Chāndogya*) and the *Brihadāranyaka*—are probably the earliest; others are in verse. Many are in dialogue form. Although the priestly or Brahmin class composed much of this literature, Kshatriyas (the warrior class) apparently composed some of them. Certainly Kshatriyas are represented as participating in the discussions. So also are women who, as in Plato's philosopher class, are clearly represented as functioning equally with men.

The upanishadic mood, however, for all the diversity of its forms, has a certain common characteristic. It is a movement away from priestly ritual and toward *moksha*, the liberation of the soul from the oppression of the body. This does not by any means imply an anticlericalism; it does mean that the value of priestly ritual and all that goes with it is seen more and more as only an instrument of the process of *moksha*. What is important for our present purpose is the fact that, in the course of discussions on how to attain this spiritual emancipation, serious philosophical questions arise and are very seriously addressed according to the temper and custom of the age. For example, some reflect a dualistic rather than a monistic solution to the basic problem to be faced, although the tendency is strongly toward monism: all is One. Whether the One is personal or impersonal is discussed and solutions to the problem are proposed, but what matters infinitely more is that in the long run ultimate reality is One.

Self-realization Asceticism is generally applauded as a way of attaining the liberation that is sought; but it is only a way, not an end in itself. What is, however, an end in itself is the realization that the *ātman* or individual soul, being part of the *Brahman-Ātman* or world-soul, finds its self-realization only to the extent that it discovers and knows its identification with the *Brahman-Ātman*. Whether the latter is mind or matter, personal or impersonal, may be a fitting topic for intellectual inquiry and the philosophical discussion that leads to tentative conclusions on such topics; but in the last resort the answer to such puzzles is subordinate to the supremely important self-realization: I am one with the Eternal One. The entire upanishadic adventure, whether seen as intellectual inquiry or mystical enterprise, is ultimately an exercise in inwardness. So, despite the preoccupation of the upanishadic writers with ontological questions, questions about the nature of existence, they are really, however unconsciously, preparing a path toward an outlook that was to become classically expressed in the teachings of Gautama Buddha in a system that is avowedly indifferent to institutionalism of every kind, including caste, and concerned only with the liberation of the individual self.

Karma and Reincarnation In the Upanishads we find well developed the great twin concepts of afterlife that have become so characteristic not only of Hinduism but also of all its offshoots, not least Buddhism: the concepts of reincarnation and karma. We have already seen that reincarnational notions are found at a very early stage in the history of religious ideas, but in primitive, magical, or quasi-magical forms. In the Upanishads, however, we find these old reincarnational beliefs transformed into a highly ethical, plausible, and well-thought-out theory of afterlife: its philosophical basis and the manner in which it works out for the individual.

The typical upanishadic doctrine of afterlife is as follows: "I," the individual self, am in the midst of an immensely long evolutionary process. What I call "this life" is a tiny slice of that process, which is in fact a gradual progression toward oneness with the All, the One, the Great Self, *Brahman-Ātman*. The progression is not a constant movement upward or forward. It may take downward turns, for it is governed by an ethical principle that works automatically, as does the "law" of gravity in the physical universe. This principle is called the law of karma.

The karmic principle is a principle of balance that is expressed in one way or another in all the great religious literatures in aphorisms such as "as one sows, so shall one reap" (compare Paul's letter to the Galatians, 6:7). If in this present life I am domineering or cruel, then in one way or another I shall be placed in my next life in circumstances in which I shall suffer the consequences. The consequences are not punitive but educational. They are a necessary part of my education. To the extent that I am generous or kind I may expect greater opportunities for the exercise of such virtues.

In a sense I may be said to "choose" the womb into which I shall enter. It may be the womb of a mother of high social standing or great intellectual gifts but by no means necessarily so, for that may not be what is most conducive to my progress. I may, rather, be born into circumstances that would by "worldly" standards be accounted miserable and unpromising, for I may need such circumstances for an evolutionary leap that I now have the opportunity of taking.

Who or what is this individual self that I call "I"? According to a Hindu teaching characteristic of the spirit of the Upanishads, the "self" is not simply my soul or spirit, contradistinguished from my body. I am much more complex than that. What for shorthand I may call my "real" self has a series of layers or sheaths of which my physical embodiment is the outer and coarsest. When I die these layers will be stripped off one by one, possibly with long pauses at each stripping, till at last I am reduced to my "naked," inmost self. In preparation for my next physical embodiment I shall spend some time during which I shall see with greater clarity than my carnal encumbrances presently allow me what I really need "next time around." I shall then replace my structure till I am ready to look for and to find precisely the right conception in the right womb for my evolutionary needs, which all along are governed by the law of karma. This journey between one physical embodiment and another may take a long time, possibly centuries, or it may be short, perhaps even almost instantaneous.

Charisma: "Amazing Grace" All this may sound very mechanical. What of that which Christians celebrate as "amazing grace"? There are indeed in upanishadic thought counterparts to what the New Testament and other Christian writers call *charisma* or "grace." As in biological evolution, so in the spiritual odyssey there are evolutionary "leaps." The karmic principle is indeed a free-will principle according to which I bear a solid responsibility for my actions and for my destiny throughout the incalculably long *samsāra*, the chain of re-embodiments, that lies behind me and before me. Yet the karmic law does not exclude help from others more advanced than I in the spiritual process. In Mahayana Buddhism, for instance, the *bodhisattva* is one who has specifically chosen to dally in his progress toward buddhahood in order, out of compassion, to help the rest of us on the path of enlightenment. Such helpers do not relieve us of the need to make our own choices and find our own paths. They do not automatically save us, nor do they do our work for us; but they provide us with conditions favorable to our progress.

In some passages in the upanishadic literature we find talk of terrible karmic consequences for transgressions in the present life: For stealing grain one would become a rat in the next embodiment and for killing a Brahmin one might be reembodied as a pig. As the doctrine developed, however, especially in Buddhism, such ferocious concepts were superseded by more benign interpretations of the working of the karmic law. These gentler interpretations provide for much less drastic forms of transition from one embodiment to another. One may be halted in one's spiritual progress in order to purge oneself of the distortions that one's sins have brought about on one's inner self, but on the whole one's spiritual progress proceeds more regularly.

What is characteristic of all forms of reincarnational theory in those traditions that have their roots in Indian thought is the underlying presupposition that separateness from the Great Self, the One, is intrinsically unhealthy, being due to self-centered desires that alienate the individual from the Great Self. The monistic presuppositions that, generally speaking, dominate this genre of thought determine the way in which the afterlife is conceived. Nevertheless, reincarnational ideas, although very notably found in Indian thought, are by no means confined to India and we shall later consider them in relation to other cultures in which they can and do arise.

Varieties of Religions with Indian Roots

Although from a Western standpoint the great religions that have had their beginnings in the Indian subcontinent tend to be seen as similar to rather than different from one another, the differences are notable. True, they do have some common features; yet even these common features are differently understood and differently interpreted. The concept of karma and its reincarnational implication exemplify these differences, as we shall presently see.

Hinduism, although describable today as a clearinghouse of religious ideas, was originally much more definable as a blood-and-soil religion: the religion, in effect, of the people of the Indus Valley. Revering its first scriptures, the Vedas, it developed the caste system that was for so long to dictate the laws and customs of Indian society. To understand how other great religions took their beginnings we must recognize a certain age that from the standpoint of the historian of religion must be regarded as the most extraordinarily significant in human history and may be said to span the seventh and the sixth centuries B.C.E. In that astonishing period emerged a most remarkable series of philosophical and religious thinkers from Greece to China. India alone cradled Mahavira (the founder of the Jain community) and Gautama (the Buddha).

The Jains The thought and practice of the Jains are distinctively uncompromising. They honor Mahavira (*c.* 540–468 B.C.E.) as the last of twenty-four *tirthankaras*. (A tirthankara is a "ford-finder": one who discovers the way out of the misery that is human life and into the condition of salvation.) In Jain thought atheism is not a mere skepticism about gods; it is a specific repudiation of the concept of deity of any kind. This atheism governs the entire Jain outlook. Jain practice not merely emphasizes but exalts as central two ideals that are both widely respected (at least in theory) in Indian thought: (1) *ahimsā* (nonviolence toward every living creature) and (2) *tapas* (asceticism). It is by the exercise of these two virtues that Jains gain the admiration and veneration of the community, which operates hospitals for rats and other such sentient beings that most would regard as detestable. Jains wear a net or shield over their mouths in hope of avoiding the danger of their inadvertently killing insects and other such entities. [1] Their extremism in devotion to the ideal of nonviolence is matched by their fanatical rigor in the practice of *tapas*, fortitude in the exercise of asceticism, which is especially admired. Jains will torment and torture themselves in ways such as lying on beds of nails, sitting motionless in blazing heat, and so forth. Their strict observance of *ahimsā* entails of course their being vegans—they practice vegetarianism in its strictest form. Some Jains practice nudism as a symbol of the disparagement of the flesh.

Why? Jainism is above all a philosophy of salvation; but from what to what? The Jain view is predicated on the fundamental mind–matter dualism that issues in the notion that matter is the supreme instrument of bondage to this world: a world of total misery. Salvation is salvation from that bondage and the bondage is the result of the inexorable working of the law of karma, on which Jains place special emphasis.

Moreover, in contrast to the upanishadic teachings of classical Hindu philosophy, which are monistic, the Jainist view is a pluralistic one. The universe consists of an infinite number of entities trapped in the misery of matter. Human beings are unique in having at their disposal the means of salvation. In accordance with the atheistic foundation of the Jain outlook, there is never any question of divine help in the process of salvation; indeed, help from any source other than oneself is excluded. Each individual must find his or her own way out of the prison. One may be helped to some extent by the example of others and by listening to the wisdom such exemplars can offer; but in the last resort only self-help can win salvation, for there is certainly nobody else, neither gods nor men, to do it for one. It is rigidly a doctrine of each man for himself.

Jain Image of Afterlife What then is the basic image of afterlife in the Jain outlook? The simple answer is the hope of achieving, over an incalculably great number of reincarnations, such a degree of mastery over all the various kinds of bad karma (there are at least 150 different kinds of such bad karma) as to enable one to obtain release from the prisonhouse of matter and entry into a condition of isolation and separation from it. There is, according to Jain belief, a realm of bliss called *Isatpragbhara* that lies somehow at the "top" of the universe. There the rare individuals who achieve this complete release live on as individuals. One must not indulge, however, in the notion that this is a norm of the human process of salvation. So rough is the road and so full of hazards that few indeed dare hope to attain it. The vast majority must simply go on trying by such feats of *tapas* and such acts of *ahimsā* as they can accomplish. The accomplishment is, however, somewhat like that of taking a hundred separate examinations all of which must be passed in the course of one life. One might in this life pass all of them except, say, examination number 53 and in the next life all of them except, say, examination number 91, and so on indefinitely.

Jainism represents an element in Hindu thought and outlook, but in an exaggerated, not to say distorted, form. The twin ideals of nonviolence and asceticism are certainly represented not only in Hinduism and Buddhism but also in other, if not all other, religions, including of course Christianity. Perhaps one might even go so far as to see Jainism as standing to Hinduism in a relationship somehow analogous to that in which Protestant fundamentalism stands to the mainstream of the Reformation heritage: a parody of, yet at the same time a pointer to, essential ingredients. In any attempt to reconstruct a satisfactory eschatology, the Jain view, with its concept of the eternity of the universe and the sense of the misery of human existence cannot be entirely ignored.

Christian Counterparts

One of the best-known of the recorded sayings of Jesus is: "If anyone wants to be a follower of mine, let him renounce himself and take up his cross and follow me" (Matthew 16:24). "To the man who slaps you on one cheek, present the other cheek too" (Luke 6:29) is no less well known. The former saying has in it something of the Jain principle of *tapas*; the latter accords with the *ahimsā* principle. Yet when the two principles are "translated" from one religion to the other the meaning is radically altered, because the bases of the two religions are fundamentally different. So with any expression of the notion of afterlife in the Jain community. Only by a far-fetched figure of speech might the Jain possibility of release from the bondage of the world and the flesh be called "heaven." The more immediately foreseeable expectation of the Jain seems to have affinities with the Christian purgatory; but even there the affinities are superficial, since only a little reflection is needed to perceive that the Jain understanding of karma and rebirth, while it looks at first blush like an Oriental counterpart of purgatory, lacks the latter's fundamental characteristic and chief joy: the certainty that one is on the way to higher and fuller life.

Gautama the Buddha

The dating of the birth and death of Gautama the Buddha is very controversial, but most Buddhist scholars would place his life somewhere between the middle of the seventh and the middle of the sixth century B.C.E. According to accounts of his early life, he was born of noble parents and reared in comfortable surroundings. Yet he experienced a strange malaise. Predictably, he followed the customary path of spiritual seekers in his Hindu culture, engaging in various forms of asceticism, including severe fasts. At last, seeing the futility of these exercises yet recognizing that they were pointing him toward a solution of his problem, he entered into a lengthy meditation as a result of which he experienced what Buddhists call the Great Enlightenment. Like Mahavira, he had started from the conviction that human life is a state of misery and that the remedy consists of emancipation from whatever it is that binds one to that which produces the misery. Unlike Mahavira, however, Gautama did not see the cure for the disease in such simple terms as emancipation from matter. Gautama saw the root of the human malady as ignorance of spiritual truths. The remedy for the disease is knowledge of how to rid oneself of the cravings that spring from that ignorance. According to tradition he formulated Four Noble Truths: (1) That all existence is *dukkha* (misery) is to be taken as axiomatic; (2) This misery has its roots in *trishna* (ignorant craving); (3) The cure consists in the abolition of the ignorant craving; and (4) This cure can be effected by means of the Noble Eightfold Path.

This path is regarded by Buddhists as a middle way between two extremes: on the one hand, the Jain prescription of extreme asceticism; on the other the pleasure-seeking life of worldlings. It is a middle way that leads to *nirvana*, a state of blessedness. The first two steps on the path to salvation consist of understanding, the acquisition of spiritual wisdom; the next three consist of living a moral life; and the last three consist of mental disciplines that educate one in the capacity to attain *nirvana*.

The Sanskrit term *nirvāna* literally means "extinguished," as one might say of a candle the light of which has been blown out. What is extinguished are the ignorant cravings in which human misery is rooted. The state of nirvanic bliss is one that may be likened to the joy of having learned truths that explain what had been the cause of one's misery.[2] The misery can no longer affect its former victim because he or she now understands the reason why it was there in the first place. *Nirvana* is an intellectual victory and a moral achievement. It is the joy of understanding what has been amiss in oneself and of having cured the malady by facing up to it and dealing with it instead of sweeping it under the rug. In this respect it would seem to be somewhat like treatment by a method such as Jung's analytical psychology, which in effect is intended to deprive the unconscious forces in the psyche of their destructive power. The liberation is through self-knowledge, but the knowledge is not claimed as ontological knowledge, the pursuit of which is discouraged in Buddhism, which is essentially psychological therapy, not philosophical or ontological inquiry.

The karmic principle and the *samsāra* or chain of rebirths associated with that principle were taken over in Buddhism as part of the ideological furnishings of the Hindu heritage. The Buddhists merely abolished their association with the traditional Hindu caste system. Nevertheless, Buddhism has affirmed many ontological assertions, notably about *maya* (the unreality of the empirical world) and the notion that there is no permanent self.[3] As Buddhism spread, however, from India to China, Korea, Tibet, and Japan, it took on many aspects and developed a variety of visions of afterlife. In the *Ching-tu* or "Pure Land" Chinese Buddhist sect, for example, the teachings of which were formulated by T'an-luan (476–542 C.E.), a central feature is belief in a "pure land" or paradise in which through personal devotion to and dependence upon Amida Buddha, including the frequent repetition of his name, one may hope to obtain a place in paradise and so bypass the *samsāra* of rebirths. Such a feature would be plainly antithetical to Jain teachings and inconsistent, to say the least, with the teachings of classic Theravada Buddhism as it is found today, for instance, in Sri Lanka.

By contrast to the "Pure Land" school's vision of paradise, an important mystical school of Chinese Buddhism, the *Ch'an* or Meditation school (which came to China through the efforts of Bodhidharma, an Indian monk, sometime about the late fifth or early sixth century C.E.) taught that through the discipline of meditation one could so overcome craving as to put oneself in the position of attaining Buddhahood. In a sense one does this by one's own efforts, yet they turn out to be not enough. In the end one must let the experience of Enlightenment supervene and take over. This Chinese school provided the roots for what became, in Japan, the form of Buddhism known as *Zen*, versions of which have been very popular in some circles in the Occident.

Generally speaking, such visions of a state of bliss as have been entertained in Buddhism are not focused on anything resembling a Christian concept of heaven or indeed any resurrection hope one might find in Zoroastrianism, Judaism, or Islam. The reason is simple. The resurrection hope in all monotheistic religions is directly focused upon God—who, as the Source of all being, is indispensable to the heavenly vision. Even in Mahayana Buddhism, the general name given to Buddhist groups and sects in China and the other countries into which Buddhism was imported and transformed, the hope of attaining Buddhahood is not to be taken as anything like a Christian hope. For a Buddha is simply one who has attained Enlightenment and, through such attainment, a kind of immortality; he is not at all to be reckoned the Creator or Source of all being. The difference is radical and crucial. Nowhere is it more striking than in images of afterlife.

Negativity in the Karmic Principle

A distinctive feature of the image of afterlife that both Jainism and Buddhism have accepted without question from their Hindu heritage is the doctrine of metempsychosis or rebirth. This doctrine is much discussed in the Upanishads, the great classic literature of Hinduism after the Vedas. There, however, as in the teaching of the religions that have issued from the Hindu parent, such reincarnationism has almost always been seen negatively, that is, as a regrettable consequence of bad karma, never as warranting hope of a future state of bliss. Also distinctive of these Oriental religions is an acceptance of the doctrine that the universe is eternal. It may be "wound" and "rewound" every so many million years with "big bangs" and "whimpers" here and there, but it never came into existence at any one time, nor will it ever go out of existence. Although it is impossible to predicate anything of Hinduism, generally, since it is so hospitable to so many different views, what we are saying here is characteristic of Hinduism itself as well as the specific outlook of the great religions that can claim a Hindu heritage.

The historical fact that the karmic principle and its rebirth implicate have been so generally interpreted in a negative way in the great Oriental religions (that is, as pertaining to human life understood as human bondage) need not exclude other interpretations, as we shall see.

Resurrection in Christian Thought

There is another and very different direction that the development of religious ideas may take: one that issues in concepts of afterlife that fit the monotheistic model briefly outlined at the beginning of this chapter. Since within this model the notion of an eventual realization of oneself as totally unified with the Great Self is uncompromisingly excluded, any concept of afterlife that may be entertained by anyone within such a tradition must follow some other line. There is no compelling reason, however, why any concept of afterlife must immediately ensue. In fact, in the case of the Hebrew tradition in which the Christian faith is historically rooted, no significant consequence did ensue for many centuries after the Hebrew prophets had established the concept of One God as the righteous and loving Creator of the universe.

The Old Testament is virtually silent on the subject of afterlife except in terms of echoes of the old, primitive image of Sheol, the shadowy underground envisioned, as we have already seen, on very much the same lines as the Greek Hades. The first clear hint of an expectation of everlasting bliss or everlasting rejection in the canonical books of the Old Testament occurs in the very late book Daniel, dating from about 165 B.C.E., in which we read that "many of them that sleep in the dust of the earth shall awake, some to everlasting life, and some to shame and everlasting contempt" (Daniel 12:2). By this time, it would seem, such a belief had at last emerged. It is also found in II Maccabees (not a canonical book of the Hebrew Bible): 7:9 and 11:23, and 14:46. (Here, however, it is only a hope for the righteous; nothing is predicted for the wicked.) Both in the New Testament and in Josephus we are explicitly told that the Pharisees believed in some form of resurrection while neither the Samaritans nor the Sadducees entertained any such belief.

A Jewish Distinction

In view of the central premise of this study concerning the intimate relation between the kind of afterlife belief that one entertains and the kind of belief in God that one presupposes, this is a convenient place to provide an example of how the principle works out. It is easy enough to see how it must work as between a monist and a monotheist, whose respective concepts of God are poles apart. Suppose, however, that we raise a question as follows. The Pharisees believed in resurrection while the Sadducees did not; could that really affect their respective beliefs in God? Or could the beliefs of two parties within Judaism differ enough to be reflected in such a difference in their afterlife beliefs?

My learned rabbinical friend and former colleague, Professor Emeritus Samson Levey, in accord with the views of his own teacher, Jacob Z. Lauterbach, provides the following observations, which support my basic premise. The Sadducees had an anthropomorphic view of God, believing that he had a humanlike face and that anyone beholding it would die. They insisted, therefore, that *before* the priest entered the Holy of Holies he must *first* start the burning of the incense so that he would not be in danger of seeing the Face of God and so being struck dead. The Pharisees, by contrast, held that, since God is a spirit, he cannot be seen, and therefore the priest should enter the Holy of Holies before censing it, for there was no reason to fear such consequences.

That points to a difference in their respective images of God; but could that difference issue in the Sadducees' disbelief in resurrection and the Pharisees' belief in it? No, not directly; but that was not the whole of the difference in their belief in God. The Sadducees did not believe in the coming of the Messiah; therefore there would have been no point in a resurrection doctrine, since there would be nothing to which to be resurrected. The Pharisees, however, believed in the coming of the Messiah and a resurrection doctrine could be fitted into that messianic expectation. In any case, the messianic expectation is much more central to Judaism than is any resurrection or other afterlife doctrine that some Jews or parties within Judaism may entertain. In no form of Judaism does resurrection function so centrally as it does in traditional Christian belief.

Returning now to the concept of resurrection itself, the general silence of the Old Testament on the subject of afterlife may be thought to make the novelty of any form of resurrection to everlasting life somewhat startling. Whence did it come? Zoroastrian and other extrabiblical influences are certainly not to be ruled out, but the concept could well have developed gradually out of intellectual reflection on the implicates of the nature of God who had lovingly guarded and guided His people through the ages and therefore would not abandon them now. In the following lines the psalmist, who also laments the proneness of the people to idolatry, exhibits his personal gratitude to and confidence in Yahweh. Again, there is nothing specifically about afterlife in this almost certainly postexilic psalm: *evermore* and *everlasting* mean only, as is common in Old Testament usage "always" or "unremittingly"; nevertheless, the psalmist's confidence is such as to open the door to a development of some form of afterlife, which eventually took shape in Judaism as a resurrection hope:

> So my heart exults, my very soul rejoices,
> my body, too, will rest securely,
> for you will not abandon my soul to Sheol,
> nor allow the one you love to see the Pit;
> you will reveal the path of life to me,
> give me unbounded joy in your presence,
> and at your right hand everlasting pleasures.

> (Psalm 16:9–11, Jerusalem Bible)

This confidence is echoed in Peter's address to the crowd on the day of Pentecost, in which he quotes from this passage in the psalm (Acts 2:25–28).

The nature of the resurrection is left obscure. What we know with any certainty about how Jews interpreted the concept in the intertestamental or any other period is based upon what we know of their understanding of the relation of body to soul. Unlike the prevailing view in Indian thought we have just considered, the Hebrews' understanding of the soul–body relation excluded the notion of a self that can be stripped of its physical sheath as one peels an orange or a banana. A man is a whole entity, consisting of body and soul, so that if there is to be any resurrection, it must be a resurrection to life: the life of that whole entity. Yet this consideration is subordinate, not to say incidental, for the all-important, all-significant concept underlying any expression of a resurrection in this tradition is that belief in some form of resurrection to everlasting life *follows* from the love of the Creator for his creatures: the love of him who cares for the fall of a sparrow, as Jesus, speaking the language of this Hebrew tradition, was to express it, according to Matthew 10:29.

The Nature of the Christian Resurrection Hope

Christian teaching on afterlife, variegated and indeed sometimes confused as it may have become, is the indubitable inheritor of that outlook. The entire notion of resurrection to everlasting life proclaimed in the creeds springs from the central proclamation that Jesus, the Christ, having died, was in some way or other "raised to life." The Christian hope of such resurrection to everlasting life is dependent upon recognition of the resurrection of Christ, through which event—however it be interpreted—the Christian's confidence is warranted. Once again, as Paul repeatedly insists, apart from the raising of Christ to life the Christian would be without hope since, in his view, we are all sinners and "the wage paid by sin is death; the gift given by God is eternal life in Christ Jesus our Lord" (Romans 6:23). How the resurrection is to be interpreted is beside the central point, which is that we, as God's creatures, are totally dependent on him as our Creator; hence our rejoicing at our discovery, through his disclosure of himself, that our Creator is infinitely loving and that therefore "we shall not be afraid when the earth gives way, when mountains tumble into the depths of the sea" (Psalm 46:2).

Resurrection in Islamic Thought

Islam inherited both Jewish and Christian concepts, including notions about afterlife and the reason for hope of it. The pre-Islamic Arabs probably did have some sort of belief in a kind of survival of death; at least such a notion was entertained by some. It was at best, however, without any convincing foundation. Death was thoroughly dreaded. This terror of death as unequivocally the ultimate tragedy is expressed by early Arab poets and even by some writing in the same tradition after the advent of Islam. The poet Ibn Qutayba, for instance, laments that not only does a man disappear after death; his inmost secrets are spread abroad. The poet even hints that in many cases it would be better for him to be forgotten, grim as that prospect might be for those who had deeply loved him. Muhammad's insistence on judgment and resurrection (*qiyāma*), although at first received with scorn, was gradually seen to be intelligible, indeed inseparable, from the extremely strong emphasis in Islamic teaching on the transcendence of God, his unity, his uniqueness, his compassion, and above all his Otherness as our Creator. Modern Muslim exegetes interpret the nature of the resurrection in various ways; but no orthodox Muslim denies the resurrection hope proclaimed in the Qur'ān. The nature of the life that is assured may or may not resemble our present human life, but whatever it is it will be cause for infinite joy. Why? Because it is the fulfillment of the promise of Allah, the Compassionate One.

In neither Judaism, Christianity, nor Islam does the notion of resurrection imply the immortality of the soul. Indeed, that concept, found in Plato and in the entire Platonic heritage of thought, may be seen as alien to the basic outlook of all the monotheistic religions. Certainly Paul lends no support for such a notion. Yet the two notions have been commingled despite the obvious fact that one can hardly find the same kind of cause for rejoicing in the hope of resurrection if one is in fact in any case by nature immortal. Indeed, if one is immortal, what need is there for resurrection as it is proclaimed in the monotheistic religions?

Envoi

Our main preoccupation in this chapter has been to show two radically divergent paths that may be taken when the more primitive forms of religion give way to serious reflection. These two forms are not, of course, the only paths one may take. One may simply renounce the entire project as misguided, being based upon unwarranted presuppositions, and opt instead for relegating religion to the dust heap and with it any hopes or fears one might be entertaining about afterlife. Plainly, at the stage we have been considering here, one would not do this in the way it would be done today or as it would have been done in say, the eighteenth century, but the general motivation would be similar. It would express itself, for example, in a professed conviction that death is indeed the end of all awareness: as much so for human beings as for beetles or mice. Along with this view would go all beliefs that could issue in either a monism or a monotheism or any other form of entity to which a designation such as *God* or *Supreme Being* or *Universal Self* could be assigned. There is nothing radically new in such a contention. Only the form of its expression changes over the centuries.

Such a stance, however, does not really address itself to the most serious questions about human life and death. It ignores, besides much else, the ethical awareness that issues in the concept that whether there be a Divine Judge to pass judgment upon our thoughts and deeds, we all are in some way "under judgment" and death stands as a crucial moment in that judgment. We now turn, therefore, to the concept of judgment, its relation to death, and the crucial role it plays in the religious consciousness of humankind.

Notes

1 Jains do not necessarily always wear such a net or shield. At an international conference of religions I attended in 1985, at which Jains were among the more than 700 participants, a Jain speaker donned such a shield only as he approached the podium.
2 Westerners tend to be repelled by the extreme and recurring emphasis on the theme of the misery of the human condition that they find in Jain, Hindu, and Theravada Buddhist language. That view of our human state is not, however, entirely alien to traditional Christian devotion, less strident though its expression there may be. For example, it is found, albeit in gentler form, in the *Salve Regina*, that beautiful Catholic prayer dating from about the end of the eleventh century and traditionally sung in Latin in the ancient monastic orders after Compline and immediately before retiring to sleep:

Hail, holy Queen, Mother of mercy,
Our life, our sweetness, and our hope,
To thee do we cry, poor banished children of Eve.

To thee do we send up our sighs, mourning and weeping in this vale of tears.
Turn then, most gracious Advocate, thine eyes of mercy toward us.
And after this our exile, show to us the blessed fruit of thy womb, Jesus.
O clement, O loving, O sweet Virgin Mary.

Job paints a gloomier picture and one bereft of hope: "Man, born of woman, has a short life yet has his fill of sorrow. . . . There is always hope for a tree; when felled, it can start its life again; its shoots continue to sprout. . . . But man? He dies, and lifeless he remains" (Job 14:1–10).

3   For an interesting treatment of the problem of the Self in Therevada Buddhism and in Christianity, see Lynn A. de Silva, *The Problem of the Self in Buddhism and Christianity* (Colombo, Sri Lanka: The Study Centre, 1975).

CHAPTER VIII

Judgment

When the mountains shall be set moving,
When the pregnant camels shall be neglected,
When the savage beasts shall be mustered,
When the seas shall be set boiling,

When Hell shall be set blazing,
When Paradise shall be brought nigh,
Then shall a soul know what it has produced.

—Qur'ān, S. 81:3–14

The association of death with judgment arises in people's minds as soon as they achieve awareness of the force of an ethical power in the governance of the universe. This awareness may be expressed in terms of the holiness and righteousness of a Supreme Being or as a karmic principle or Kantian moral law. Death is a traumatic event even for an observer, even indeed for the least morally sensitive of observers. When, however, one has developed any clear sense of the significance of the ethical dimension, death calls attention to something from which one is normally shielded by the bustle, the cares, and the enjoyment of human life. Not only does death confront one with a recognition of the brevity and precariousness of human life; it seems to bring into relief whatever ethical awareness one has so far attained. When such ethical awareness has reached the point of affecting one's religious outlook, that outlook is radically changed. For instance, one is no longer in fear of the power of the dead to return to haunt and torment the living, but one may be troubled by fear of judgment that may bring painful consequences. The entire mind-set will have been radically changed by the new focus of one's religious outlook.

Egyptian, Zoroastrian, Hindu, and Other Sources

We may well look first at ancient Egypt, noted for an intense interest in immortality for which the mummification process was regarded as a preparation. In the so-called Pyramid Texts, which date from about 2350 B.C.E., entry into immortality is presented as a sort of combination of military conquest and diplomatic success, both achieved more or less by cunning and deceit. By contrast, at a later period in Egyptian antiquity we find that admission to the Kingdom of Osiris, the realm of bliss, is by a moral examination. Many pictorial representations depict the soul brought by the jackal-headed Anubis, who guards the cemetery, into the great Hall of Truth for this examination. Osiris himself, king of the realm of bliss, presides over the process, attended by Isis and Nephthys. The deceased person pleads his or her own case to the judges. Then Anubis places on one side of the Scales of Judgment the dead person's heart and on the other an ostrich feather. If the heart is lighter than the feather, the soul is deemed worthy to enter the kingdom of bliss. If, however, the scales show the soul to be heavier than the feather, the fact is taken to be evidence that it is encumbered by evil, whereupon the soul is taken immediately for punishment. The nature of the punishment varies from one account to another. According to some reports the soul is flung into a fiery furnace; according to others it is eaten by a ravenous monster lying in wait for such opportunities. By all accounts the soul's fate is determined by success or failure in the examination in the Judgment Hall.

As noted in an earlier chapter, judgment also played a prominent role in the Zoroastrian concept of afterlife: predictably, for Zoroaster saw all human life as a constant struggle between the good spirit of Ahura Mazda and the evil spirit of his enemy, Angra Mainyu. Zoroaster, whose dates are very uncertain but whom scholarly Iranian tradition has generally placed in the seventh century B.C.E., taught an ethical monotheism. He believed that Ahura Mazda, despite the immense power of his Adversary, would in the long run prevail. He taught that in the end a general resurrection would take place and all persons would have to pass through a terrible fire. In some versions of the Zoroastrian judgment, the righteous will pass through this fiery ordeal unharmed and without pain, while the unrighteous will find the fire a cruel agony.

As in Christian and other conceptions of afterlife, however, much confusion attends Zoroastrian accounts of the ordeal of judgment. For example, each individual is judged either immediately upon death or on the fourth day thereafter and an examination somewhat analogous to the Egyptian procedure is administered. Each individual is confronted with the Chinvat Bridge, which lies across the abyss that is hell and leads at the far end to the realm of bliss. The righteous, being morally straight and upright, will have no difficulty in crossing the bridge. The others, stricken by their own awareness of the evil within them, will falter as they reach the middle of the bridge, lose their balance, and fall, plunging into the Zoroastrian hell, often called "The House of the Lie": a dark and foul place in which each individual will be forever alone. Although according to some accounts the individual is first judged before passing across the bridge, one really brings upon oneself the bliss of heaven or the misery of hell, as the case may be, as surely as if there were no formal judgment. Justice automatically ensues as surely as if the souls were chemical compounds being analyzed in a spiritual dimension of being. We should perhaps note in passing that the funeral practice of exposing the dead in the Towers of Silence (traditional to this day among most Parsees and other Zoroastrians, although some now resort to cremation) expresses a distaste for contaminating the soil of the earth with the decomposing body of the deceased. The Towers of Silence consist of an elevated platform on which the bodies of the dead are exposed so that the flesh will be promptly stripped from the bones by waiting vultures.

Hinduism encompasses and is hospitable to such a vast and variegated number of religious ideas that we need not be surprised at any conception of afterlife that may be found there, ranging from the most primitive to the most thoughtful. Nevertheless, among well-educated Hindus and Buddhists, some form of reincarnational teaching, developed in the light of a highly ethical understanding of the karmic principle, pervades all teaching about the long pilgrimage of the individual self and its destiny. Judgment is automatic and ongoing, but it occurs specifically between embodiments.

Practical Consequences Before we go on to consider other forms of the concept of ethical judgment in relation to afterlife, it will be convenient and profitable to pause here to contrast the practical results of such highly developed ideas of judgment based upon ethical principles of one sort or another with the notions that prevail in those primitive cultures in which no such ethical concepts have been developed. Compare, for instance, what we have already found among the ancient Egyptians and in the Zoroastrian tradition, as well as in Hinduism and its Buddhist offshoot, with the absence of such an element among, for instance, the Dieri aborigines of Australia. Elaborate rites attended the funeral arrangements prepared for a dying member of this tribe; none, however, seems to have had any discernible ethical reference. Such rites refer, rather, to the fear of the dead that we considered briefly in Chapter VI. The relatives of a dying man of the tribe separated into two groups. One group, consisting of his father, his uncles, and his uncles' children, together with certain women who, according to totemic rules would have been possible wives of the deceased, hovered nearby and flung themselves upon his corpse as the breath left his body. The other group, comprising his mother, her sisters and brothers, and various other relatives, remained at a distance lest the dead man should so long for them that he would draw them to himself and so cause (as they apparently supposed) their deaths. The men of this latter group then dug a grave for the deceased, while those of the former group painted themselves white with gypsum as a token of their mourning. One of the older men entered the grave and cut off as far as possible all fat from the various parts of the corpse. These fatty parts were then distributed and eaten in turn by the relatives according to a cannibalistic tribal rule. Various rites and ceremonies expressed the terror that the tribe felt at the possibility of the deceased's attempting to return to haunt the living, even draw them to the land of ghosts. They might tie his feet together, for instance, and then, the day after the burial, they would check the surrounding ground for evidence of tracks.

At such levels, fear of the dead is often mingled with respect and veneration for ancestors—attitudes that often persist when the society has advanced far beyond primitive, magical notions but may well continue to lack any content of the sort that could be hospitable to ideas of judgment such as could be expected to affect the course of the future life of an individual.

Chinese Religion

Ancient Chinese religion, for instance, which far antedates Confucius, Lao-tzu, and the Buddha, seems to lack a sense of the *kind* of divine judgment that we have seen in one form or another in ancient Egyptian religion and in the Zoroastrian tradition: no perilous bridge poised above a valley of fire arranged to receive miscreants; no scales for souls to be weighed by balancing against a feather. Chinese attitudes to religion are, however, notoriously syncretistic. Since the advent of new sages such as Confucius and Lao-tzu and the considerable influence of Buddhism, sharp distinctions such as are customary in the West between, say, a Roman Catholic church and a Jewish synagogue or even between a Baptist and a Methodist church have been alien to the Chinese temper. So one need not be surprised to find, as one often finds today, temples hospitable to two or three or even almost all of the various forms of religion that have found adherents among the Chinese. A sign announcing Taoist-Buddhist Temple or the like is quite common; I have seen many such signs in the Orient. Moreover, ancestor worship, as Westerners traditionally call it, has a pervasive influence on all Chinese, irrespective of the demands of the various religious options. The ancestors are generally recognized to have notable powers to visit their anger on those who fail to give them the respect that is their due, but such consequences arise in the way in which living people may obtain vengeance upon one another for real or imaginary wrongs. That is neither the kind of moral judgment that springs from beliefs such as underlie Christian and other attitudes toward death and afterlife; nor yet is it that which is at the heart of, say, acceptance of the karmic law as an eternal principle of all things.

Yet the concept of punishment for vice and reward for virtue is found very clearly in Chinese religion. Anne Swann Goodrich reports in detail her study of a temple in Bejing that had been built possibly in the Yüan dynasty (1279–1368 C.E.) and certainly no later than the Ming dynasty (1368–1644 C.E.) in which eighteen "hells" are represented, each portraying a different form of torture (see illustrations on pages 106 and 107).[1] This scenario reflects Taoist and Mahayana Buddhist concepts that had by then exerted considerable influence in Chinese thought and lore. The concept of judgment that pertains to it springs of course from an interpretation of the karmic principle.

Westerners should note a radical difference between what are called "hells" and the traditional Christian concept of hell: The former, horrific though they are, are not everlasting. Through prayer and other spiritual exercises those suffering in a Chinese hell may be released or their torments mitigated. True, one may suffer for an enormous length of time; nevertheless, not everlastingly. Ideologically, the Chinese hells may be said to correspond to the more penal of the concepts of purgatory in Christian tradition.

Superstitions abound: Feng-tu Tati is the supreme god of hell and people passing by the city of Feng-tu are reported to have heard the cries of those being whipped inside the cave that is believed to be the entrance to hell. An ancient ordinance required the people of that city to provide ten bundles of rods every month to be placed in the cave on the first day of the new moon and to take away the discarded ones that had been already used to whip the inmates.

The Confucian element in Chinese religion, on the contrary, is, although highly ethical, notably inhospitable to "supernatural" concepts. Ideas such as divine judgment and the working out of the karmic law are alien to it. A notable Confucian, Hsün-tzu (*c.* 298–238 B.C.E.) specifically rejected ideas of this sort. Wang Ch'ung (*c.* 27–100 C.E.) even more pointedly renounced all "supernatural" notions. The spirit of Confucius, which expresses what is most characteristic of Chinese civilization and culture and is a potent force in the history of human development, is rich in ethical awareness, yet its focus is sharply directed to this-world concerns. Death-and-judgment themes are as alien to this immensely civilized society as they were to some of the most primitive tribesmen of whom we have any knowledge.

So while ethical awareness constitutes an essential *condition* for the development of the concept of a spiritual power far beyond the narrow confines of the human condition and in the long run effectively redressing wrong and establishing righteousness, it is by no means sufficient for the development of any such concept. What more, then, is needed? The answer that spokesmen of all the great monotheistic religions give is clear and unwavering: the disclosure by God the Creator of his own fundamental nature, which leads ineluctably to a recognition of the concept of judgment. This divine judgment is inevitable. It must be seen to be so once we find ourselves confronted by the ethical demands of our Creator, which are absolute. Yet, because so also is the love of God absolute toward his creation, God's justice is unlike anything that passes for justice in the regulation of human affairs. It is not merely tinged with mercy; it *is* mercy and it discloses the superhuman quality of divine mercy. The manner in which all this is revealed to human beings is infinitely varied. The one element that seems constant in all the varieties of its manifestation is that of surprise.

Fig. 7. One of the Chinese hells: the Hell of the Saw. *From Anne Swann Goodrich,* Chinese Hells: The Peking Temple of Eighteen Hells and Chinese Conceptions of Hell, *Plate XXIX. Reprinted by kind permission of the author and the publisher, Monumenta Serica, by whom all rights are held jointly. Original photograph by Professor Robert des Retours. Generally speaking, the punishments in the various Chinese hells are designed to fit the crime: liars have their tongues cut out by hot pincers; women who paint their faces and dress seductively will have their skin stripped off; those who waste oil may expect to be boiled in oil.*

Fig. 8. Another of the Chinese hells: the Hell of Cold Ice. *From Anne Swann Goodrich,* Chinese Hells: The Peking Temple of Eighteen Hells and Chinese Conceptions of Hell, *Plate XXXI. Reprinted by kind permission of the author and the publisher, Monumenta Serica, by whom all rights are held jointly. Original photograph by Professor Robert des Retours. One should note that the basic motif underlying Chinese concepts of hell is that one creates in one's own heart the hell together with the character of the punishment. The Hell of Cold Ice, for instance, has some similarities to (although also some dissimilarities from) the punishment of traitors in the ninth circle of Dante's hell. Callousness is a basic sin in Taoist, Buddhist, and Confucian ideologies and is at the root of treachery.*

Judgment and Eschatology in the Bible

Nowhere before in the history of religion and religious ideas do we find this more dramatically than in the unfolding of the disclosure in Hebrew thought. The Hebrew people emerge in a manner not notably different from that of many others in the course of human history. They have their own ways, of course, but so does every tribe and group, every nation, every empire. Even their traumatic experience of going into exile in Babylonia, although it drove home to them a spiritual dimension in their religion that had hitherto been dormant, was not in itself enough to distinguish them from the general history of humankind. Their prophets, from the eighth century B.C.E., such as Amos and Hosea, pointed their attention to the nature of Yahweh, their traditionally recognized deity. More and more he was to be perceived as no mere tribal or national deity but as the Creator of the universe.

Amos told of his righteousness, his universality, his supremacy; Hosea, in a beautiful allegory, spoke of his love. It would seem from the biblical text that Hosea had married a woman called Gomer who bore him three children. Eventually, Hosea discovered that she had been unfaithful to him. The Bible indicates that she had become a temple prostitute. According to Hebrew law the judgment on an unfaithful wife entailed her divorce. Hosea, in conformity with the law, was in process of putting the standard judgment into effect when suddenly he was inwardly impelled to seek her out and through love of her to "buy her back," forgiving all her waywardness and her infidelities. The message conveyed in the Book of Hosea is that the prophet was led through this personal experience to perceive that if he, a mere man, could exercise such forgiveness, how much more would God's judgment be saturated with a forgiveness far beyond our human dreams.

Isaiah, a great contemporary of Hosea and the author of the first thirty-nine chapters of the biblical book that bears his name, upheld a similar vision of divine judgment. He saw, moreover, in his own way, that for forgiveness to be effectual it must be accepted and that to be able to accept it one must have the loving disposition that issues in trust in the One who forgives. So Jesus (Luke 7:47) assures his hearers that the many sins of the woman of ill repute in the town, who had given him such a loving welcome, pouring out her tears on his feet and wiping them away with her hair, must have been forgiven, for otherwise she could not have been capable of such love. Divine judgment, while it issues from the Eternal One, is multifaceted, appearing to the loveless as wrath and to the loving as mercy.

Such is the theme that is gradually unfolded in the thought of the great prophets of Israel and both inherited and, in Christian eyes, immensely developed in the proclamation of the apostles of the Christian Way who saw in Jesus the superlatively surprising fulfillment of Hebrew prophecy. Indeed there would be a day of reckoning, the Last Day (*dies irae*, the Day of Wrath, as it was to become known in medieval Latin piety); yet those who attached themselves in spirit to the Risen Christ are assured of rising to "new life" with him.

The preoccupation with finality that we find in the earliest expressions of the concept of judgment in the writings of the Hebrew prophets is so strong as to seem almost obsessive. In the midst of the trials and sorrows and above all the outrageous injustices in the world around them they urged their people to trust in God who, because of his power and righteousness, would one day establish a new arrangement of human affairs, a new kingdom in which evil would be punished and righteousness rewarded. This new order would be ushered in dramatically. In the apocalyptic literature of Judaism, also inherited by Christians, the imagery followed the same theme and elaborated it. Representations of judgment as taking place suddenly in an immediate upturning of all things served to instill hope in the future but must have tended to blind the average person to the ongoingness of divine judgment.

The emphasis on finality is expressed in what has come to be called in Christian theology the Éschaton, from the Greek *ta eschata*, "the last things." The use of the term *eschatology* to designate that discipline within theology that treats of final judgment and the afterlife is comparatively modern. A standard dictionary for scholars edited by Sir William Smith and published in London in 1893 calls it "the name that has of late become common for doctrine concerning both the future state of the individual . . . and the end of the world with its accompanying events." The concept, however, seems to be of great antiquity. Even in the eighth century B.C.E. Amos takes for granted (Amos 5:18–20), as part of the conceptual scenario of his audience, the notion of a day of reckoning. He assures the people that the sun on that day is to be eclipsed (Amos 8:9). Isaiah warns that on that terrible day Yahweh will cast down what is now exalted. Zephaniah foretells the punishment of crimes and speaks of cries being heard all over the land. The New Testament writers take over the traditional Hebrew language almost without change, except that the role of divine Judge is assigned to Christ, whose Second Coming on that day will ensure the establishment of justice and with it the inevitable overthrow of injustice and the dethronement of evil powers. In the Christian apocalyptic (e.g., Revelation 16:14) a battle is to be pitched between the forces of evil and the armies of God. So horrendous are the events that are to occur on that day of wrath that even the heavens are to be destroyed (II Peter 3:12) and a new heaven and a new earth are to replace the present arrangements.

The date of the awful Day is known only to God, who will not announce it. Even Jesus disclaims knowledge of it. It will come "like a thief" (I Thessalonians 5:2, 4). In Christian eschatology it is also and aptly called the *parousia*, a Greek word by which the early Christians designated the Second Coming in terms of the ceremonial visit of a king to a city within his domain, with perhaps hinted connotations of a tour of inspection. Jesus never so much as suggested a period of time within which the Day might come; on the contrary, because not even he knew the date he emphasized the importance of being ever ready, ever on the alert for it. The designation of Jesus as king (perhaps a little strange to modern ears) was apposite, because one of the most characteristic and basic functions of the Hebrew king was that of judgment (I Samuel 8:5; II Samuel 8:15). The king was the final court of appeal. In Solomon's palace he exercised his judicial function in a room called the Hall of Judgment. So the imagery of Jesus returning as king, the King of Righteousness, come to judge the world and everyone in it, was apt.

Literalism and Allegorization How literally did the ancients and the people of the Middle Ages take such language? On the one hand, there can be no doubt that some people would take it quite literally, as some do to this day. There are people in every age who are for one reason or another mentally incapable of understanding and appreciating allegorical language. On the other hand, it is true and easily demonstrable that far more people in antiquity and in the Middle Ages instinctively interpreted biblical language allegorically. Even today countryfolk, being close to nature, are generally less prone to fall into the literalistic trap in which the modern metropolitan dweller is so easily caught. True, it was in Alexandria, one of the great centers of life in the ancient world, that allegorical appreciation of the Bible and of religious concepts generally was conspicuously well developed by both Jews and Christians, but not even Alexandria was a megapolis in the sense in which New York or Los Angeles is so called today. Today, a worker in Manhattan who lives in one high-rise building and works in another day after day in a world of computers, telephones, typewriters, and fax machines is so estranged from the realm of the spirit that he or she can hardly be expected to understand biblical language. Learning this language is, moreover, a far more difficult enterprise than an American's learning, say, French or German or even Japanese. The thought-mold is radically different from that of the marketplace of today. The barrier to understanding is a "barrier beyond words."

While today, not least in our great urban sprawls, the peril we face is that of approaching literature such as the Bible in an excessively literalistic way, the danger in the Middle Ages was the reverse: that of overallegorization. Not only was the thoughtful peasant in the time of Dante less likely, in hearing the priest's homily at Mass, to be caught in the trap of the literalism that so easily ensnares the well-educated accountant or engineer today, but biblical scholars in the Middle Ages were more likely to be entrapped by a web of fanciful allegorization of the Bible—so much so, indeed, that from time to time they were summoned (by the Victorines, for instance) to beware of such fancies and to work instead under a banner bearing the salutary watchword "Back to the text!"

In interpreting the Day of Judgment we must not entirely exclude the vision of a cataclysmic event at what the New Testament and other early Christian writers call "the end of the age." All ages must end and are indeed ending all the time, and presumably we are warranted in expecting that planet Earth itself will not survive forever. The universe itself may come to an end, if only to be supplanted by another heralded by yet another "big bang." The concept of divine judgment, however, is not to be restricted to any such remote event. It is to be understood, rather, as running through the course of history and even including individual human life, although the rhythm of God be so different from ours that we cannot see it except in rare flashes of insight with which our Creator may sometimes favor us. Such, at any rate, are the lines on which the operation of divine judgment must be understood within the monotheistic tradition.

Judgment in Islamic Thought

Nowhere is this monotheistic climate of thought more vividly felt than in the great civilization of Islam, in which the promise of resurrection (*qiyāma*) from the dead and divine judgment runs right through the Qur'ān. Some sort of vague notion of afterlife seems to have been not entirely alien to the pre-Islamic culture that flourished in Southern Arabia from possibly as far back as about 1000 B.C.E. Archeological evidence of special care for the dead indicates a concern such as is common in primitive societies all over the world; yet it seems to have consisted largely of an idolizing of famed or beloved "men of old" and notions somewhat similar to those of Hades and Sheol—a far cry, to say the least, from the vigorous preaching of Muhammad about the eschaton as he portrayed it. In classical Islam the belief in resurrection and judgment, which no doubt was ridiculed at first by Muhammad's fellow Arabs, came to be central to the Islamic faith, inseparable indeed from the emphatic, not to say strident, emphasis on the unity of Allah and his sovereignty over all his creatures. At the resurrection, Allah would personally retrieve the bodies of the dead and join them to their respective spirits, giving them new life as at the first he had given life to Adam and Eve.

Despite much confusion about the resurrection so vehemently insisted upon in classical Islam, one point is unwaveringly taught: none will escape judgment. Descriptions of the nature of the judgment vary from one interpreter to another, but the Qur'ān itself alludes more than once to a principle of balance (mīzān) and to the plural form of that term (mawāzīn). The latter suggests the scales of justice, the "weighing" that we have seen in ancient Egyptian religion. Is it fanciful, however, to see in the use of the singular form (mīzān) a hint, at least, of the idea of karma that is, as we have seen, so central to Hindu thought about judgment and afterlife? No two of the great religions of the world are so sharply opposed in so much and at so many points as are Hinduism and Islam; yet the karmic principle seems clearly to be at the root of their respective concepts of the reckoning or judgment associated with death and re-embodiment, vastly different though their respective uses of imagery may be.

While Islamic thought on judgment and other afterlife questions allows for great diversity of interpretation, one fundamental principle governs the Muslim outlook in a very distinctive way. It is this: Islam, although it entails individual submission to the will of Allah, is first and last a *community*. Muhammad intercedes for the community. Whatever the hope of afterlife and however it be interpreted, it is inseparable from the community that is Islam. The important implications of this basic element in Muslim thought are well brought out in Professor Jane Smith's Ingersoll Lecture at Harvard in 1977.[2] To attempt in any way to detach oneself from the community is to detach oneself from whatever is promised in the Qur'ān, which is the revelation of Allah to the community of Islam. As in a certain stage in the development of the people of Israel, God made his covenant not with individuals but with the whole people, so such an emphasis on the Islamic community persists in Muslim thought.

Classical Islamic teaching never really deviated from the basic imagery of

112

resurrection that it drew from the Qur'ān. Such traditional teaching reflected an uncritical reading of the Bible, resulting in a fundamentally unintelligible picture of the eschaton. Nor could we expect otherwise. True, the Islamic world, in the heyday of its missionary success and intellectual leadership in mathematics and the natural sciences, was so far-famed that Jewish and Christian scholars were frequenting Muslim seats of learning. (As late as the twelfth century the most revered Jewish thinker in the Middle Ages, Moses Maimonides, did so.) Nevertheless Islam, despite its prowess in certain fields of human inquiry, was for one reason or another insulated from the *kind* of critical thought that was then about to burgeon in the West, where it would eventually bloom and transform Western thought. Gradually, however, Muslim scholars, while remaining faithful to the Qur'ān, began cautiously to reinterpret it at certain points.

An interesting and important example is the interpretation given by some Muslim scholars in modern times to the term *barzakh*, which is used at least twice in the Qur'ān and has traditionally been understood as a barrier between the realm of the living and that of the dead: a barrier that makes communication between the one and the other impossible. In more modern times, however, Muslim commentators have offered a variety of interpretations subtly affecting the traditional thrust. Among the most interesting are those that recognize an evolutionary principle that breaks down even this barrier. This evolutionary principle is not only biological; it is ethical and spiritual as well. Even death cannot halt the evolutionary process. So, on such a daring hypothesis, we may find at least hints of a sort of Islamic doctrine of purgatory. Through continuing education and purification the soul continues its progress beyond death and before resurrection. This stage is more a slice of the soul's pilgrimage than a state. Some have even likened it to a period of gestation in the womb leading eventually to a new kind of birth. Many, especially in Egypt, have been deeply influenced by parapsychological studies in Britain, Europe, and the United States and have applied them within the parameters of Islam. The *barzakh*, in the thought of such modern interpreters, might even be said to designate the spirit world through which one passes en route to the eventual resurrection. It is a closed "area" to those on this side of death and so is in a sense a veil; nevertheless (and here is a crucial provision) some in the spirit world may be granted, for special reasons, God's permission to become available to help those on this side of the veil who seek such help. With this proviso goes, however, the prudent warning that not all communication with the spirit world is desirable, for besides the spirits who are willing to help us and capable of doing so are

Fig. 9. Muhammad's Ascent into Paradise. *Reproduced by permission of the publisher, Anton Hiersemann Verlag, Stuttgart, from J. Christoph Bürgel and Franz Allemann,* Symbolik des Islam *(Symbolik, vol. 20), p. 131. The Prophet's countenance is veiled. The angel Gabriel and he are enwrapped in the prophetic flame. Angelic hosts and houris attend the Prophet, bringing him a variety of dishes.*

Fig. 10. A Muslim Vision of Paradise. *Reproduced by permission of the publisher, Anton Hiersemann Verlag, Stuttgart, from J. Christoph Bürgel and Franz Allemann,* Symbolik des Islam *(Symbolik, vol. 20), p. 134. A benevolent spirit* (jinn), *enthroned in a tree accessed by an ornamental stairway, is served by houris and watched over by a god. This miniature (c. 1500 C.E.) is from West Turkestan.*

others who are not only malignant but also eager to enter into communication with us for our hurt. Therefore one should be extremely cautious in attempting to open up any lines of communication with the spirit world, since by the laws of probability one is more than likely to be besieged by a Pandora's box of evil spirits that may well hamper rather than promote communication with the loving and friendly ones whom we would so much welcome.

Such notions bear a remarkable resemblance to those proposed by some of us in the Christian tradition who are hospitable to the work of psychical research. Aware of the dangers of two-way traffic with those on the other side of the veil, we pray the ancient Catholic prayer that they may rest in peace: *requiescant in pace*. Nevertheless, if they are willing and have the blessing of God on the enterprise, we may open the way for them insofar as God is pleased to grant safe conduct for them and to us freedom from harm.

Above all, however, *barzakh*, the "barrier" that is essentially governed by the same principle of spiritual evolution that governs life as we know it on this side of the veil, is part of the ongoing process of judgment. It is, so to speak, judgment in another key. In that spirit world Allah reigns as he reigns here. He likewise continues to protect those who are faithful to his commands and responsive to his love. Some of those in the spirit world may be too busy with their purification to spare us much time, if any, so we may be unable to feel the vibrations of their presence. Others may be ready and able to manifest themselves to us in such a way as to promote our welfare. All this seems remarkably conformable to enlightened Christian views of purgatory as an intermediate state of purification. Anglican scholars affected by Tractarian interpretations of the concept of purgatory have long entertained such hypotheses. In Islam, as in the Christian Way, all is under the judgment of Him who is Sovereign over all. Even in such dangerous terrain the faithful may walk as fearlessly as the Psalmist (Psalm 23:4) proposes to walk through even the darkest of valleys, fearing no evil, because God himself is there to guard and guide him.

This intermediate state, however its nature be interpreted, is a prelude to the resurrection, which is attended by judgment of a more decisive order. Although modern Muslim scholars may interpret the resurrection in varying ways also, the finality of the judgment associated with it generally remains inviolate. What is distinctive of Islam is of course the sacrosanct authority of the Qur'ān. No matter with what ingenuity the commentators may handle the sacred text, it remains unique as the lodestone of Islamic faith.

Nevertheless, conceptual imports from non-Islamic and extrabiblical sources are to be found, introduced no doubt to give life and color to the central teachings of the Qur'ān. For instance, the notion of a bridge (*ṣirāṭ*) spanning the fires of hell, over which all must pass on the Day of Judgment, is almost certainly a Zoroastrian import, although industrious interpreters may invoke two references in the Qur'ān (S. 36.66 and 37.23f.) as providing at least an appearance of authority for such imagery. Muhammad himself leads the faithful across the bridge, which they find wide and well lighted, while for the evildoers it shrinks to the thinness of a sword's edge even as they are engulfed in darkness so that they inevitably lose their balance and drop to their doom.

Judgment and Reincarnation in Islam

The fearsome finality of Judgment-Day imagery, in which the reckoning is made on the basis of one life that is of unpredictable duration, is mitigated, as we have seen, in the proposals of those modern commentators who provide opportunities for spiritual development between death and resurrection. Such views, however, are aberrant from the mainstream of Islamic theology. Even more aberrant in Islamic thought is the concept of re-embodiment or reincarnation in our present human state on this planet Earth: a widely held notion and one that is virtually universal in Hindu and Buddhist thought and has a considerable history within both Judaism and Christianity, albeit an underground movement in these two religions and in the West generally.

Despite the striking adaptability of a reincarnational scenario to the aims of those Muslim scholars who have tried to introduce into Islam some means of spiritual advancement in the afterlife between death and resurrection, reincarnation (*tanāsukh*) has found little favor, generally speaking, even among those who have been so ready to entertain ideas of evolutionary progress beyond the grave. Even the Sufis, who may be said to represent the mystical wing of Islam, have generally rejected reincarnation no less than do orthodox Muslims, although with some exceptions.

Reincarnation is vital to the teaching of the Druze. The Druze, however, although evolved from the Ismaeli faction of the Shi'a branch of Islam, would be regarded by orthodox Muslims as having moved beyond both the Qur'ān and the Hadith (the corpus of traditions that play a very important part in the interpretation of Islamic law and the way in which Islamic practice has evolved) and therefore cannot, from any orthodox Muslim stance, be re-garded as within the Islamic community. Still, they do represent an extraordinarily interesting development in the history of religious thought. Moreover, their reincarnational theory includes the concept of immediate re-embodiment with no interval between one incarnation and another; that is, one passes directly from the moment of death in one's last embodiment to the moment of one's conception in the present one. For the Druze, judgment is an ongoing process throughout these uninterrupted re-embodiments.

The Concept of Self-Judgment

The concept of automatic judgment or self-judgment is present in all religions that have reached a stage in which ethical factors play a fundamental role. In the monotheistic religions, however, the nature of judgment is transformed by the profound belief that the ethical factor itself flows from God and so takes its very nature from him. Jesus stressed the inwardness of the ethical: an inwardness that the Law itself can do no more than express. The Pharisees were great upholders of the Law, the Torah. In the eyes of Jesus that was good, but not good enough. He reminded his hearers that the Law forbade, for example, adultery. On the view that he presented, however, "if a man looks at a woman lustfully, he has already committed adultery with her in his heart" (Matthew 5:27f.). This reflects a far higher and much more difficult standard to maintain than that of merely abstaining from an adulterous act. It is also a standard of moral judgment that entails a positive, inward, and individualistic element in which intention is all-important.

What counts before God's throne of judgment is not what one has done or said or even thought; it is, rather, what one has inwardly become. So in the afterlife, when God's judgment is more fully revealed, there will be many surprises, causing much astonishment to those unaccustomed to computing morality by such inward methods. Such injunctions to inwardness are not really alien to any religion that has developed a radically ethical stance; they certainly could not have been alien to devout people, Jews or Gentiles, among those who heard Jesus talk.

According to the Gospel account, however, Jesus emphasized inwardness in a very distinctive way. He used the conventional mode of his time and circumstance in talking about judgment and the coming of the Kingdom of God, but when the Pharisees asked when, precisely, the Kingdom was to come, he answered that the Kingdom of God "does not admit of observation" (Luke 17:20); the Kingdom of God is within you (*entos hymōn*, "within" or "inside" you) (Luke 17:21). It is not a spatially extended area such as Arabia or Gaul. So don't look east or west for it; don't try to plot the latitude and longtitude of God's Judgment Throne. If you do you will be in the wrong dimension.

Judgment in Hinduism, Jainism, and Buddhism

We have been considering at some length how the idea of judgment works out in the various monotheistic religions: wherever, indeed, belief in God as Creator and Supreme Being is established. We ought not to leave this subject, however, without comparing and contrasting the notion of judgment as it emerges in such an ideological climate with the notion of judgment that is so powerful in and central to the very different climate of monistic pantheism so characteristic of the mainstream of religious traditions such as Hinduism, Jainism, and Buddhism. These religions differ in important respects from one another but also share, especially as seen from a Western standpoint, certain common aims that presuppose an outlook radically different from that of the monotheistic religions, from the standpoint of which they seem classifiable as atheistic. Most striking to Western eyes is the fact that they generally see man as having a basic spiritual task: the attainment of *moksha*—release from his present condition. This present condition they see as enslavement of one kind or another. In the Jaina (sic) system the enslavement is seen as enslavement to matter; in Buddhism it is seen, rather, as enslavement to desire; in Hinduism we might say it is seen as enslavement to self-centeredness. All this is an oversimplification, but it will serve for the present purpose. *Moksha* is nevertheless the common aim: liberation from our present condition, making possible our rising out of it to a higher form or state of being. This presupposition is worked out in such a way that it is treated as a fact of "spiritual chemistry"; it requires no "faith" or anything of the sort, being taken as self-evident.

Mahavira (*c.* 540–468 B.C.E.) the founder of the Jaina system, is notably explicit in his repudiation of gods of any kind. Matter is eternal, but it comes in varying densities. The subtlest form is what is called karma-matter, which directly affects the purity of the soul and inhibits the latter's liberation. *Moksha* is impossible without the severe practice of *tapas*, which consists of ascetic renunciation of all thoughts, words, and actions that tie the soul to karma-matter in such a way as to cause it to be, so to speak, stuck into it as if with a sort of glue. *Ahimsā* (nonviolence to any living entity) is first among the five vows that a Jain ought to take, because such violence damages the soul, "glueing" it to karma-matter and therefore making *moksha* all the more difficult to attain. Gluttony, even the mildest form, is obviously also detrimental to one's prospects of liberation. Anger, avarice, and all else that even in the slightest way adversely affects one's self-control must be avoided. Sexual activity is especially dangerous to the soul, because such is the strength of sexual passion that it makes the soul, so to speak, so bonded to matter as to become "thick and sticky" in such a way that liberation becomes supremely difficult. Any sensual pleasure is detrimental, but such is the strength of the sexual instinct that men and women find it often so totally uncontrollable that they must root out all sexual preoccupations with a severity great enough to conquer even the force of their sexual instincts.

What is vital to an understanding of the Jaina attitude here is that it does not issue from a specific ethical principle and certainly not, of course, from any divine command. It is presented, rather, as a descriptive account of a factual situation, as a physician might warn an overweight patient to undertake dietary reform, not because there is anything unethical in being fat but simply because it is dangerous to one's health. Yet underlying the therapeutic language is a perhaps unspoken and even unconceptualized belief that it is morally wrong so to destroy one's health.

Buddhism expresses the process of *moksha* in other terms. The impediment consists in desires and the cure in detachment from all desires. Theravada Buddhism especially resembles, at least to perceptive Western eyes, a therapeutic program rather than an ontological or theological system. It is about salvation (understood as *moksha*, liberation), yet there is in the program an implied ethical injunction: One ought to seek health; one ought not to settle for psychosis.

One need hardly say that in practice of course all these three great religions go far beyond such parameters. Nevertheless, the manner of their focus on *moksha* is such as to invest their concept of judgment with a meaning different from that which it has in Western thought and in the monotheistic religions that have such deep roots in it, including Judaism, which from before the time of Jesus had been so much affected by Hellenistic modes of thought. In all those three Oriental religions *karma* is a central concept entailing a concept of judgment that permeates all such religions, affecting them at every point. Yet the karmic principle is often treated in those religions, not least by their most notable thinkers and leaders, more like a chemical result than anything that could ordinarily be understood as a judgment. The fact that water boils at a certain temperature results from a natural "law," but only by a somewhat contrived sort of metaphor could nature be seen as "passing judgment" on the situation as water comes to a boil. It would be like talking, as we sometimes do, of an angry sea: a fine, if overworked, poetic conceit, but not one that helps much in elucidating the nature of anger. Judgment, in any well-developed ontological or theological system, must be in one way or another independent of any mere analysis of the "laws" of the human psyche.

If, then, the karmic principle is to be adopted into the ideological furnishings of any monotheistic religion, it must undergo a certain transformation in meaning. Indeed it is judgment and must be discussed as such, but in the process of its "naturalization" it will have been transformed. It can function well within its new environment and indeed (as I have argued elsewhere) can abundantly enrich any monotheistic system that embraces it. Its meaning, however, will be changed by the ideological structure of the system into which it has migrated, more especially in face of the sovereignty of God that is at the heart of any monotheistic system.

Notes

1 The lack of the kind of judgment that we find in so many of the great religions of the world does not exclude the idea of afterlife punishment. See illustrations on pages 106 and 107. Anne Swann Goodrich, *Chinese Hells* (St. Augustin, Germany: Monumenta Serica, 1981).
2 Jane I. Smith, "Reflections on Aspects of Immortality in Islam," *Harvard Theological Review*, 70, 1–2, January–April 1977.

CHAPTER IX

Modes of Afterlife

Life is pleasant and I have enjoyed it, but I have no yearning to clutter up the Universe after it is over.

—H. L. Mencken

Here is my Creed. I believe that . . . the soul of man is immortal and will be treated with justice in another life respecting its conduct in this.

—Benjamin Franklin, letter to Ezra Stiles

We have considered at some length the concept of judgment as it appears in various forms and both as ongoing and as final. Final judgment implies entry into a new *kind* of life. On the view presented in the New Testament and in other early Christian literature, the situation is very confused. Traditional Christian thought on this subject is, however, highly informative and thought-provoking, not least since it inherits, directly or indirectly, many different strands of human thought about afterlife. We shall leave aside for the moment what happens between death and resurrection, which is a separate question with its own difficulties, and attend to the question: after the Final Judgment, what?

The Christian Doctrine

There is no doubt at all that resurrection is at the very heart of the Christian hope. But what precisely is resurrected? And to what sort of condition? The followers of the Christian Way were discouraged, generally speaking, from engaging in philosophical speculation about such matters. Such was their belief in the imminence of the Second Coming of Christ and of the Last Judgment that would accompany it that on the whole they seem to have been content with being told, in effect: "You'll know soon enough; perhaps even tomorrow, so don't trouble your heads. Prepare for the Great Event by attaching yourselves more and more resolutely and lovingly to the Lord Jesus Christ. That is all you need to know." Paul tells the Corinthians that some people may ask "How are dead people raised and what sort of body do they have when they come back?" He tells them that these are stupid questions and they should know that when one sows a bare grain of wheat into the ground, God makes it emerge from the ground with the kind of body proper to that particular kind of grain. In the resurrection, what is sowed is perishable; what rises from it is imperishable. When the Last Trumpet sounds our present perishable nature must "put on" imperishability; our mortal nature must "put on" immortality (*athanasia*) (I Corinthians 15:35–53).

So resurrection, whatever it is, is to bestow on us an immortality that is alien to our present life, which is by definition mortal. We do not know and we need not know precisely how the seed will flower, but by analogy we can easily see how much more glorious will be the flower than was the seed. Jesus had been asked by the Sadducees, who did not believe in the resurrection, a "trick" question involving marital relationships in the resurrected state and presupposing by implication that matters are arranged "in heaven" somewhat as they are "on earth"; for example, that men and women marry and copulate. No, he assures them, in the resurrected state "men and women do not marry; no, they are like the angels in heaven." Matthew tells us that on this "his teaching made a deep impression on the people who heard it" (Matthew 22:23–33).

Resurrection and/or Immortality? Notions about immortality (*athanasia*) abounded in the Mediterranean world and could not but at least affect the thought of the early Christians as they had affected, to some extent, the thought of Jewish scholars by the time of Jesus. That most perceptive of twentieth-century Jewish scholars, Harry Wolfson, tells of a great rabbi who died in a village some thirty miles from Jerusalem about half a century after the Crucifixion of Christ. This rabbi, when he was dying, told the bystanders that the tears that flowed from his eyes were due to the sorrow that he felt "because his soul, which would survive his body, would have to face the inscrutable judgment of the supreme King of Kings, the Holy One, blessed be He." Early Christian thought could hardly escape the influence of Mediterranean and other "foreign" ideas that had already invaded Judaism. Nor did it.

The Christian Fathers, even as early as Justin Martyr, made a distinction between the "pagan" (e.g., Plato's) concept of immortality and the Christian one. The idea of immortality was of great antiquity, both in popular religion and in philosophical thought. In popular religion the gods were immortal. To be immortal was to be, in effect, godlike. Since the Greeks called any sort of fleeting and local wonder or mysterious force *theos* (god), some confusion attends the use of such language. It is easy enough to see that while every man and woman is bound to die, since that is human destiny, the same cannot be said of a goddess such as Aphrodite or her Roman counterpart, Venus. Such a goddess does not die as do mortal women. She, the very principle of sexuality, lives on through innumerable generations, surviving all their lusts and longings, all their copulations, all their births, as she survives the sexual acts of the myriads of men that are born and die from generation to generation.

It is more difficult to see that every *theos* is immortal. Some *theoi* are nine-day wonders or less. Even today we give some natural phenomena such as hurricanes the names of women: Hilda or Bertha or Kate. They appear briefly and exhibit their stormy temper, their petulance, their rage; they may leave behind them a trail of destruction; but fortunately they do not last forever and so seem to lack the essential character of immortal deities. Still, the principle of which they are but manifestations does have some such immortal quality: hurricanes, like earthquakes, are recurrent phenomena of nature on our planet.

Plato, although he had no less intellectual disdain for popular religion than that associated with his master Socrates, bequeathed to us one of the most impressive of classical arguments for the immortality of the soul. Whatever may have been the ancestry of this concept, it implies some sort of notion such as is expressed in the Stoic idea that the human soul is a spark of the divine fire and so, sharing the immortal nature of that divinity, it is *intrinsically* immortal. The idea that the human soul, although wrapped in perishable bodily "clothing" is thus by its nature immortal, is one that the Greeks could understand, whether they accepted it or not. They could not, however, understand the idea of resurrection. When Paul mentioned it to the Athenians, some of them burst out laughing (Acts 17:32). The Jews, by contrast, were ideologically programmed to take seriously the concept of resurrection, whether (like the Pharisees) they accepted it or (like the Sadducees) they did not. They were not prepared for the idea of immortality, at least not as understood in the pagan world. It was suspect, to say the least, since it implied the notion that they accounted blasphemous: that man has some sort of divinity in him. God had indeed breathed on Adam and so given him life, but that life is mortal; that is, susceptible to death.

True, one of the creation accounts in Genesis seems to presuppose that if Adam and Eve had not eaten the fruit of the forbidden tree they would not have died; but that did not mean that they would have been incapable of death, which is what the "pagan" understanding of immortality means. What Satan, in the guise of the serpent in the Garden of Eden, promised Eve was that she and Adam, if they ate the forbidden fruit, would "be like gods" and therefore immortal in the "pagan" sense of being incapable of death.

With this inheritance of emphasis on the creatureliness of man the Christian Fathers generally contended that the soul is not immortal by its own nature; it can, however, *partake* in the immortality that God wills for it. Through sin it has lost this capacity, but through the resurrection of Christ it has regained it and those who truly adhere to Christ will attain it in the resurrected state of the hereafter. They will attain the immortality that God wills for them. For any biblically oriented thinker, everything, of course, depends upon the will of God to which all is subject. Tertullian, Origen, and Augustine, each very different from the others and all affirming the doctrine of the immortality of the soul, make the distinction between a "profane" immortality doctrine that is widespread and fashionable and a Christian one that takes into account biblical presuppositions. They are in effect reiterating the biblical celebration of the Sovereignty of God.

Confusion in Christian Afterlife Doctrine Nevertheless, it is not very long until this all-important distinction comes to be overlooked. Alongside the still-central Christian proclamation (*kerygma*) of the resurrection of the redeemed we begin to hear not only intimations of the immortality of the soul in its more generally accepted sense but the expression of notions such as that there are sins so grave that they are to be called "mortal" because they "kill the soul," notwithstanding the soul's immortality.

Compounding such confusions, we find the development of the notion that we, as finite beings, are to win "eternal" life. True, the great creeds, both the so-called Apostles' Creed and the Niceno-Constantinopolitan (commonly known as the Nicene Creed although not formulated till 381, more than two generations after the Council of Nicaea in 325), affirm simply belief in "life everlasting" (*zōēn tou mellontos aiōnos*). But most people recite or sing the creeds without entertaining distinctions such as the radical one between eternity and time. Eternity, in the biblical tradition, is an order that pertains to God; time is an order pertaining to man and God's other creatures. In the eternal order of God there is no room for change, development, or growth. So the individuals who "go to heaven" are plunged into perfect bliss (it is perfect because the presupposition is that it cannot be improved upon), while those who "go to hell" are likewise plunged into total torment. It is total because, according to the theologians' formulation, it is *poena damni*, the sense of the total loss of God and, in the more colorful imagery of the popular preachers, it is physical pain so excruciating from the beginning that it cannot ever get worse. Both the bliss and the punishment are changeless. This is not only beyond anything in our experience; it is also, I would submit, inconceivable in a human being who is by nature finite, limited, and in process of evolution and growth even apart from the fact that such outrageous cruelty is contrary to all the believer's experience of God's ways.

The medieval schoolmen made a useful distinction that ought eventually to have precluded such imagery: a distinction between *aeternitas* (the eternal order beyond the temporal that pertains to God alone) and *aeviternitas* (an indefinitely ongoing series in the temporal order). This latter is what is characteristically envisaged in the language of the New Testament in its talk of "the end of the age" and "from ages to ages" and in the creeds of the Church with their affirmation of belief in "life everlasting." The eternal order does not "last," for it is beyond duration.

Must Not Creation Be Eternally Ongoing? How, then, did such a scenario ever come to be presented at all? The traditional answer not only provides a clue to how the muddle arose; it also helps to show why the act of creation must be an ongoing one (although it is a view traditionally accounted heterodox), as must also be life in the resurrected state, whatever it is.

The traditional answer has been that God, being alone and perfectly happy and self-contained in the eternal order suddenly (if there can be a "suddenly" in eternity) decided to create. When theologians were asked the by no means unreasonable question "Why?," the reply was that, although God cannot ever be said to need creatures to love him, he willed, out of his superabundant love, that others should enjoy him by returning that love, for it is of the divine nature to love. True indeed, but might not one ask, in a paraphrase of the celebrated words of Golda Meir in a less theological context, "What took him so long?" (if eternity may properly be called "long"). Why was not God eternally doing what it is his eternal nature to do? Why was he, so to speak, sitting alone in his heaven, needing no creatures and then at a certain point in time (if indeed there could be such a point in eternity) changing his mind?

To love is, inter alia, God's métier. Then why did he take so long (if eternity can be long) to exercise it? Moreover, on the traditional model we begin with a universe consisting solely of God and end a few thousand or a few billion years later (it matters not which) with a startlingly new but no less eternal state of affairs in which the universe consists now of God plus two categories of finite creatures, the one in unchanging bliss, the other in unchanging misery.

Such imagery seems to have arisen from a natural error in the reading of Genesis 1:1, where we read that "in the beginning God created. . . ." The Septuagint has the Greek verb *epoiēsen*, which in Latin becomes *creavit* and in English "created": the past definite tense that is part of the tense structure of Indo-European languages. The Hebrew tense structure, however, is different. The Hebrew verb *bārā* used in Genesis 1:1 does not fix a time when creation "happened." It does not justify translation into a tense that specifies a moment in time in which an action was performed and once-and-for-all completed as, for instance, when one reports that a man was shot and killed at eleven minutes past ten on a certain Monday morning. As used in the opening verse of Genesis it summarizes the creative process that is recounted in the rest of the chapter, which sets forth the author's evolutionary understanding of the creative process. (It *is* portrayed as evolutionary, for it takes a "day" to do this and a "day" to do that. The only possible exception might be the case of light, which is represented as the instantaneous result of the divine *fiat*.) The verb can mean "was creating," and a modern Jewish translation does in fact render the opening words of Genesis by "When God was creating. . . ." The Old Testament uses the verb *to create* only of God; it is his characteristic act: as characteristic of God as is breathing of us. Yet God's creation does not emanate from God as sunshine from the sun as in a Neoplatonic arrangement; he continuously and benevolently wills to create.

Moreover, the words *In the beginning* must not be understood in the sense in which we understand them in phrases such as "in the beginning of the twentieth century" or "in the beginning of my first day at school." The

Septuagint opens with the words *En archē*, which would be more appositely rendered in English by the adverb *archetypally*. The Vulgate latinizes the words *In principio*, "In principle," which is far less a betrayal of the original intent than "In the beginning."

Why then, have we inherited such a different picture? Aristotle had argued persuasively from within his own system that God as *Actus Purus*, Pure Act, must be eternally creating. Thomas Aquinas knew this, of course, and agreed that reason dictated Aristotle's view. Nevertheless, St. Thomas, holding that revelation in Scripture must take precedence over even reason, concluded that he must follow what "the Bible" surprisingly says. In this case, however, Thomas, despite his extraordinary acumen, was wrong in his interpretation of what Scripture says and does not say. His exegesis was eminently excusable in his day, when even among the best of Christian scholars Hebrew was much less well understood than it can be today. It is not at all so excusable today. Either God is always creating or he is not creating at all. God's order is the eternal one and his creativity is ongoing. Our order is temporal and implies growth and evolutionary change. It is because our order as finite beings is temporal and evolutionary that the traditional interpretation of the nature of heaven and hell cannot possibly work.

Immortality by Participation in God's Love

There is, however, a way in which the concept of immortality can be intelligibly introduced into a Christian vision of afterlife. It can be won by acceptance of God's grace as a divine gift granted to those whose gratitude to Jesus Christ for his redemptive, sacrificial love is such that they return that love by conforming to God's will. Through the spiritual power of Christ's resurrection one can accept the forgiveness that God, in his loving mercy, bestows and so eventually *participate* in the immortality that belongs to God alone.

A notion of this kind lies at the heart of the medieval Catholic concept of heaven as the *visio beatifica*, the vision of God, the essence of which consists in a fuller knowledge of God: one that is not possible for us in our present state. As Paul puts the concept that was later developed into that of the *visio beatifica*, the Beatific Vision, now we see "through a glass, darkly" but hereafter we shall see "face to face" (I Corinthians 13:12). This vivacious vision of afterlife joy is very ill represented in popular images of pearly gates, and streets of gold, where even the rivers are solidified into crystal.

When a human soul is conceived as immortal in its very nature the way is open to what did in fact become a horrific doctrine of hell. This doctrine arises because of the notion that the soul, being indestructible, cannot be by any means extinguished; therefore, if it fails to attain everlasting bliss it must continue its existence otherwise. Such an existence bereft of God was described by the learned in the Middle Ages as *poena damni*, the pain of loss that comes with awareness of having forever renounced the love of God and his mercy. In popular preaching the notion was expressed in terms of everlasting torture, most commonly torture by fire.

Limbo

In classical Christian doctrine Heaven and Hell were not the only possible final destinations of the soul. There were many souls, indeed, who had never had the opportunity of qualifying for either. Yet, being supposedly immortal by their very nature, they were no less inextinguishable. Who were they, these souls disqualified for both heaven and hell, and what happened to them?

The theory was that two classes of people were so disqualified, through no fault of their own. One consisted of those who, having lived before the coming of Christ, had had no opportunity of responding to the grace he was to make possible. These included not only Moses and the great Hebrew prophets so much venerated by Christians as well as by Jews (e.g., Amos, Hosea, Isaiah), but also the great thinkers of pagan antiquity such as Plato and Aristotle and noble poets such as Virgil. Such great and good souls, according to Scripture (e.g., I Peter 3:18–20), had been waiting for Christ's appearance, but could not yet profit from his redemptive work. They were in limbo, a pleasant place or state of "natural" happiness but incapable of enjoying the supernatural bliss of heaven.

Much vagueness, however, attended the exposition of this theory of the afterlife of such persons. The general view, following that allusion in the first letter of Peter, was that Christ, between his death and his resurrection, visited the saints and great ones of old, drawing up such men as Abraham and Moses; exactly how many and on what principle they were selected was never clear. Even the purpose of his "descent," which in England was widely and popularly known as "the Harrowing of Hell," and often depicted in art under that title, was left very vague indeed. The question of what would happen to saintly men and women in distant lands such as, say, China and Japan,

Fig. 11. Limbo. *From Gustave Doré's illustration for Dante's* Vision of Hell, *1866, Canto IV. Illustration 11. The souls in limbo, although they do not enjoy the bliss of paradise, do not suffer. They are afflicted only in the sense that they desire paradise yet cannot hope for it. Virgil himself, who conducts Dante, is among the multitudes of those who, only for lack of baptism, cannot hope for paradise. Dante grieves sorely, for he knows how many worthy and noble souls are here, longing without hope.*

probably did not arise in the minds of many in the Latin world, but if it did it would have exacerbated the difficulties.

There was, however, another problem that was not at all remote but, on the contrary, a very present and practical difficulty. What of a child who had died at birth or perhaps a few days afterwards and before having been afforded an opportunity for receiving the sacrament of baptism: the entry into the mystical Body of Christ? Without this sacrament the child, through no fault of its own, could not attain heaven; nevertheless, at any rate according to the prevalent theological opinion, it merited (by reason of its innocence) everlasting "natural" happiness: the quality of happiness of which such a child was capable of enjoying.

So there came to be two categories of limbo: the *limbus patrum* (the "limbo of the Fathers") for Plato, Moses, and the like, and the *limbus infantium*, "children's limbo." The latter would be a solace, at least, to the child's parents. Both forms of limbo arose, of course, through the introduction into early Christian thought of the notion that the human soul is intrinsically immortal. The Greek Church, happily, never seems to have become so involved in such theological muddles on the Christian view of afterlife.

The **"Harrowing of Hell"** Calvin provides a characteristically confident exegesis of the article in the Creed that alludes to the descent of Christ into hell (*descendit ad inferos*—to Hades, the underworld). Calvin says that for Christ to have died a "physical death" would not have been enough to accomplish salvation for humankind; so he had "to grapple hand to hand with the armies of hell and the dread of everlasting death" (*Institutes*, II, 16, 10). Christ not only suffered visibly but in his soul; he suffered even "the terrible torments of a condemned and forsaken man." So Calvin aligns this concept with Christ's cry of dereliction on the Cross, "My God, my God, why hast thou forsaken me?," a direct quotation from Psalm 22. Luther seems to have been more literalistic on this point, contending that Christ actually entered into hell. The question was much discussed by many of the Reformation Fathers.

Consequences of a Non-Evolutionary Ideal

Much of the labyrinth of confusion attending traditional Christian conceptualizations of the "final" state of everyone in the hereafter is due to static understandings of the nature of existence itself. Since the universe was perceived so generally in nonevolutionary terms, there was no powerful reason to see the dimension of the spirit as in that respect radically different. So heaven, hell, and limbo are all seen in a uniformly static way. The present life is transitory, but that is merely a defect in our present mode of existence ("Change and decay in all around I see," as the popular hymn puts it). The life hereafter, by contrast, will not be so encumbered; it will be changeless. All will perceive, whether in heaven or in hell or even in limbo, each in the way proper to one of these future modes of being, that changelessness. None of these states is to be like anything now experienced "on earth"; it is to be radically different: different in that the balance sheet of the universe will have been drawn up. God will have settled his account at last, to the dismay of evildoers and to the joy of his saints.

The presuppositions underlying this way of looking at the Church's traditional images of afterlife make these images at best puzzling and at worst unintelligible. In Catholic tradition, however, there is one element in the hereafter that we have not so far discussed: one not subject to objections that images of heaven, hell, and limbo all invite. I refer to the concept of purgatory, sometimes called "the intermediate state."

Purgatory Purgatory, despite its having been too generally depicted in the Middle Ages and later Roman Catholic tradition in penal and therefore fearsome terms, is by no means necessarily so understood. It has, moreover, counterparts in other religious traditions outside the Christian Way. It works because it provides for education and growth, the process of evolution common to all human experience at every level. It also recognizes that there is some good in the worst of us and some bad in the best of us. Punishment, however painful, however severe, may be borne if only it is presumptively corrective and educational. All education, indeed, entails some element of pain. There is no "algebra without tears." One accepts the tears if only they exhibit a purpose. Every form of growth, including even the process of biologically growing up, entails some sort of pain: growing pains of one sort or another. Purgatory, however, as an "intermediate state," does not belong to "last things." Even though it last for the equivalent of millions of years, it is still on this side of what we might call the great eschatological divide. It pertains to afterlife but does not belong, strictly speaking, to the final state of affairs. We shall therefore postpone further consideration of it and of similar afterlife concepts till the next chapter.

Other Concepts

Afterlife in Medieval Judaism In medieval Judaism various concepts of heaven and hell were developed, some picturesque and evocative in their imagery, others intellectual and philosophical, others again a mixture of both ingredients. For example, in rabbinic eschatology we have a picture of the world to come (*Olam ha-Ba*) expressed in the prediction that in the world to come "the righteous shall sit with their crowns on their heads and enjoy the splendor of the *Shekinah*." The Hebrew word *Shekinah* (literally, "dwelling") is not found in the Hebrew Bible, but came to be used by the rabbis to denote the visible presence of God conceived as dwelling among men and often, to avoid anthropomorphisms, as a periphrasis for the sacrosanct, unutterable name of God. It is the "glory" that is echoed in John's prologue (John 1:14), where it is rendered by the Greek word *doxa*. This rabbinic promise of heaven might be understood simply as the eternal enjoyment of God's presence, with connotations in some ways similar to the Christian hope of the Beatific Vision. Saadia (892–942), however, interpreted this prediction as signifying that the life of the world to come will consist of a specially created luminous substance that sustains and delights the righteous while at the same time burning and torturing the wicked. In this perception Saadia, who has been called the father of medieval Jewish thought, adumbrates an insight of Boehme, Swedenborg, and Blake many centuries later: The wicked would be unhappy in heaven and the righteous happy in hell, for the joy of the latter and the misery of the former both spring from their own interior condition.

Neoplatonism much affected Jewish as well as Christian medieval thought and where Jewish eschatology came under this powerful influence the joy of heaven was understood in notably different terms. It was seen, rather, as the climax of the soul's process of disentanglement from matter and ascent to union with the divine light. As in medieval Christian thought, one might enjoy a foretaste of this eternal bliss even in the present life, by the special favor of God enabling one to withdraw from the allurements of the flesh and the influence of lower elements destructive of the ascent to God.

Solomon ibn Gabirol (*c.* 1022–*c.* 1051 or 1070), the greatest of the medieval Jewish neoplatonists, who was more philosopher than theologian, followed much the same line of thought. The soul, liberated from the captivity of nature, is purified by the contemplative life of the intellect and by the practice of moral virtues, and these combined purifications lead it to the highest level of contemplation. Beyond that, however, it can attain, not by its own efforts but by the special favor and gift of God, communion with the divine light.

The author of what is easily the best-known Jewish philosophical work produced in the Middle Ages, the *Guide to the Perplexed*, was Moses Maimonides (1135–1204), so revered that he has been called "the second Moses." By his time Jewish thinkers, under the influence of Aristotle, were divided on the possibility of individual afterlife. Some denied entirely any such possibility. Whatever bliss is attainable must be attained in this life. Others, however, held that such bliss is possible both in this life and in afterlife. Maimonides, unfortunately, is unclear on this question, sometimes denying individual immortality, sometimes admitting it. Those who upheld the notion of individual immortality perceived heavenly bliss as knowledge of God, so adumbrating the Thomist perception of heaven as the Beatific Vision, which consists in direct knowledge of God. Predictably, many Jews found the philosophers' treatment of the subject too intellectual and saw piety and the love of God as the way to heaven. Similar differences of opinion on the subject of eternal felicity prevailed in Islam.

Mormon Concept of Afterlife Mormons believe that there will be a regeneration of nature that will entail an event analogous to death and resurrection and that as part of this cosmic rejuvenation a resurrection of all living entities who have ever existed on earth will take place. This resurrection, however, will be in two steps. First will be a resurrection of the righteous, which will include both all who have ever lived lives in fidelity to the laws of God as known to them (including children as well as adults ignorant of the Bible) and those who are to be on earth at the time of this dramatic event. Then will come later a second resurrection in which those not eligible for the first resurrection will be restored.

Resurrection is understood very literally as a reunion of the spirits of the deceased with the bodies with which they were "clothed" during their time of probation in mortal life. The transition from mortality to immortality will take place in the course of the resurrection event. Those who are alive on earth at the time will have the additional bonus of escaping the "sleep of the grave," being granted the transition from mortality to immortality without facing the death and burial that will have been the lot of the vast majority both of the righteous and of the unrighteous.

Since Mormons see baptism, which they practice by immersion, as a requirement for salvation, symbolic of burial awaiting resurrection, they provide a form of baptism for the dead who have not had the opportunity to be baptized during their period of life on earth. Moreover, although polygamy, which was practiced by the Mormons at first on the ground of its having biblical warrant, has been abolished, it is still promised to Mormons in the future life. For there are two ways in which marriages may be entered into here and now: (1) for time and eternity and (2) till death do part. A man or woman may marry consecutively as often as he or she chooses according to the second form, till death do part. While, however, a man may do so as often as he pleases according to the first form (for time and eternity), a woman may enter into this form of marriage only once. In the Mormon heaven, therefore, a man may have several wives but a woman no more than one husband. Moreover, when a woman reaches an age when she is not expected to be married she may be "spiritually" married to a deceased man, so indefinitely enlarging the number of wives he will be able to claim at the resurrection. Such warrant as may be missing in a literalistic reading of the Bible is provided in a literalistic reading of the Book of Mormon, which Joseph Smith claimed to have reconstructed from gold plates he had seen in a stone box on a hill described to him by Moroni, one of his angelic visitants.

The Baha'i Alternative to Heaven and Hell By way of contrast, we may usefully look at the afterlife beliefs of the Baha'is, another important religious movement that emerged about the same time as the Mormons, having been founded in Iran in 1844 and now claiming some four or five million adherents with its headquarters in Haifa, Israel. (It has temples throughout the world, including an important one in Evanston, Illinois.) Although rooted in Islam, adherents of the Baha'i movement do not account Baha'i a Muslim sect. Following the teachings of their founder, Mirza Husayn Ali, Baha'u'llah (1817–1892), Baha'is believe that all religions are fundamentally one and that from time to time God raises up teachers or prophets (Baha'is call them "manifestations") to guide humankind to spiritual fulfillment, among whom Baha'u'llah is the most recent.

Baha'is teach, in accordance with their scriptures, that the soul has its beginning at conception and is endowed with immortality. Life here and now in physical embodiment provides an opportunity for spiritual progress for which the physical body serves as an instrument. Baha'i is reluctant to sketch any chart or blueprint of afterlife, much less to enter into pictorial details of the pilgrimage in which it is to consist. Nevertheless, it is plainly to be fundamentally a pilgrimage and one in which our present identity shall be maintained, because that identity depends upon the mind of the individual, not the body. Further spiritual growth after death will occur both through the divine mercy and through prayers and labors, our own and those of others. Heaven and hell as traditionally portrayed in Christian eschatology are ruled out; yet they may be seen as representing respectively whatever is directed toward God and whatever is moving from him.

In short, Baha'is renounce the concept of permanence as a category of afterlife, whether a "heavenly" permanence or a "hellish" one. The afterlife, as an unending pilgrimage toward greater and greater spiritual perfection and understanding, cannot be understood in terms of a final state, for *stasis* is radically at odds with *dynamis*, the life of the spirit. By salvation a Baha'i understands a journey through openness toward an endless variety of possible attainments. The process of this evolutionary development in the afterlife is unending. The individual, being immortal, cannot ever be extinguished; yet one may halt one's own progress and so be "as if" dead. Even such an unfortunate blockage of one's progress, however, need not be without remedy. One may always be restored to the path of spiritual development that is the healthy condition of the soul in the afterlife as in life here and now. Whatever good we do here and now will enhance our prospects of success in the afterlife and enrich our capacity for the openness that such success requires.

Most striking in Baha'i teaching on afterlife is its total repudiation of final, permanent states, notably the Christian images and perhaps even more specifically their Islamic counterparts. The Qur'ān repeatedly and graphically depicts the everlasting domains of the righteous and the unrighteous: the lush and delectable garden (*jannah*) of paradise, with its abundant fruit, cool shade, gentle conversation, and beautiful apparel for the righteous on the one hand and, on the other, roaring flames, rivers of boiling water, stifling smoke, and other unspeakable tortures for the wicked. All such concepts of a final and permanent state, either of torture or of bliss, are alien to the Baha'i vision.

Machiavelli Both heaven and hell have been the butt of innumerable jokes throughout the ages: jokes that sometimes have the merit of pointing indirectly to what is wrong with traditional representations of these concepts. Niccolò Machiavelli (1469–1527), notorious for the worldly-wise outlook for which he is famous, would seem to be almost the last person to have any interest at all in afterlife concepts. Sebastian de Grazia, however, a modern writer, in his delightful *Machiavelli in Hell*,[1] shows that Machiavelli did not by any means entirely forget or ignore the notion of afterlife. Predictably he pokes fun at the traditional imagery of hell, as in *The Ass*, which echoes *The Golden Ass* of Apuleius. He also parodies Dante. In this literary mood he suggests that, while heaven has the edge in climate, hell can offer more interesting company. Yet he does not merely reduce the idea of afterlife to literary fun. He seems to have had an ambivalence in his psychological makeup that caused him to tend to oscillate between irreverent satire and intellectual seriousness. In his serious moods he showed signs of recognizing God as both all-powerful and all-compassionate and, moreover, he appears to have thought of death as the gateway to another dimension of being: a spiritual realm the arrangement of which, although we can know nothing about it, must be radically different from the manner in which affairs are ordered in our present life. We often find, in the history of human thought, that even the most skeptical of thinkers, while ridiculing the ways in which concepts of God and afterlife are commonly understood, nevertheless see in them important and profound truths. They reject only claims to greater knowledge of the celestial and infernal geography than could possibly be justified.

Note

1 Sebastian de Grazia, *Machiavelli in Hell* (Princeton, N.J.: Princeton University Press, 1989). See especially Chapter 13.

CHAPTER X

———————————————————◼———————————————————

Purgatory

For a rational but finite being, the only thing possible is an endless progress from lower to higher degrees of moral perfection.

—Kant, *Critique of Practical Reason*

The Christian concept of purgatory as an "intermediate state" has very ancient roots. Not only is it expounded as educational by both Clement of Alexandria and Origen; it can be traced back to pre-Christian Judaism. In II Maccabees, written in the second century B.C.E. almost certainly by an Alexandrian Jew of the school of the Pharisees, we read (12, 43–45) of a "sin-offering" for the dead. Judas Maccabaeus had sent about two thousand drams of silver to Jerusalem for Jews who had been slain in battle. The writer much approved of this action, perceiving it as expressive of a "holy and devout" thought. By the earlier part of the second century C.E. prayers for the dead had become part of the regular worship of the synagogue. By about the end of that century we find Tertullian referring to the practice as well established among Christian communities. Oblations for the dead were made, he tells us, every year on the anniversaries of their deaths. Wherever we find the practice of prayers or offerings for the dead we have found at least the emergence of some form of intermediate state, for there can be no

———————————————————◼———————————————————

point in praying for the dead if their destiny for good or for ill is already sealed forever in heaven or in hell.

Purgatory as Spiritual Development

If we are to entertain any image of an afterlife at all, the most intelligible form is on purgatorial lines. I do not mean that the model must necessarily be Purgatory as traditionally conceived or depicted in the Middle Ages. Dante's great epic, the *Divina Commedia*, does provide, however, a singularly pictur-esque literary representation. [1] The learned in the Middle Ages expected great religious truths to be expressed in allegorical terms. They were in more danger of overallegorizing the Bible and other texts than of taking them too literally. Even the unlearned were far less likely to treat what they knew of the Bible or other religious literature as literalistically as urban dwellers today tend to treat it. They were, for one thing, too close to nature for that. Dante provided a conceptual model that they could understand.

The *Commedia* was immensely popular in its day before it became, as it is

Fig. 12. The Proud in Dante's *Purgatorio. From John Flaxman's illustrations in Cary's English translation (Oxford, 1916). Those who must expiate the sin of pride are bent down under the weight of the heavy stones they must carry.*

Fig. 13. The Gluttonous in Dante's *Purgatorio. From John Flaxman's illustrations in Cary's English translation (Oxford, 1916). The gluttonous are punished by being situated under a tree bearing the most tantalizingly luscious of fruits for which they vainly clamor, for it is just out of their reach.*

now, a classic in the literature of the world. Parts of it were read in the Duomo of Florence. The ordinary person could hear it and adjust to it in such a way as to fit the model into the parameters of his or her own imagination. What such a person would rightly see as of unique value in the concept of purgatory was that, however painful it might be, at least it provided one with a second chance. Once you "woke up" in purgatory you knew that, however short or long your sojourn there and indeed whatever "purgatorial time" might mean, you were earmarked for salvation.

No doubt many people did see purgatory too much in penal and too little in educational terms. Some, however, notably Catherine of Genoa (1447–1510), who appears at the end of the Middle Ages, were able to see it as a choice by the individual at the point of death. I shall have more to say later in the present chapter on this remarkable woman.

This was the purifying and educational aspect of purgatory that the English Tractarians in the nineteenth century developed and emphasized. Purgatory is, in their view, essentially a state of growth. It is evolutionary, and that they should so have seen it is all the more remarkable in light of the fact that they were active in decades immediately preceding the publication of the discoveries by Darwin and Wallace of the principles of biological evolution in Darwin's epoch-making *On the Origin of Species* (1859). The Oxford Movement that the early Tractarians had fostered continued to exercise its immense influence on Christian thought long after the publication of that work. Evolution was in the air. Biological evolution, as theologians no less than physicists and others were more and more to perceive, is by no means the only aspect of the evolutionary process.

Human Frailty and the Love of God

Purgatory, so interpreted, takes for granted human weakness, folly, and occasional sheer wickedness, while at the same time providing a remedy reflecting belief in God as creative, loving, and merciful. Such a God does not constrain his creatures, for constraint is destruction. He lets them be. So he leaves each of his creatures free to work out his or her salvation. He lets them develop themselves so that each works out his or her victory in his or her own personal struggle. Yet can one imagine that such a loving God, despite the unlimited freedom he accords his creatures in the making or marring of their destiny, would permit any of his creatures to advance far up in the realm of the spirit and then, because of a creature's grievous error and sin, stand by to watch that creature plunge headlong to everlasting destruction? Of course not. On the contrary, he hastens with his "amazing grace" to aid his beloved ones, as a good shepherd comes to rescue the sheep that has taken a wrong turning and has fallen into a hole in the ground. Such a God, despite his nonintervention that assures the freedom his creatures need to win their battles, will save them.

Such an afterlife belief is at the heart of the Christian understanding of God's nature: an understanding that is by no means without parallel in other religions, although notably central to the New Testament and historic Christian tradition. According to that document and that tradition Christ is the full and final expression of the loving nature of God in his relation to humanity. While he graciously lets his creatures be, giving them the freedom necessary for their moral and spiritual development, he no less graciously is ever ready to save them through the innumerable instruments at his disposal and most amazingly through the power of Christ. His nonintervention and his intervention are opposite sides of the same coin of his love.

Consider a situation that is in fact almost a literary commonplace. A boy grows up to be not merely a responsible and honest citizen but also a man of courage, sensitivity and (though he would not so think of himself) authentic holiness of life. At some point, however, things go wrong. Circumstances seize and paralyze him in such a way that he becomes involved in actions that lead him to commit an act that horrifies others and deeply shames himself: an act diametrically opposed to the standards he has set and has for so long notably upheld. It might be an adultery, an embezzlement, perhaps even a murder. According to traditional Roman Catholic theology, if he should die in such a state of alienation from God, which is very possible, since genuine penitence cannot be turned on like a faucet but may take much time and many heartbreaks to achieve, he who up to then has led a blameless, even saintly life becomes instantly a lost soul and destined for the awful punishment of being forever cast from God's grace and condemned to everlasting torment in hell. The question is not whether the torment is physical, as in popular preaching, or mental, as in the more learned interpretations; what really matters is that it is everlasting.

That such a view could have been developed under the banner of a loving God is not so astonishing as it may at first appear. It was plausibly argued that if one truly loved God one simply could not displease him by acting in flagrant opposition to his revealed will. But is not that precisely what, at the human level, every lover says: "If you had really loved me you could not have been unfaithful." Such, however, alas, is human weakness that we do not love enough even at that human level, let alone in our feeble attempts at loving God. Only God can so totally love his creatures as to forgive them repeatedly. When Peter asked Jesus the question (Matthew 18:21f.) "Lord, how often must I forgive my brother if he wrongs me? As often as seven times?" Jesus answered "Not seven times, I tell you, but seventy-seven times," or, as we might say, "umpteen times." Jesus, in urging Peter to forgive without limitation, was giving him a preliminary lesson in the cost of love.

So much for one side of the case: the oddness, not to say cruelty, of the notion that what a person is thinking or saying or doing at the moment when, as we might say, God snatches his or her soul by sudden death should determine the destiny of that person in the afterlife. We have considered how outrageous such a notion sounds in terms of everlasting punishment in hell or everlasting bliss in heaven. But even if we think in terms of purgatory, consider this notion: A man or woman who has led an admirable moral life in all respects, including a marriage of exemplary fidelity for twenty years or more, becomes so infatuated and so overwhelmed by sexual desire as to commit adultery in a frenzy of sheer lust in total disregard for his or her marriage partner's rights or feelings. Overtaken in the very act by death (for instance, in an earthquake or other unpredictable disaster), is such a man or woman to be earmarked for an especially long and arduous stay in the seventh story of Dante's purgatory, where the lustful are tortured by fire till the lust is burned out of them? Is no credit to be allowed to such a person for the years of fidelity that he or she has displayed and that have contributed so greatly up to this point at least in producing an eminently happy home and conjugal relationship? Is it not somewhat as if a schoolboy, noted from first to twelfth grade for exemplary industry in his work, were to turn in a sloppy piece of work in the last term of school and be severely penalized for his unusual behavior as if it were his norm?

A moment's reflection will show that there is something psychologically flawed in these images of crime and punishment. We have been talking as if virtuous and vicious acts were monads each unrelated to the others. In fact, neither virtues nor vices are so singularly "committed"; each is built up, the virtues often very painfully, the vices usually through indolence, until at length a habitual disposition, good or evil as the case may be, is attained. The good disposition does not totally rule out the commission of an act not in keeping with it. A moral disposition, however, is only gradually created and gradually achieved.

If souls may be said to have attained a condition of spiritual health without being thereby totally immunized against every possible evil invader, may not the opposite also be true? May not one become so spiritually shrunken, so morally warped, that one's case looks hopeless, yet, if only there were time for whatever it takes for restoration to health, that restoration could be achieved? This does not make a purgatorial conception of afterlife in the least easy-going. If with the best will in the world I have still a long way to go as well as a long way to grow, how much longer and how much more terrible my prospect if I am stunted and obdurately resistant to the love of God?

Such ideas, essentially Alexandrian in their roots, have the great merit of treating "moral disease" as remediable without underestimating the serious-ness of the diseased condition. There is an infinite difference between saying that my spiritual condition is terminal and hopeless and saying that its cure will take an unimaginably long time. In traditional discussions of purgatory in a Catholic context, much is often made of the notion that purgatorial time is somehow different from "our" time as measured on earth in the present life. But even in "ordinary" experience there is more than one kind of time. Time as I experience it does not keep pace with "clock" time. When I am happy, time flies; when I am sad, it drags. Notoriously children experience time in slow motion while older people find that Christmas is hardly over when the next Christmas is being heralded. Some people experience their entire lives as rushing past while others perceive their lives as a huge and tedious slice of history. Above all, when one has the sense of making progress in whatever one is aiming at, time will race by, but when one is fumbling and muddling one's way through a task the process is wearisomely long, whatever the clock may say. So purgatory, which is a state of consciousness, would be of course notable for this aspect of awareness of time.

Love Surmounts Death

Also associated with the Catholic doctrine of purgatory is the alleged efficacy of prayers by the living for the "holy souls" in purgatory. How, one may ask, can your prayers do my penance for me? Is not that like the notion that you can learn your child's lesson *for* your child? The point seems well taken till one reflects that what is really at the heart of the issue here is the power of love.

Omnia vincit Amor, wrote Virgil: "Love conquers all." If there is an afterlife at all, a deep and genuine love will surmount whatever barrier may lie between those on this side of it and those on the other.

If, as Paul wrote to the Romans, "neither death nor life . . . nothing that exists, nothing still to come, not any power . . . nor any created thing can ever come between us and the love of God made visible in Christ Jesus our Lord," then the concept that the prayers of a loving relative or friend can help a soul in the afterlife is not at all so far-fetched as it might at first appear. But in what way might it help? Not by any means by "doing the other's task for him" but by the sense of encouragement that the almighty power of love can convey across even the barrier of death. Moreover, the love of God that works in that direction can work in the other too. It is not a one-way street. Those in the afterlife can encourage us by our awareness of their love. Nor need such benefactors be restricted to those officially recognized on the Church's calendar. In what the Church traditionally calls "The Communion of Saints" there are no border guards in either direction so long as one is traveling by the freeway of God's love.

In traditional Catholic language, the Church encompasses three states: (1) the Church Militant, the faithful soldiers of Christ struggling here and now; (2) the Church Suffering, the "holy souls" in Purgatory; and (3) the Church Triumphant, those who, having gained final victory, are already in possession of their heavenly state of everlasting bliss with God. It is a neat, tripartite arrangement, which the Western mind tends to like. But of course its neatness is artificial. For the Church Militant is suffering too and the Church Suffering is engaged in battle: the battle of evolution and growth. Both enjoy, nevertheless, the presence of God, at least in some measure here and now, so both already participate, copiously or meagerly, in the Vision of God, which, according to the model, is the ultimate goal of the soul's pilgrimage.

The Image and Shape of Purgatory

The Christian Church has never given the image of purgatory any clearly defined shape and has usually been reticent in giving the concept any unambiguous content. All that can be said of the traditional Catholic understanding of purgatory is that it pertains to the afterlife, is transitional, and includes suffering. Within these parameters it could be interpreted in innumerable ways.

It can be envisioned, for instance, as Dante presents it, as the arduous ascent of a seven-storied mountain in the course of which one's spirit is purged of its wayward tendencies and dispositions. Or it might be conceived as, say, a chilly waiting room just outside the gates that lead to heavenly bliss. Or again it can be presented in much more horrific imagery such as we have encountered in the Chinese hells that are horrifyingly long purgatorial processes, with a particular form of terrible torture assigned to each. Once again, the soul may be purified simply by being forced to look at itself as in a mirror that faithfully exhibits the various diseases it has allowed to make it the way it has become: an examination of its own conscience, a nightmare of the soul. There is really no limit to the ways in which the purgatorial process may be interpreted and symbolized.

Serious thinkers—Jewish, Christian, and Muslim—who have written on the concept of the "intermediate state" as it occurs within the framework of the monotheistic way of understanding the nature of God, have been wisely reticent, as a rule, on the form that it might take.

True, picturesque symbolism, as used so effectively by Dante and others, abounds both in literature and in the visual arts. Homilies on purgatory generally depict it as a very painful process. The commonest imagery is that of fire, symbolizing the burning heat of thirst, longing, and desire that is the soul's interior anguish as it struggles to attain a sought stage of perfection. The literature is pervaded by hints and suggestions and indeed, as in Dante, clear affirmation of discipline fitted to purge the soul from its special forms of weakness, whatever these may be. The proud have to carry large stones, forcing them to bow their heads and bend their backs as a sign of the humility they must inwardly cultivate (see Fig. 12, p. 139). This physical mortification, however, is a mere backdrop for the interior growth in which they must engage to root out their besetting sin of pride. The gluttonous are tormented by luscious fruit just out of their reach (Fig. 13, p. 140) and again this is a mere stage prop, so to speak, for the painful inward struggle of controlling their piggish craving for overfilling their bellies. Only those unaccustomed to the depth and subtlety of Dantesque allegory are really satisfied with interpreting such figures merely as "punishment fitting the crime." Their significance is much more profound. No words, no pictures can tell of the interior torture of the soul as it engages in authentic spiritual growth: the kind of growth that requires the rending of the heart by instruments more painful than whips or prison bars. Such interior anguish is inexpressible or at best only feebly so by metaphorical devices.

Purgatory as a Series of Re-embodiments

I am going to propose an interpretation that I find for more than one reason especially apposite and helpful. Why might not purgatory take the form of a series of re-embodiments from each of which the soul would learn something of the nature of the spiritual dimension of existence and by discipline have its faults rooted out and supplanted with more benign dispositions to fit it to enter God's living room? Why might not the soul, by such educational discipline, mature sufficiently to understand and enjoy the finer kind of heavenly music that lies ahead?

Among ancient beliefs about afterlife, one of the most widespread and persistent is, we have seen, that of transmigration or reincarnation. It occurs, we have also seen, at every level of religious development, from the most primitive to the most reflective. It is an outlook that has pervaded Indian culture and thought from very early times and flourishes today not only in modern Hinduism but also in the numerous offshoots of that great Oriental clearinghouse of religious ideas. It was apparently one of the central teachings of the Pythagorean brotherhood and by its wide dissemination throughout the Mediterranean world it affected Greek thought, including Plato's understanding of the nature of the pilgrimage of the human soul, in the immortality of which he clearly believed. Through its influence in the Mediterranean world it affected the thought of learned Christians in the first centuries C.E., especially those of the Alexandrian school. It has at various times appeared in one form or another within Judaism, and although generally accounted alien to Muslim teaching has occurred even there and is a prominent part of the beliefs of the Druze.

The ancient doctrine of transmigration of souls functions in so many ways as does the doctrine of purgatory that we should seriously consider whether the two doctrines may be different formulations of the same fundamental concept. Reincarnation, although it has entered into the history of religious thought in the West to a greater extent than is generally supposed, is historically more connected with Oriental than with Occidental modes of thought. It is not specifically taught in the Bible, despite some references that hint at or suggest some form of it; but then neither is the doctrine of purgatory explicitly taught in the Bible; nor, for that matter, is the doctrine of the Trinity, that most widely accepted symbol of Christian orthodoxy.

More to the point, however, there is nothing in the Bible specifically against either the doctrine of purgatory or that of reincarnation. An allusion in the letter to the Hebrews (9:27) to the effect that men die only once and that after that comes judgment (misused by some literalistic readers of the Bible against the compatibility of reincarnationist ideas with the biblical text) has no such force if read in context, where it appears in a sort of parallelism with the appearance of Christ once and for all. Indeed the writer's purpose in the entire passage is to affirm the uniqueness of the work of Christ, which is fulfilled in one life. The allusion to the death that ends every human being's life once and for all (*hapax*) is by way of illustrating the theological affirmation about Christ's accomplishment of human salvation. It is not a theological statement in itself but merely a truism that in mortal man life ends in death, for that is what it means to be mortal: death is the singular end of every mortal life. There is no evidence at all here that the writer of the letter to the Hebrews (whoever he was—or perhaps she, for some New Testament scholars have included Priscilla among the possible candidates for authorship) had any intention of making a statement for or against the transmigration of souls.

The kinship of the two doctrines, purgatory and reincarnation, is strikingly brought out by the fifteenth-century saint Catherine of Genoa in the *Treatise on Purgatory*, where she describes how the soul accepts (one might even say chooses) the purgatorial state needed for its purification and progress. "The soul," she says, "so seeing that it cannot, because of the impediment [in itself], attain to its end, which is God, and that the impediment cannot be removed from it, except by means of purgatory, swiftly and of its own accord throws itself into it." Catherine is writing in Italian and the word here translated is *volontieri*, which warrants the notion that at least in some sense the soul actually chooses the form of purgatory that matches its specific needs, somewhat as, ideally, one would choose the school that fitted one's educational needs.

The resemblance of this notion to that of some versions of the Hindu concept of how the self, between embodiments, "chooses" the next one in conformity with its needs for development and growth is striking. Of course it may be argued that in both notions there is an element of predeterminism. One may prefer to say that the soul or self spontaneously moves toward the rebirth it needs to remedy its present shortcomings. Such an interpretation is available in any claim to the making of a free choice. The important feature in both interpretations is that, having been impelled toward or having chosen one's course of action, one has settled one's karmic condition for one's next embodiment. One has to work out how one will use, endure, profit from, or grow in terms of what one now has as one's karmic circumstances. That is how the karmic principle works alongside the reincarnational *samsāra* or chain of embodiments.

According to Catherine, the purgatorial instrument is best symbolized by fire, the traditional symbol. Fire consumes the dross but cannot destroy the gold. While the dross and the gold are mixed, the fire, which is God, is experienced as pain. When the dross has been consumed by the fire the pain has gone and is replaced by joy: the joy of victory. The fire is painful while we resist it, failing to perceive it as God. Once again the parallel with a reincarnationalist interpretation is uncannily striking: according to the karmic principle, the sufferings we endure in life are brought on by ourselves. They may seem to have been imposed upon us by an external force, but they are essentially the result of our own karmic buildup. The external circumstances remain the same; it is I, the diseased soul or self, who changes by the use of the medication that the successive embodiments provide.

To appreciate that such is the case is at the same time to perceive that I am already *in* purgatory, that I have been in it for an incalculable period, and that I am likely to remain in the purgatorial process for a no less incalculable time. This is simply to say, in one or another of two ways, that I am growing and am suffering from growing pains. Growing pains, although they can be terrible, are not unmitigated, so long as they are accompanied by a sense of growing out of an attenuated life and into a fuller one.

A standard objection to all forms of reincarnationist teachings is that (apart from some exceptional and often suspect claims) the memory of past lives is lost. This poses several kinds of question and invites several sorts of objection. A common one is that I am held accountable for past misdeeds or waywardnesses that I cannot even remember. Is not it ethically unacceptable that I should be "punished" for what I cannot even recall? No, indeed, for much of the evil that men and women do issues from states of unconsciousness. Drunk drivers exemplify that. They had no intention of causing such terrible consequences upon their victims, but it is precisely through their having become drunk in the first place that they have become such instruments of evil.

Some deprivation of memory is, moreover, essential to spiritual growth. A person of advanced age is burdened with such a vast array of memories that he or she would be paralyzed by them were it not for nature's merciful mechanism for forgetting. If one remembered everything even in one life of eighty or ninety years one would be stifled. Think what it would be to remember in similar detail hundreds, perhaps millions, of previous ones. One would be buried under the oppression of the load.

Plato, in his treatment of the ancient myth of Lethe, the waters of "unmindfulness," presents a vision of souls having first crossed the hot wasteland of "forgetfulness" and of their then being brought to Lethe, where they must drink of its waters. Thirsty, most of them drink too much and so forget all; the wise, however, drink moderately, preserving thereby enough memory of their past lives to enrich their upcoming new embodiment with greater self-understanding than is enjoyed by the majority of men and women. These minorities are they who would be called, in theosophical language, "advanced souls." In terms of a Catholic vision of purgatory we might say that for them the pains of the purgatorial process are tempered by the fuller understanding they enjoy of the reason for their sufferings. This understanding would equip them to see their sufferings as having a value far beyond any penal interpretation of them. As at school, a task imposed on one by way of punishment is always much harder than the same task perceived as leading to one's advancement or general betterment.

The fact that the Oriental concept of the reincarnational process obviously functions so similarly to the functioning of the purgatorial process in Catholic tradition does not mean that they are interchangeable. The one is fitted to rendering the self able to realize its identity with the Great Self; the other has a radically different goal: to purify and so develop the soul in such a way as to make it capable of the Vision of God. The Vision of God is available to all in the sense that a symphony concert is available to all comers, but one may need some musical training to enjoy it and if one is completely tone deaf no amount of training will help. (Such is presumed to be the case of those whose souls are in hell: They are totally incapable of hearing the heavenly music.) A transmigrational doctrine designed for Hinduism or Buddhism must be adjusted, therefore, to fit any of the monotheistic religions, since their goal is so differently conceived. This can well be done, however, as I have shown elsewhere.[2] When so adapted, the series of embodiments or chain of rebirths can be seen as functioning so much like the Christian purgatory as to be a perfect expression of the purgatorial pains which, despite the intensity of their anguish, are by no means without joy, for they are the pains of love, which entails both the sharpest of sufferings and the most ecstatic of joys.

All authentic education, all professional or other training, demands perseverance and entails tears. Training for a higher stage in the evolutionary spiral must be expected to entail both in the most eminent degree. For good reason have theologians suggested that "purgatorial time" is different from clock time. It is different if only in being incalculably long and therefore immeasurable.

Yet when all that is said, is not the idea of re-embodiment so alien to Western modes of conceptualizing the afterlife as to make it ill adapted, if only for psychological reasons, to the Occidental mind, Plato and so many others notwithstanding? To that question we shall attend in the next chapter.

Notes

1 For a scholarly and persuasive argument for extensive Islamic influence on Dante's *Commedia*, including the *Purgatorio*, see Miguel Asin y Palacios, *Islam and the Divine Comedy* (London, 1926 and 1968). The author was a Roman

Catholic priest and Arabist. The Spanish original was *La Escatología musulmana en la Divina Commedia* (Madrid, 1919).

2 For example, in my *Reincarnation as a Christian Hope* (London: Macmillan, 1982), *Reincarnation in Christianity* (Wheaton, Ill.: Quest Books, 1978, 1986), and *The Christening of Karma* (Wheaton, Ill.: Quest Books, 1984).

CHAPTER XI

∎

Resurrection

Someone may ask, "How are dead people raised, and what
sort of body do they have when they come back?" They are
stupid questions . . . each sort of seed gets its own sort of
body.

— Paul's first letter to the Corinthians, 15:35–38.

The idea of resurrection occurs in all the great monotheistic religions.
Zoroaster taught that at the end of the present "age" or "world order" a
general resurrection would take place, at which time the good and the evil
would be separated. Although the dates of Zoroaster's life are disputable and
some very extravagant claims are made for their antiquity, we can safely put
his time frame at least as early as the seventh century B.C.E.

As we have seen, this idea was alien to the beliefs of the Hebrew people
until comparatively late, but in the Book of Daniel, for example, which in its
present form may be dated between 167 and 164 B.C.E., although it may
have had antecedents of greater antiquity, we find a definite allusion to
resurrection, similarly in connection with the "end of the age." Michael is to
arise and there is to be a time of unparalleled distress. At that time, however,
those whose names are "found written in the Book" will be spared. "Of those
who lie sleeping in the dust of the earth many will awake, some to everlasting

∎

life, some to shame and everlasting disgrace. The learned will shine as brightly as the vault of heaven, and those who have instructed many in virtue, as bright as stars for all eternity" (Daniel 12:2–3). A similar apocalyptic vision is found in the Second Book of Maccabees, which cannot be dated so precisely, although it was written in Greek and almost certainly by an Alexandrian Jew, probably in the first century B.C.E. Here, however, resurrection is restricted to the righteous (see II Maccabees 7:9, 11, 23; 14:46). Both in the New Testament and in the Jewish historian Josephus we are told that the Pharisees believed in resurrection while other parties in Judaism, such as the Sadducees, did not.

So central to Christianity is the concept of resurrection that we shall leave it aside for the moment and note that when, early in the seventh century C.E., Muhammad began appearing in the courtyard of the Ka'ba in Mecca preaching what seemed to his hearers a new and strange doctrine, which at first they ridiculed, he taught from the first that along with a coming judgment day there would be a "resurrection of the body."

What exactly was understood by this promise of resurrection that we find emerging in such varied circumstances and in the context of an emphatically monotheistic understanding of God? While it is impossible to determine what was exactly in the minds of those who talked of the resurrection of the body, we may be fairly sure that they were vague about the nature of it. They could not have asked the kinds of question that would come so naturally to our minds today, such as: Exactly how is this rising from the dead to take place and precisely what is to happen chemically to the skeletons of the dead to re-embody and re-animate them? It would seem that in some miraculous way the constituents of the bodies of the dead would be brought together again and no less miraculously "come to life." This is also, as we shall presently see, how many Christians in early times conceived of the resurrection process. No wonder that the Athenians laughed at Paul and that, some six centuries later, the Meccans mocked Muhammad for announcing so incredible a prediction. Their minds were not prepared to conceptualize in such ways. Yet we cannot dispose of the matter so lightly, for although those who scoffed at Paul in Athens and at Muhammad in Mecca were presumably for the most part unlettered audiences, groups such as the Pharisees certainly were not; nor was Paul, who had been trained in the Pharisaic tradition.

The Central Christian Proclamation

The chronologically earliest allusion to the central Christian proclamation and to some Christians' disbelief in it occurs in Paul's first letter to the Corinthians, in which Paul asks how those who disbelieve in the resurrection of the dead can do so, in view of what, he affirms, has been consistently preached about the resurrection of Christ? "If there is no resurrection of the dead, Christ himself cannot have been raised, and if Christ has not been raised, then our preaching is useless and your believing it is useless" (I Corinthians 15:12–14). This passage follows his reminder that what he is teaching is what he had been taught himself, that Christ was raised to life, that he appeared to Cephas, later to the other disciples, then to more than five hundred witnesses at the same time, most of whom were still living at the time of Paul's writing; then he appeared to James and finally to Paul himself (I Corinthians 15:3–8).

Paul's letter was written from Ephesus about 52 C.E., at least twenty years before Luke wrote Acts, which contains both the account of Paul's vision of the Risen Christ who had appeared to him on the road to Damascus and abundant testimony that the resurrection of Christ was the central proclamation (*kerygma*) of the apostles of the Christian Way. So we have literary testimony dating from about two decades after the death of Jesus that the universal and central teaching of the Apostles was that Jesus Christ truly died on the Cross and was truly raised from the dead on "the third day"—the first day of the week. The resurrection of Christ is, according to Paul, what warrants belief in the possibility of resurrection for those of the Christian Way.

Paul's Teaching on Afterlife Belief in the resurrection of the dead is not incompatible with the concept of the immortality of the soul that Plato expounds, but the latter doctrine is not what Paul teaches. He expressly says in his letter to the Romans, datable about 58 C.E., that death is what must be expected to issue from our sinful nature; nevertheless God has given us, as a pure gift, through the resurrection of Christ, the capacity to be resurrected with him (Romans 6:20–23).

By the time of Paul's earlier letter to the Corinthians he had apparently already been asked for more precision about the kind of body we might expect when we are resurrected. Paul calls such questions stupid. They are, of course, by no means stupid in themselves; they are very intelligent questions.

Paul, however, denigrates them by way of expounding a fundamental principle that he wishes to establish. He reminds his audience that you get what you sow: "Whatever you sow in the ground has to die before it is given new life and the thing that you sow is not what is going to come; you sow a bare grain, say of wheat or something like that, and then God gives it the sort of body that he has chosen: each sort of seed gets its own sort of body" (I Corinthians 15:35–38). He clearly teaches in the rest of this chapter that the resurrected body will therefore be different from our present flesh-and-bones body. It will be *pneumatikos*, a "glorious" or "spiritual" body. In "the twinkling of an eye" as the "last trumpet" sounds, our bodies will be transformed from perishable, "flesh-and-bones" structures into imperishable bodies suited to our transformed state of imperishability (I Corinthians 15:39–53).

Paul was plainly teaching a view incompatible with one that was widely taken by theologians both in patristic times and in the Middle Ages. In the fourth century C.E., the learned and original thinker Gregory of Nyssa, in discussing the respective merits of a reincarnationist and a resurrection view of the afterlife, prefers the latter. He does so because the reincarnationist view presupposes the notion of the soul's "alighting" on one body after another, while on the resurrection view one gets back (according to his interpretation) "the same body as before, compacted around the soul." This understanding of resurrection seems to have had much acceptance both to theologians in the ancient world and to those in the Middle Ages. Some ecclesiastical councils supported it, notably the Fourth Lateran Council (1215), which in its first canon affirmed that both the elect and the reprobate would arise *in their own bodies, the bodies that they now have*, to receive their reward or their punishment as the case might be (*Omnes cum suis propriis resurgent corporibus, quae nunc gestant*: All shall rise with their own bodies, the bodies that they now bear). This tenet seems to have been acclaimed with the Albigenses in mind: a movement that taught reincarnationist ideas of afterlife and was so feared by the Church because of its immense growth in and influence over much of the south of France and north of Italy that the Church planned to root it out in one way or another and eventually undertook what amounted to the genocide of its numerous adherents.

Such insistence on so primitive an interpretation of the resurrection doctrine at the heart of the apostolic *kerygma* was singularly unfortunate. Not only is it contrary to all that we know of physics and biology today; it was precisely the outlook that had made the notion of resurrection seem so ridiculous to Paul's hearers at Athens and to Muhammad's at Mecca. Moreover, if applied to the resurrection of Christ on which the notion of the possibility of the resurrection of those who followed the Christian Way depended, it would mean that Jesus Christ's resurrected body would have been also "the same body as before, compacted around his soul," and that this was the body that walked through closed doors (John 20:19, 26) and appeared to Paul on the Damascus road (Acts 9:3–9).

Resurrection as Re-embodiment The concept of resurrection is of course a form of re-embodiment, as is that of reincarnation. When baldly stated, both doctrines present philosophical and scientific difficulties fatal to their intelligibility. Notoriously, the references to the resurrection of Christ give a very confusing picture. The resurrection event is nowhere *narrated* in the New Testament. What is found in the New Testament documents is (1) reference to the empty tomb and (2) reports of the apparition of the risen Lord Jesus Christ. The Gospels themselves report that the disciples doubted the resurrection of their Master, despite his having explicitly foretold it according to the testimony of all the three synoptists, Matthew, Mark, and Luke, who also report that the disciples found the predictions unintelligible both at the time that Jesus made them and later in the resurrection itself. If it is to be taken as a real fact, as is unequivocally affirmed by all orthodox Christians, it must be a real fact in a dimension of being beyond the empirical. That is precisely what Paul implies in his letter to the Corinthians in calling the resurrected body *pneumatikos* and in using the analogy of the seed sown in the ground, producing the kind of fruit proper to such a kind of seed. It is a way of enunciating the karmic principle without pinning upon it any specific theory, hypothesis, or doctrine by way of explaining how the principle works.

Re-embodiment as the Conquest of Death What is proclaimed in the New Testament and the Christian creeds and celebrated in Christian worship is not any particular form of "rising from the dead" but, rather, the conquest of death. Death has "lost its sting," having been conquered by the power of Christ. The Risen Christ has indeed a body: one far more powerful than the one made of flesh and bone that had been his embodiment during his life on earth. The earthly body of Jesus was of flesh (*sarx*); his body as the Risen Christ is indeed an embodiment (*sōma*), an organizational whole, visible and tangible to those equipped to see and touch in a dimension of existence beyond the empirical one. Such is the nature of the body promised to those who share in the glory of his resurrection. The vision of it that Paul so eloquently portrays in his letter to the Corinthians is often obscured for us by the complicated mixture of Hebrew and Greek ideas about body, soul, and spirit.

"Flesh and blood" (*sarx kai haima*) is a Hebraistic periphrasis for "human nature," or "a human being." Sometimes it is contrasted with *psychē*, sometimes with *pneuma*. In Greek thought *sōma* also is distinguished from *psychē* and *pneuma* and can refer to the human body. *Sarx* can refer to the physical aspect of man without any allusion to its weakness or other pejorative idea; but Paul often applies it to that aspect of human nature that tends to rise up and dominate the human being when it ought to be under the control of the higher self. In this usage it is often associated with weakness and sin. All these and other confusions contribute to the obscuring of what is meant by resurrection as the idea is applied to what happened in Jesus Christ after his death on the Cross and what is predicted for those who ally themselves to him and so share in his risen glory. No clear enunciation of what is meant by saying that "Christ is risen" is provided; but the total picture as presented in the New Testament documents makes clear that, in modern terms, the simplest way of expressing the resurrection event is to call it embodiment in a higher and fuller dimension of existence than that in which we are normally confined.

The concept of resurrection is not necessarily related to that of immortality; nevertheless, historically it is closely connected with the latter. Although immortality is not the central image of the Christian teaching on afterlife, it soon came to be interwoven with it in the development of Christian thought. The relation between the two concepts as well as their independence of each other must now be considered.

Immortality and Re-embodiment

Immortality is historically an attribute of divinity, however divinity be conceived. We mortals are contrasted to the great gods by our mortality. So it was with the gods on Olympus. Ultimate reality, whether conceived in the Indian manner or as in the monotheistic religions, is by definition eternal, imperishable, immortal. Any notion about the immortality of the individual soul springs from some theory of its participation in or derivation from that divinity: the notion that the human soul is a spark of the divine fire trapped in a human embodiment and therefore immortal or else, as in the monotheistic religions, the belief that God the Creator has bestowed upon or infused into humanity, in contrast to the brutes, the gift of immortality, or again that human beings partake in some way, as rational beings, in the imperishability of a rational principle that governs all things. Individual immortality is always in some way derived from the immortality of divine Being.

To the Greeks of antiquity, the rational element in man seemed to have a kinship with a rational principle in the universe so that in some way it partakes of or participates in the immortality of that principle. Plato, in harmony with that general outlook, went on to infer the pre-existence of the individual human soul and so also its survival of the death of the body. The process of learning is therefore largely the recovery or remembrance (*anamnēsis*) of knowledge acquired in a previous life. In the *Meno* Socrates asks a slave boy various mathematical questions and the boy, although untrained in mathematics, works out the answers by himself. Where we would call such a slave boy unusually intelligent, Plato explains his skill by the theory that he is remembering what he already had learned in a previous life. The soul, in this view, has an existence independent of the body that is at once its instrument and its prison. Intelligence, in this view, can be seen as the ability of a particular soul to function well despite the impediment of its being embodied. This view, very influential in the ancient Greek world, implies a reincarnationalist interpretation of the pilgrimage of the soul. It stood in sharp contrast to the popular conception of afterlife in Homer's Hades or the biblical Sheol, which we considered earlier, in which the soul, being understood as a sort of by-product, an epiphenomenon of the body, survived in a shadowy way as a pale ghost or even a puff of smoke that eventually would just blow away. Indeed, some critics were jestingly proposing that in this traditional, popular view, it would be prudent to try to die on a windless day rather than on a windy one when one's ghost would be more expeditiously dispersed in the air.

As we have seen, the central apostolic Christian teaching was not an immortality doctrine but was, rather, that those who were made one with Christ would share, through his resurrection, in his triumph over death. The focus was on victory over death, which through Christ's rising had lost its power, its "sting." The concept of immortality was from this stance a philosophical one. Not only was it apart from the central focus of the Christians that they expressed in their customary salutation (*Christos anestē*: Christ is risen); human destiny was more than the survival of the human soul as of its own nature immortal; it was the granting of everlasting life *with Christ*. The early Fathers of the Christian Church commonly understood the

Christian hope of immortality only in relation to the resurrection of Christ that warranted such a hope. As Christian thought developed in the midst of a climate of Greek philosophy, however, the tendency, especially among Gentile Christians, was to treat the human soul as an entity separate from the body, a view alien from the classical Hebrew understanding of body and soul as a unity such as makes the notion of a disembodied soul absurd. Predictably, however, Christian thought was very much influenced by Platonism down to the twelfth century, the time of the recovery of Aristotle in the Latin West. Even the great thirteenth-century Christian thinker Thomas Aquinas was no doubt a Platonist at heart, but since Aristotle in his age represented what today we would call the natural sciences, Thomas molded his thought in Aristotelian terms. In Aristotle's system everything other than God consists of "form" and "matter." The soul is the "form" of the body of the human being and cannot subsist on its own; it must have embodiment of some kind. This Aristotelian mode of thinking happened to fit perfectly with the theological doctrine of the resurrection of the body and some kind of re-embodiment could be seen as necessary, in Aristotelian terms, for any sort of afterlife.

The notion of a disembodied mind or disembodied soul is by any reckoning extremely difficult. Whether indeed anyone ever really accepted the implications of any such view is doubtful. The embodiment need not be our present one, but some organization of one kind or another seems to be necessary for individual consciousness to exist. One might imagine various possible forms of embodiment not visible to the human eye or tangible to the human touch, but one cannot really imagine what it would mean to talk of a disembodied soul or mind. Even in the unique case of God, the notion (largely inherited from Aristotle and "baptized" by Thomas) is not without philosophical difficulties, although perhaps not insurmountable ones.

Be that as it may, the concept of immortality has been gradually woven into Christian thought about the afterlife, despite the fact that in apostolic times it was taken to be a consequence of the resurrection of Christ rather than a condition of the human soul. The specific doctrine that the human soul is not intrinsically immortal but may attain immortality conditionally upon how it behaves in the course of its life in the body was held by some notable religious thinkers in the nineteenth century such as Edward White and the Unitarian James Martineau. The distinguished Anglican thinker Charles Gore (1853–1932) was sympathetic to this view. It has appealed to some in modern times as a way of avoiding both the traditional but horrific doctrine of everlasting torture in hell, on the one hand, and Origen's teaching, on the other, that in the end all, including Satan himself, are to be saved. Somewhat surprisingly, the view that immortality is an attainment (a view sometimes nowadays called "conditional immortality") has had comparatively few supporters in modern times and perhaps only a single representative in the patristic period and the Middle Ages—the early fourth-century Arnobius, a Christian apologist who, according to Jerome (*c.* 342–420), was originally from proconsular Africa.

What makes this circumstance especially surprising is that Paul clearly implies such a view in his letter to the Romans (6:23) in which he affirms that the reward of sin is death but God's gift is "eternal life in Christ Jesus our Lord." To anyone familiar with what was actually taught in Christian pulpits for centuries, both in the Catholic tradition and in the Reformation heritage, Paul's teaching here is attractively benign and one would have thought that his immense authority might have influenced the thought of the Church on this point. Instead, what prevailed among the learned in Catholic tradition was a very confused notion that the human soul, while in a state of grace, is immortal but, when it loses that state of grace through "mortal sin," is "killed" yet remains capable of everlasting suffering in hell. In Reformation theology the basic concept remained: The immortal soul must go somewhere and if not to heavenly bliss forever, then to everlasting torture in hell.

Immortality and the Soul

In the seventeenth century, two of the greatest thinkers in human history—René Descartes and Gottfried Wilhelm Leibniz—each in his own way vigorously upheld the justification of belief in the individual immortality of the human soul. Immanuel Kant's metaphysical skepticism prevented his claiming to prove the immortality of the soul on metaphysical grounds; nevertheless, in his *Critique of Practical Reason* he sought to establish it on moral grounds and his contentions from that standpoint enormously affected the temper of philosophical thought on the subject through the nineteenth century and beyond. The force of Kant's treatment of the immortality of the human soul depends, however, on his postulate of the existence of the kind of God who stands behind our moral experience and its expectations.

Kant's argument for individual immortality rests largely upon the fact that human beings are confronted with the obligation to perform certain duties the performance of which cannot be accomplished within any human lifespan and that therefore there must be an afterlife to provide the individual with the opportunity of performing them. For on the basis of his maxim "If I ought I can," I cannot be said to have a duty that I do not have time to do. Since my moral experience shows me that I have such a duty, I must have some means in an afterlife to fulfil my obligation. Kant's argument, when fully expounded, is eminently persuasive to those who believe in God and the reality of the moral law that such a God entails and who also have developed in themselves the sensitivity of moral awareness that makes Kant's vision of an afterlife a vivid reality to them. Otherwise, however, Kant's "moral argument" and its consequences for the afterlife will not seem nearly so plausible, to say the least.

Belief in the immortality of the soul has become, nevertheless, widely assumed by orthodox Christians to be part of the basic teachings of the Church. Despite the early history of Christian attitude to afterlife we have traced here, much can be said in favor of the view that the two ideas of immortality and resurrection were assimilated at a fairly early stage in the development of Christian thought. Professor Oscar Cullmann, in his Ingersoll Lecture for 1955, made a very strong case against the view that the immortality of the soul is anywhere taught or implied in the New Testament and therefore cannot be saddled upon Christianity. Indeed, he goes so far as to contend that the teaching of the New Testament is, on the contrary, that the soul is *not* immortal. In the Ingersoll Lecture for the following year, however, Professor Harry Wolfson, out of his rare combination of patristic learning and rabbinical scholarship, undertook to show that the two beliefs are "inseparably connected with each other," although the one is as scientifically unverifiable as the other. In short, both depend upon belief in the kind of God envisioned in the biblical documents.

In the intellectual climate of today we must also raise another question in regard to the concept of the immortality of the human soul. The early Christian Fathers, with some exceptions, such as Tertullian and possibly Origen, generally regarded the human soul as not immortal by its own nature but through some sort of participation. The Fathers and likewise the medieval schoolmen were able to think of humanity as a species, while today, from our evolutionary approach to the universe, including man, we must think of it, rather, as a slice in the evolutionary process of life. Not only must we find difficulty in the notion that we are each immortal by our own nature simply in virtue of being human; even the notion of individual immortality by participation presents more of a problem to us than it would have generally presented to our forefathers in antiquity and the Middle Ages who could think of "man" as a universal and "Socrates" as an exemplar of that universal humanity. We might postulate, for example, that Mother Teresa has a soul that is immortal, but her postulated immortality would be because of her being that individual, Mother Teresa and of her special relation to God. One might go on to say that it is possible that a criminal lunatic might have the capacity to attain such immortality in some distant age and in another embodiment but that such a joyous development is unlikely to occur soon, in view of the slow speed with which the mills of God grind. We who have learned from archeological and other evidence of the enormous ranges of time that are involved in the evolution of even the comparatively recent ancestors of Homo sapiens (more than three million years, for instance, even since "Lucy" appeared on the scene), must accustom ourselves to expecting to find, as we do find, vast differences in development and capacity within what has been traditionally called the human species.

In the apocalyptic vision in the Book of Revelation, John sees the redeemed as clothed in robes washed white and standing with palms (the emblem of victory) in their hands. Because of their victory (the victory made possible because of God's redemptive act) they are never to hunger or thirst again, nor be plagued by heat or storm or any other force of nature. God will take care of them and "wipe away all tears from their eyes" (Revelation 7:9–17). John's reference here is plainly to the passage in Isaiah in which the prophet envisions a banquet at which Yahweh will provide the best of food and wine and *destroy death for ever* and "wipe away the tears from every cheek" (Isaiah 25:6–8). The destruction of death plainly entails the hope and expectation of immortality for those invited to that banquet, but it is an immortality that has been attained. It does not inhere in any mortal man or woman either by nature or by participation. It can be best interpreted as a stage in human development: one that, according to Christian teaching, has been made possible by the blood of Christ, which "is to be poured out *for many*" (Mark 14:24).

We must conclude, then, that the meaning of the concept of immortality, no less than that of resurrection or other re-embodiment, is modified by the conception of God, which varies not only in expression but also in content according to the teaching of the religious society that uses such terms.

CHAPTER XII

Problems with Traditional Christian Images

Men have fiendishly conceived a heaven only to find it insipid, and a hell to find it ridiculous.

—George Santayana, *Little Essays*

I saw when, at his word, the formless mass,
This World's material mould, came to a heap:
Confusion heard his voice, and wild Uproar
Stood ruled, stood vast Infinitude confined;
Till, at his second bidding, Darkness fled,
Light shone and order from disorder sprung.

—Milton, *Paradise Lost*

We have seen in what sometimes haphazard ways images of afterlife have arisen in the history of religious thought. We have also been forced to recognize the malaise, intellectual and emotional, that issues from such confusion. For although groping for an intelligible view of the subject may sometimes guide us toward a belief or disbelief in this or that kind of God, once our concept of God has been formed in principle, whether by way of denial or affirmation, we need a view of afterlife that can sit with whatever our type of belief or disbelief in God may be. Instead, we too often find, in Milton's celebrated phrase, "confusion worse confounded."

What are the sources of that confusion? Can we sort out its constituents and have at least an intelligible vision of afterlife that would do justice to the rich imagery we have inherited and yet be intelligible enough for us to decide for or against?

Resurrection

For example, take the concept of resurrection. Not only is it absent in almost the whole of the Old Testament; when it does appear in the Maccabean period (e.g., II Maccabees 7:9, 11, 23 and 14:46) it seems something of a novelty, yet in Daniel, the latest book in the Hebrew Bible, it is presented as a belief already recognized (Daniel 12:2). Moreover, it is often a highly ambiguous term, sometimes used figuratively to refer to the survival of Israel. Yet as we have noted, belief in individual resurrection is attested by both the Jewish historian Josephus and the Christian Gospels as a belief held by the Pharisees. Since there is no way in which its roots can be traced with any plausibility from within biblical literature, we must see it as a foreign import. Furthermore, it seems to be associated in some way with the messianic hope, itself a concept with a very complex history in Hebrew thought.

When it became the central focus of the Christian expectation its meaning was modified if not radically changed. Now it was firmly anchored in belief in the resurrection of Christ: the basis of Easter joy. Because Jesus was reported as warning his followers that the Day of Judgment was at hand, Christians in the first century seem to have generally assumed that it might come any day (a supposition that inevitably affected their outlook on everything) and that a general resurrection would be among the events of that great and terrible day. Yet the apocalyptic vision in the Book of Revelation does not seem to harmonize with the general Christian expectation of that time. For according to Revelation 20:1–10, the Devil is to be bound for a thousand years and during this millennium the righteous are to rise with Christ and reign with him. At the end of this millennium, however, the Devil is to be released. Being released he makes war with God, besieging the holy city, the New Jerusalem; but he loses the war. Only then comes the general resurrection of the dead and the final judgment in which the wicked are to get their deserts.

This curious conception does have some literary ancestry in a Jewish apocryphal book written in Greek before 70 C.E. and called *The Secrets of Enoch*. (This is sometimes known to scholars today as the Slavonic Enoch to distinguish it from another composition relating to Enoch on which to some extent it depends.) In this book is a passage that canvasses the highly speculative notion that the world, having been created in six days, would endure for six periods of a thousand years each, after which would ensue the seventh and final millennium at the close of which the world would end. This fanciful apocalyptic vision was entertained by some of the early Fathers of the Christian Church as well as by some sectaries, among whom the belief was sustained that the sixth millennium had begun with the birth of Christ and that the seventh would therefore begin in the year 1000 C.E., ushering in the New Age. As the year 1000 C.E. approached, there was in fact a revival of such millenarian expectation that the Second Coming of Christ would take place in that year.

From all this one can easily appreciate that even the notion of resurrection could be variously conceived, both in Judaism and in Christianity and in the former of course it could very well not be entertained at all. In Christianity, where it was central, all ambiguities notwithstanding, it gave rise to intolerable problems, as we saw earlier, about what happens to the individual between death and resurrection. Did the dead sleep to be awakened by the Last Trumpet, as was generally supposed in the first century C.E.? Such a notion would seem highly plausible when the Last Day was so imminently expected; when it seemed indefinitely postponed, difficulties proliferated. Was there a particular judgment for each individual at death and a temporary resurrection body to serve till the Last Day, whenever that might be, when it would be exchanged for the permanent resurrected body? Or what? For the majority of Christians, who believed in some form of intermediate, purgatorial state, the problems might be removed to another level, but they were by no means solved.

Background Whence came, then, in the first place, the concept of resurrection that was to play so central a role in Christian faith? Whence did Ezekiel, for instance, get his vision of a gloriously rebuilt Jerusalem? Whence did he get his vision of a vast plain covered with "dry bones" to which he was commanded to address a sort of resurrection promise?

Ezekiel was prophesying during the Babylonian Exile and sometime between 585 and 568 B.C.E. He was living near a region populated by Elamites and Persians. He could hardly have failed to know about Zoroaster and the

Zoroastrian custom (still observed) of exposing the bodies of the dead rather than burying them. The point of this custom was and is to let the vultures eat their flesh and then to let the bones dry out to provide a framework for the restoration of their bodies. The Zoroastrians taught that God, who had created the bodies in the first place, would eventually reassemble them. Simplistic as some might find the idea today, no doubt it fitted the age and the circumstances. If, as seems likely, Ezekiel adapted it for his own use, he did with it what any good preacher today does with what he takes to be a good idea for a sermon: He painted a picture and then interpreted the picture for his own purpose. His purpose was to talk of the restoration, the resurrection of Israel: a Zionist hope for a return to a glorified homeland.

When the resurrection idea reappeared much later in its cosmological and theological form it had to be fitted to a Judaism (and later to a Christianity) that had become far more complex than either the Zoroastrianism or the Judaism of Ezekiel's day. Moreover, there may well have been other ingredients in the idea of re-embodiment when it eventually came into late Judaism and thence into the heart of the teaching of those who followed the Christian Way. Such ideological adaptations often fit the new scenario no better than would a Baroque extension fit an English Perpendicular church. Such architectural feats may be felicitously accomplished from time to time, but they need more skill and ingenuity than one is likely to be able to muster when talking, as rightly one may feel a duty to talk, under the influence of divine inspiration.

Traditionally inseparable from the resurrection hope in Christianity has been the concept of everlasting life. Christianity, true in this respect to its Jewish heritage, was not generally hospitable to the notion of everlasting life in a disembodied state. God is indeed Spirit, but in that he is unique. There were some who entertained the notion of disembodiment, but it was difficult to square it with the concept of resurrection. The angels, according the medieval angelology of Thomas Aquinas, are disembodied, being, in medieval language, "separate substances." Resurrection, then, could not apply to them since, having been created without bodies, they have none to resurrect.

Such theologians today as are willing to talk seriously of heaven and hell are generally inclined to insist that these are names of states, not places. The notion of heaven as a place is widely regarded, even by conservative, traditionalist theologians, as a superstition to be discarded. Yet if there is any sort of resurrection of the body, "glorious" or otherwise, surely it implies some sort of extension in space. Moreover, apart from what the resurrection hope imposes on Christians, the notion of disembodied consciousness is, as we saw earlier, philosophically difficult, to say the least. Some eminent philosophers in recent times have valiantly tried to uphold the notion (among them H. H. Price), but most would find it inconceivable. So where do these resurrected bodies, redeemed or reprobate, go eventually after death? Why, to heaven, of course, since that is the traditional name for it, wherever it may be.

The earlier biblical writers had little if any difficulty locating the place whither one might go if righteous enough to be received into God's company on a permanent basis. Such a privileged person would go to heaven. Where else? There were only three possibilities in the universe: (1) the Earth, (2) the Underworld (Sheol), and (3) the Heavens, where God dwelled. Such communication as there might be was between the Heavens and the Earth. The Underworld was cut off. Such, at any rate, was the basic model the biblical writers inherited from their ancestors and their neighbors. When, however, anyone did go to the Heavens to be with God, it was a most exceptional event. Enoch and Elijah seem to have escaped death and to have been "translated" or "assumed" into the Heavens. It had to be a bodily assumption, since deprivation of the body would have meant diminishment, not the extraordinary reward that these uniquely favored holy men received. Normally, people went at death to Sheol and its attenuated form of existence.

As time went on, however, the situation became more complex and confused. The Exile in 586 B.C.E. had been a catastrophe to those Jews with nationalistic sentiments and profound nostalgia for their ancient homeland. Their noblest hope was for a return thither to a new, victorious Jerusalem, center of a revived, restored, and transmogrified Israel; it was a political aspiration rather than a spiritual hope. Not all dispersed Jews, however, shared that outlook. Many, especially the more philosophically minded Jews of the Diaspora, took an individualistic stance. They recognized the fact that the wicked seemed to prosper while the righteous suffered here on earth; but, full of trust in the power and righteousness of God, they looked forward to a reversal of these injustices. The tables would be turned; God would let the arrogant wicked perish in Sheol but reward the righteous by removing them from the power of Sheol and drawing them to himself. "Why should I be afraid in evil times . . . of men who trust in their wealth and boast of the profusion of their riches?" asks the Psalmist-Sage, who goes on to assert that prosperity seems to dull intelligence. "Do not be afraid when a man grows rich . . . when he dies he can take nothing with him." One has no reason to be overawed by these arrogant parvenus who put such trust in their wealth. Sheol is all they will have in the end. By contrast,

God will redeem my life
from the grasp of Sheol, and will receive me.

[Psalm 49]

The author of this psalm seems to recognize that the parable he is enunciating (really a part of the Wisdom literature of the Bible, although set to be sung with musical accompaniment) is novel. It is not in the mainstream of classical Hebrew thought. Yet it is along the lines of the central theme of Job: Why do the wicked prosper and the righteous suffer? The Psalmist's answer lies in the future when these inequities shall be corrected, as each individual is to find out. Clearly, here is a radical departure from the traditional expectation associated with death. No longer are the Enochs and the Elijahs extraordinary cases whose blessed lot in the afterlife is as much beyond the hope of ordinary mortals as would be the desire of a beggar to become a king. No, there is an afterlife in which the righteous will be "received by God" and not go down into the darkness of Sheol.

The theme of the author of Psalm 37, which also belongs to the Wisdom type of literature, is very similar. Yahweh, the Psalmist-Sage concludes, will deliver the righteous from the wicked, because the righteous trust in him. Yahweh will not abandon the righteous to the machinations of the wicked. This psalm probably was composed in the third century B.C.E.

The author of Psalm 73, in a similar spirit, looks back with regret on the time in his life when he felt bitterness at the thought of the arrogant pride of the prosperous.

Envying the arrogant as I did,
and watching the wicked get rich.

He now perceives that he had been an ignorant brute till he learned the true nature of Yahweh, whom now he recognizes as "my heart's Rock, my own, God forever!"

Such was the mood of many Diaspora Jews who had politically acclimated themselves to their adopted land and no longer thought of themselves as exiles. They might well have affection for their ancestral land. That was only natural, but it was not part of their vision of salvation. Emancipated from dependence on a mere nationalistic heritage, they more fully realized a vision of themselves as individually standing alone before God. They could now see more clearly than could any of their ancestors before the Exile that in Yahweh alone could they put their trust and he alone would save them from death and draw them into closer union with him. As we have now seen, this could only be in some sort of afterlife, a life made fuller through gratitude and love.

Immortality

Such developments in the mind of the Diaspora Jew brought him in some ways into closer sympathy with the outlook of the most enlightened of his Gentile contemporaries who had been influenced by Plato and the Stoics. There was, however, a difference. Both might talk of immortality, but while the Platonists and other Greeks thought of it as a condition of the human soul, along with reason, courage, and much else, the Diaspora Jew was predisposed to think of immortality as a special gift from God. How radical was that difference depends on one's point of view. In both cases, at any rate, heaven was the locale. In Hebrew, the word for heaven is a plural— *šamāyim*—so Hebrew writers could think of stages or levels in heaven, varying in number from three to five, from seven to ten, according to the writer's schema. This is reflected in Paul's claim (II Corinthians 12:2) that he was taken up into the third heaven. In both Hebrew and Greek thought in this later period, heaven is still "up," but Jewish thinkers, now deeply influenced by Hellenistic ways of thought, were inclined to take "up" more allegorically than had their ancestors. The ordinary person, however, Jew or Christian, continued for centuries to think in terms of the three-storied model (Heaven, Earth, and Underworld) that had been long abandoned by the learned. It mattered not whether heaven was the Elysian fields or the Isles of the Blest, both favored ideas in the Greek arena of imagery. They could be at least poetically located "up there," since *up* is a basic human metaphor for what is noble and lofty and good, contradistinguished from what is low and base.

A remarkable variety prevailed in this increasingly syncretistic climate of thought about the afterlife of the redeemed, whether the redemption was attributed to God's direct action or to the refinement of the soul by its own exertions or to a combination of these and other outlooks.

The view of the Essenes, for instance, with their strong emphasis on "monastic" virtues, such as poverty, through the renunciation of private possessions, and celibacy, entailing the suppression of sexual needs, encompassed the notion that the body is corruptible while the soul is by nature immortal: a very "Greek" view, alien to the classical Hebrew outlook. The

Pharisees' view of afterlife is more obscure. Josephus tells us that while they took for granted the immortality of the soul they also taught the interesting doctrine that only the souls of the righteous would receive a new embodiment. Thus, despite their obviously different criteria for righteousness, with their intense emphasis on the observance of the minutiae of the Torah and their respect for legalistic tradition in general—for which Jesus, according to the Gospels, uncompromisingly attacked them—the Pharisees seem to have incorporated into their outlook on afterlife two elements characteristic of the Platonic tradition on it: the immortality of the soul and some form of re-embodiment.

Philo (c. 20 B.C.E.–c. 50 C.E.), who belonged to a prosperous priestly family of Alexandria, was a Jewish thinker who exercised an enormous and beneficial influence on both Jewish and Christian thought. He was syncretistic (perhaps, more accurately, eclectic) in his handling of the various ideas he treated, thus giving us some notion of the extent of the options that educated people of his time could entertain concerning the subject of afterlife.

But what of the teaching of Jesus on the subject of afterlife? This is a question of extraordinary difficulty, not to say enigmatic. Behind it is a scholarly and highly controversial question about how much and how little we know of the teaching of Jesus himself, distinguished from the reports handed down by the New Testament writers, more especially the Evangelists. Even setting aside this superlatively difficult question, however, and looking only to what is actually reported in the Gospels, we are left with a puzzlingly complex set of views attributed explicitly or implicitly to Jesus himself.

What we find in the phrases copiously used in the Gospels and attributed to Jesus on the concept of heaven is mostly very traditional Jewish language. Heaven and earth are frequently conjoined as cosmological elements in the universe (see Mark 13:31 and Luke 21:33). In conformity with Jewish custom, he often used *heaven* as a stand-in term for the word *God*, which was so sacred as to be unutterable. When the disciples asked him why he talked in parables he replied that it was because the mysteries of the Kingdom of Heaven were revealed to them but not to those bereft of understanding (Matthew 13:11). Yet he enjoined his hearers to seek first the Kingdom of God (Matthew 6:33). He often talks of heaven as above and beyond, yet he tells the Pharisees, when they ask him when the Kingdom of God is to come, "you must know that the kingdom of God is within [or among] you" (*entos hymōn*). Jesus lived as head of a celibate community, yet his manner of life is contrasted with that of John the Baptist, for—unlike the latter, who lived on what he could gather in the desert—Jesus partook of good food and wine. Jesus spoke of God as "in heaven" but clearly in allusion to God as the source of all: "heavenly Father" contradistinguished from "earthly father." His vision of the resurrected state is distinctive: Men and women, when they rise from the dead, do not marry; no, they are "like the angels in heaven" (Mark 12:25). That is, either they are incorporeal or they are corporeal but asexual. In the teaching of Jesus as reported in the Gospels, the Kingdom of Heaven is both beyond and right here. It is both a process in the spiritual dimension and a state to be attained.

Sheol, Gehenna, and Hell

What is translated in English as *hell* can also lead to misunderstanding. Jesus tells Peter that the gates of hell (*Sheol, Hadēs*) shall not prevail against his Church (Matthew 16:18) and he warns against that which can destroy both body and soul in hell (*geenna*); that is, Gehenna, the place of destruction and punishment, named in Hebrew *ge-hinnōm*, shorthand for the valley of the son of Hinnom (probably the name of the original Jebusite owner of the property), today the Wadi er-Rababi and at one time a cultic shrine where human sacrifice had been offered. To Jesus is attributed the notion of the punishment of the wicked by destruction, although by no means necessarily an everlasting punishment. As time went on, however, hell became the most fearsome image of afterlife within Christian tradition.

Visions of Hell

In popular preaching on both sides of the Reformation curtain full use was made of the concept with all its terrifying implications and unspeakably blood-curdling imagery. The English Methodist catechism designed for "children of tender years" defines hell as "a dark and bottomless pit, full of fire and brimstone." The punishment is depicted: "Their bodies will be tormented by fire, and their souls by the wrath of God." To the question "How long will their torments last?" the answer prescribed is "The torments of hell will last for ever and ever."

A sort of crowd sado-masochism seems to have pervaded the pulpit and other instructional agencies of the Church, irrespective of its polity. William Booth, founder of the Salvation Army, wrote in 1854 to his future wife that people "must have hell-fire flashed before their faces, or they will not move." About 1850 a pamphlet by a Redemptorist priest, published in Dublin with ecclesiastical approval, tells of a child who was given sixpence from his father to buy bread. The child bought instead "sugar-sticks and other foolish things." The same child had also often neglected the opportunities for grace afforded by the Church: prayer, good books, and of course the sacraments of the Church. The child dies and when it sees what is happening it falls down on its knees before Jesus, begging for mercy and imploring Jesus not to send it to hell. "I was a poor ignorant child," it cries; "I knew no better." Jesus then carefully rehearses with the child the opportunities it has had and has neglected, while the child trembles in fear of the terrible sentence that it knows only too well, from such instruction as it has received in catechism and the like, must be everlasting punishment in hell. Then the pamphlet goes on to describe the scene that ensues: "Jesus Christ now orders the cross to be taken away" as a sign that mercy is no more. "Oh, how the child roars and screams when it sees the cross going away." Then Jesus, having pronounced sentence, tells the devils that the child now belongs to them to do with it as they please. The whole sky becomes dark with millions of devils. At last the child is in the "red-hot oven" of hell, burning and screaming in agony. "The wicked child has been burning in Hell for years and years."

Since according to the evidence provided in the pamphlet its turpitude surely could not have warranted by any reckoning more than a sound whipping followed by being sent supperless to bed (the customary treatment in those times and circumstances for such conduct as is described in the reported indictment), even some years of the horrors of hell-fire roasting seems already excessive even by the social standards of the age. The narrator, however, goes on relentlessly to depict the moment when all hell becomes silent as a trumpetlike shout goes forth: "Arise, ye dead, and come to judgment." The child is among the rest who move out to receive the final, irrevocable sentence of God's Supreme Court. The gates of hell then close it in with all the other writhing, roaring, and screaming denizens of the damned. "The wicked child is in Hell for ever and ever." Although the tract is entitled "Books for Children and Young Persons," it was no doubt also intended to reinforce the terror of hell that had been designed to deter the faithful from improper behavior. It could hardly have been ineffective in its purpose even with the grossest and most inveterate of sinners, to say nothing of its effect on "children and young persons."

G. G. Coulton, a notably careful Cambridge historian writing in 1930, assures us that that Dublin tract was still in circulation within the lifetime of people then still living. My purpose in citing it here as an example of the way in which in comparatively recent times hell was almost routinely represented in such terrifyingly concrete and colorful ways is to show that the idea of the immortality of the human soul is not always such a benign concept as it may sound when propounded by philosophers as a hypothesis supportive of the grandeur and dignity of man.

Let us not suppose that Christianity was alone or even preeminent in the presentation of such sadistic horrors. As we have seen, in China, both in Taoism and in Buddhism, eighteen hells are recognized. (Eighteen is a symbolic number in Chinese lore, hence presumably the choice of it here.) To list them all would be tedious, but a few will show that the Chinese imagination is by no means behind the West in visions of afterlife torture. The punishments seem designed to fit the crimes. T'ang-huo, for instance, the hell of burning oil, is for those who waste oil or meat in cooking. Kai-shan is a hell in which one is frozen inside a block of ice as a punishment for having wasted heating fuel or worn more clothes than needed while having no pity on those who shivered in the cold. Pao-p'i is specifically a hell for those women who wear seductive clothes and adorn their bodies with powders and paints to tempt and entice men. They are skinned alive. There is, however, one major (indeed infinite) difference between the Chinese hells and the Christian one: They are not everlasting. They are suffered between one incarnation and another and sometimes leave their mark on the victims on the rebirth of the latter. Those who have gone to Pao-p'i, for instance, may be recognized in their next incarnation by the pockmarks on their faces. The word *Ti-yü*, generally translated "hell," is conceived as a prison where wrongdoers imprison themselves and in fact create their own self-torture appropriate to their sins. It lacks the awful hopelessness of the Christian hell; nevertheless, being continuously skinned alive for even a year or two is terrifying enough. [1]

We can see, then, an immense variety of sources of confusion in the Judeo-Christian heritage of teaching on the afterlife. Besides, no doubt other ideas about afterlife current in Mediterranean thought on the subject were entertained even though not all of them were necessarily recorded, and these could have had in their turn indirect influence on what both Jews and Christians have since the time of Jesus included in their range of views on the afterlife.

Heaven

In both Christian literature and Christian iconography in the Middle Ages, heaven, the ultimate goal of all life and striving, was presented as an everlasting joy in the endless adoration of God. This image enabled people to perceive God as the central focus of all striving. The present life and the intermediate state that (in the case of most people) followed it were largely deprivations of that joy: the first state overburdened by work, the second overstrained by purification. In both of these states the hope of peace and joy forever in the knowledge of God in which the heavenly vision consists was for the majority of people on the whole as close to perfect bliss as one could conceive. The learned liked that image because it emphasized the sovereignty of God, which the masses, in a religious culture replete with a cornucopia of angels and saints, could be in danger of losing sight of.

Renaissance art introduced new and sometimes very different images of heaven that contributed much to European culture but little to support the theological focus that the Golden Age of medieval scholasticism had achieved. In the Reformation heritage, however, theologians were well content with the theocentricity of the medieval concept of heaven and equally satisfied with the medieval concept of hell. Indeed, perhaps these two images of afterlife were the only ones that pleased the Reformers.

The Shorter Catechism, which emanated from the Westminster Confession of Faith, ratified by the General Assembly of the Scottish Presbyterian Kirk on August 27, 1647, was designed as a popular summary of that larger confessional document. It opens with the question "What is the chief end of man?," to which the appointed answer is "Man's chief end is to glorify God and to enjoy him for ever." Thomas Carlyle, writing in 1876, stated in a lamentation against what he took to be the crass materialism of his age that the older he had grown (and he remarks "I am now upon the brink of eternity") the more he had come to appreciate the depth of the meaning of this first question and answer of the catechism he had learned as a child.

Predictably, this very Protestant document also denounces the "Romish doctrine" of a purgatorial state between death and resurrection and explicitly affirms in the answer to Question 37 that "The souls of believers are at their death made perfect in holiness, and do immediately pass into glory; and their bodies, being still united to Christ, do rest in their graves till the resurrection." Such was the emphasis on belief in God and his redemptive act in Christ as the ground of the "blessed assurance" of the faithful that excludes

Fig. 14. The Highest Heaven. *From Gustave Doré's illustration of Dante's* Vision of Paradise, *1868, Canto XXXI. Illustration 59. Dante, having been taken by his beloved Beatrice into the Empyrean and having had his sight strengthened by her aid to the point at which he can behold even the divine essence, now stands with Bernard of Clairvaux contemplating the joy of the angels and above all that of Mary, Queen of Heaven.*

the need for any works or any purification of the soul, which in that climate of theological opinion would have been taken as derogating from the all-sufficient redemptive act of Christ.

At the same place the catechism, in its insistence that the souls of believers *immediately* pass into glory, conforms to the express teaching of the Westminster Confession (Chapter xxxii), which states that "Besides the highest heavens and hell, besides these two places for souls separated from their bodies, the Scripture acknowledgeth none." An implicate of this image of afterlife is plainly that the soul can not only exist independently of the body but enjoy the glory of God from the moment of death till the day of resurrection, whenever it may come.

According to Calvin's teaching, however, the souls of believers, although they "no longer contend with the lusts of the flesh," being beyond even "the reach of a single dart," they "do not enjoy the felicity and glory which they have hoped for," so it is not improper for them to be spoken of as "in the way of advancement" pending the Day of Resurrection.

Calvin testifies that "Many torment themselves overmuch with disputing as to what place the souls occupy and whether or not they already enjoy heavenly glory." Such speculation he pronounces "neither lawful nor expedient." He also regards inquiries about the whereabouts of the soul between death and resurrection as futile, because "the soul does not have the same dimension as the body" (*Institutes*, 3, 25, 6). That it should have any dimension at all is remarkable, since that notion would be consistent with the concept we considered in Part One according to which one might identify the soul with one's "astral" embodiment. No doubt this was far from Calvin's mind, but his talk of a different dimension suggests that he was well aware of the problems connected with the concept of the soul's independent life between death and resurrection. His notice of them does not only reflect his own indisputable theological genius; it witnesses to the dissatisfaction he must have encountered among thoughtful people of his time.

This dissatisfaction was only one element in the spectrum of the malaise that people on both sides of the Reformation curtain were already feeling about the traditional images of afterlife. Renaissance artists were happily able to address themselves, at least obliquely, to the widespread puzzlements. For instance, for all the logic of the medieval imagery (and let us not forget that the classic Reformers were in many ways medieval), people naturally wondered what sort of heaven it would be without a renewal and continuation of their relationship with their loved ones. The classic Christian doctrines on afterlife did not seem to provide much ground for hope of this kind.

True, the ancient doctrine of the Communion of the Saints did address itself to this aspect of popular concern. At prayer a faithful Christian, bereaved of his or her parent or spouse, could feel assured of being in communion with the one who had meant so much and was now gone beyond the veil of death. After all, the living and the dead were united in their being alike waiting for the Day of Resurrection. When, however, that glorious day arrived they would be wholly taken up with the adoration of God. Richard Baxter, author of *The Saints' Everlasting Rest* (1649), is not only decidedly emphatic in his theocentricity; he also provides an image of heaven somewhat reminiscent of a perpetual church service. In New England, John Cotton had already (in 1640) written of the joy of singing "eternal hallelujahs" in heaven.

Little wonder that Lloyd George, second in renown only to Churchill among twentieth-century British statesmen, reported that as a little boy in a Baptist Sunday School in Manchester more than two hundred years after Baxter was writing, he was more terrified of heaven than of hell, thinking it would be like an everlasting church service with every exit closed and guarded by an angel preventing escape! Joseph Hall (1574–1651), an English bishop, specifically repudiated the notion of meeting one's loved ones in heaven, remarking (not without theological consistency in terms of his age) that when we chance to meet a brother or a son in the presence of a great prince, we are too much in awe of him to be paying courtesies to them. Therefore, thought the bishop, it must be so a fortiori in the presence of the Almighty.

Whatever bishops and theologians thought about such matters, no doubt the average person's heart was kindled with the hope that in the life of the world to come we should meet our friends and find inexpressible joy in companying with them as together we were to enjoy the Vision of God. Perhaps bishops had fewer friendships of the kind that so stir the hearts of others.

So crucial is the question of meeting or not meeting loved ones in the hereafter that the next chapter of this book will be devoted to a fuller consideration of it.

Dissatisfaction with Concepts of Heaven and Hell

If there was such dissatisfaction with the traditional teaching on heaven, there was even more about the teachings on hell, probably because educated people perceived and even uneducated people at least suspected that the

Fig. 15. Last Judgment: The Good Death. *Courtesy of Professor Samuel K. Cohn, Jr., from his book,* Death and Property in Siena, 1205–1800: Strategies for the Afterlife *(Baltimore: The Johns Hopkins University Press, 1988; reproduced by permission). This painting is by Lorenzo Vecchietta (mid-fifteenth century) in the old sacristy, Santa Maria della Scala, Siena. Those blessed souls who have made a "good death" are being lifted up gently by angels by whom they will be conducted to everlasting bliss.*

tremendous emphasis that popular preachers gave to the horrors of everlasting torture in hell often sprang from less than healthy motives. It provided a tremendously ferocious instrument for the Church to wield, one that provided an outlet for the worst aspects of the power mania for which some clergy are notorious. It is one thing to warn evildoers of the grave consequences of their acts and that if they do not mend their ways they will reap bitter fruits and sorely regret their impenitence. It is another to dwell upon and openly gloat over images of endless torture that give free rein to indulgence of the most monstrously sadistic impulses not only on the part of the preachers but perhaps hardly less on the part of their hearers who identified the tortures of hell as the afterlife of those for whom they felt a desire for personal vengeance.

Underlying the concept of hell lay a confusion of ideas that equaled the confusion behind the concept of the traditional heaven. The results in practice, however, were far more vicious in the case of hell. The images of hell

Fig. 16. Last Judgment: The Bad Death. *Courtesy of Professor Samuel K. Cohn, Jr., from his book,* Death and Property in Siena, 1205–1800: Strategies for the Afterlife (*Baltimore: The Johns Hopkins University Press, 1988; reproduced by permission*). *This painting by Lorenzo Vecchietta (mid-fifteenth century) in the old sacristy, Santa Maria della Scala, Siena, shows the damned tortured by venomous snakes, fire, and other torments that will be everlasting.*

were infinite in their variety. Both Catholic and Protestant writers dwelt on images of the most extravagant kind: One would be roasted on the left side for twenty million years and then turned to be baked on the right side for the next twenty million. While the burning process was going on, serpents would be perpetually stinging the victim and each sting would produce an agony greater than that of all the stings that all the vipers in the world could produce if they all were able to sting at the same place at the same time. Yet not even all this endless reveling in such absurdly sado-masochistic images of inconceivable physical torment could exhaust the extent of the pitilessness of popular preaching on hell, for by far the worst ingredient in the horror was that it is everlasting. Moreover, not a single tear would be shed by anyone in heaven over the everlasting torture of the denizens of hell.

On the contrary, even the generally moderate and judicial temper of Thomas Aquinas did not prevent his endorsing the view, by then widely held, that the blessed in heaven will be granted a perfect view of the punishment of the damned and will have no pity on them; indeed, the punishment of the damned will be an indirect result of the joy of the blessed, since it is part of the fulfillment of God's justice.[2] On the Reformation side very similar views prevailed. Jonathan Edwards (1703–1758), for instance, one of the most celebrated of American divines, said very much the same sort of thing, and his earliest biographer, Samuel Hopkins, who much admired Edwards for his originality both as a philosopher and as a theologian,[3] wrote that if the fires of hell were to cease it would "in great measure obscure the light of heaven, and put an end to great part of the happiness and glory of the blessed and be an irreparable detriment to God's eternal kingdom."[4]

If hell is everlasting torture, then heaven is its opposite: everlasting bliss. But in what does the bliss consist? The emphasis on putting God, the Eternal One, at the center of heaven was salutary and a welcome safeguard against the extravagances of the imagery that artists and others suggested to the people. What was wrong was not the theocentricity but the concept that the blessed in heaven, having reached their final goal, have nothing further to do except to praise God. This image of heavenly bliss in effect demolishes the gulf between God and his creatures, which we have repeatedly seen to be the cornerstone of all the monotheistic religions. It either divinizes the blessed (in the sense that they are no longer finite beings but quasi-divine choristers around the Throne of God) or else it makes them into a horde of celestial loafers as envisioned by the legendary old and overworked charwoman who on her deathbed cried out:

> Don't mourn for me now, don't mourn for me never;
> I's gonna do nothin' forever and ever.

Unlike the angels, many of whom were seen as tirelessly busy ministering to men and women and guarding little children from misadventure, the re-deemed in heaven seemed to have no comparable ministry of grace. Far from being humans perfected and re-energized, they could not but seem to be, rather, distorted and dehumanized. This was a difficult enough image to fit into the thought of Catholics and Eastern Orthodox with their merciful concept of the intermediate state of purgatory (merciful even in its excessively penal form), but in Protestant thought it meant that the old woman whose deathbed wish is celebrated in the couplet just quoted would be forthwith sealed on that deathbed as washed in the Blood of the Lamb, put to sleep till the Day of Resurrection, and then suddenly transformed into a perpetual chorister in the heavenly choir. Such also would be the destiny of each of the rest of us: the newborn baby and the centenarian alike.

Swedenborg, Boehme, and Blake

With the approach of the eighteenth century, the age of the *Aufklärung* or Enlightenment, the educated classes of Europe were ill disposed to take seriously *any* medieval religious ideas and certainly unwilling to accept traditional ideas of heaven and hell. Even the spiritually minded in the Age of Reason could not accept anything so flagrantly incoherent as the images of afterlife that were presented with the rest of the "package deal" of Christian doctrine either in its Catholic or in its Reformation wrappings.

Probably the first to offer a serious alternative image of afterlife about this time was Emanuel Swedenborg (1688–1772). Swedenborg, born in Stockholm and educated at Uppsala, soon displayed his extraordinary genius as a scientist and mathematician. Influenced by Locke and Newton, he made, early in life, important scientific discoveries (among them nebular theory and magnetic theory), and he may be regarded as the founder of the science of crystallography. In 1716 he was appointed to an important position on the Swedish Board of Mines. In 1734 he published a Latin treatise in which he sought to show, by strictly scientific methods, that the universe has a spiritual basis. Ten years later he found himself in direct communication with a spiritual dimension in which, he claimed, he was enabled to discourse with angels. He died in London and was buried in the Swedish church there, but such was his fame that in 1908 his remains were removed to Stockholm by an arrangement with the Swedish government. His remarkable system of philosophical and religious thought is most comprehensively presented in his *Arcana Coelestia*, a work in eight volumes published in 1756. Most immediately relevant to our present study, however, is his *Heaven and Hell* (1758).

Swedenborg's entire system of religious thought has at its center the concept of love. Moreover, he saw us here and now living on the edge of the veil of death and able, if we work at penetrating that veil, so to pierce it that we can cross to it any time at will. At death we enter into an afterlife that is a fuller life than our present one but not essentially different. Human love continues to play a vital role on the other side of the veil and, far from being in any way diminished in importance, assumes an even greater role and develops an even more profound rationale than it has in our present state.

Above all, afterlife in Swedenborg's heaven is a continual engagement in increasingly energetic activity, more and more inspired by love, which is expressed in acts of love toward our fellow creatures, yet is at the same time fundamentally the love of God. Heaven is anything other than static. The spiritual voyage never ends. One experiences spiritual progress forever. Heaven is not so different from earth as has been traditionally supposed. God casts no one into hell; on the contrary, it is man who turns his face to hell and takes up his abode in it. But most fundamental in Swedenborg's thought about afterlife is the view that what is everlasting in it is everlasting progress toward the fulfillment of love of God. Since God is infinitely great there can be no question of total fulfillment in the sense of reaching a point where there is nothing left to do. Swedenborg sometimes uses traditional language such as "eternal rest," but the "rest" is that which we feel in the joy of acting more and more efficiently, overcoming obstacles more and more easily.

So similar is the afterlife to the present one that some, Swedenborg alleges, do not know they are dead. His concept of afterlife is basically more like an adumbration of the Tractarian view of purgatory as a state of growth and development than like the traditional view of heaven and hell. The perceptive reader of Swedenborg who is already familiar with the karmic principle and its reincarnational implicate will notice a certain resemblance, although Swedenborg's vision of the afterlife is nothing if not highly distinctive. It has also been very influential on many thoughtful people, so exhibiting the extreme dissatisfaction of deeply spiritual minds with the traditional images and showing the intense longing of many for a more intelligible view of the life of the world to come, a view not entirely detached from the highest forms of love that we know in society and family life. Swedenborg, who never married, had a very high regard for the sanctity and grandeur of romantic love, such as binds a man and a woman together in a life of ever-deepening loyalty.

Among those who fell under the influence of Swedenborg was the mystical and theological visionary, William Blake (1757–1827), the English poet and artist whose works include *The Marriage of Heaven and Hell* (1793).

Blake was also influenced by Jakob Boehme (1575–1624), whose background was notably different from Swedenborg's. The son of a German farmer, Boehme had worked first as a shepherd, then as a shoemaker. With education limited to what he was able to learn at the town school of Seidenberg in Upper Lusatia, he claimed to have received mystical illumination. The publication in 1612 of his first work evoked the ire of the chief local Lutheran pastor, who denounced it as heretical. The town council ordered

Boehme to write no more, but he continued to do so. He wrote in a very difficult, obscure style expounding what he felt he had learned from his mystical experiences. His writings reflect a neo-Gnostic, theosophical outlook. He was read with interest by important thinkers in the German-speaking world, notably by Hegel and Schelling and not least by Carl Jung. According to Boehme, heaven is in hell and hell is in heaven, yet the one is not manifest to the other. The Devil might go millions of miles to see heaven and not see it because he would be in hell wherever he went. In effect every spirit is confined within his own principle, good or evil as the case may be.

This concept is echoed in Blake's work, literary and artistic, in which he represents the Devil as blind and therefore unable to see a good angel. They cannot ever see one another because the good angel is bathed in light and the evil one blackened by a burning fire. Blake was indebted to Swedenborg too but seems to have lost interest in him as the years passed. He drew from many sources, yet (as William Butler Yeats pointed out) he always transformed them into the special mold of his own distinctive imagery.

At any rate, both Swedenborg and Blake exhibit an important aspect of the dissatisfaction felt by so many concerning traditional Christian ideas of afterlife, and they represent, or are among, the first "modern" attempts to sort out the jumble of received images from traditional Christianity relating to afterlife. Even to this day a remarkably large number of people show interest in the concept yet cannot find meaning in the maze of the traditional imagery. They are lost in the maze not because they are particularly alienated from their ancestral faith or because they are peculiarly blind to the things of the spirit, but rather because Christian teaching on the afterlife has become in fact insupportably muddled. In our final chapter I hope to provide at least some pointers to the direction in which one must go for an intelligible presentation of how the Christian hope may be understood. Meanwhile, however, we must consider an important and much-asked question: "Is meeting loved ones in the afterlife a part of the Christian hope?"

Notes

1 See Chapter VIII, note 1, and Figs. 7 and 8, pages 106 and 107.
2 *Summa Theologiae*, III, Suppl., 94, 1.
3 Samuel Hopkins, *The Life and Character of the Late Reverend Mr. Jonathan Edwards* (Boston, 1765).
4 Samuel Hopkins, *An Enquiry* (Newport, R. I., 1793), pp. 154f.

CHAPTER XIII

Meeting Loved Ones in the Afterlife

I'm wearin' awa', Jean,
Like snaw wreaths in snaw, Jean,
I'm wearin' awa'
    To the land o' the leal. [*loyal*]
There's nae sorrow there, Jean,
There's neither cauld nor care, Jean,
The day is aye fair
    In the land o' the leal.

Ye aye were leal and true, Jean,
Your task is ended noo, Jean,
And I'll welcome you
    To the land o' the leal.

Then dry that tearfu' e'e, Jean,
My soul langs to be free, Jean,
And angels wait on me
    To the land o' the leal.
Now fare ye weel, my ain Jean,
This world's care is vain, Jean,
We'll meet and aye be fain [*fond; in love*]
    In the land o' the leal.

     –Carolina Oliphant (Baroness Nairne),
          The Land o' the Leal

At the outset of this book I took the stance that "this or that kind of belief or disbelief in afterlife is a corollary to this or that kind of belief or disbelief in God." If then one believes in an infinitely loving God, love must play a central role in our conception of the afterlife. "No one has ever seen God," writes the author of the first letter of John; "but as long as we love one another God will live in us and his love will be complete in us. . . . God is love and anyone who lives in love lives in God, and God lives in him" (I John 4:12, 16). He continues with even sharper rebuke: "Anyone who says 'I love God' and hates his brother is a liar, since a man who does not love the brother that he can see cannot love God whom he has never seen" (I John 4: 20). Surely then an afterlife that excluded meeting again those who have first shown us the meaning of the sacrificial love that first pointed us toward an understanding, meager though it be, of the infinite love of God toward his creatures, could not be reconciled with the central focus of one who believes in such a God.

The concept that God would create us and make possible our evolution into our present state as human beings only to let us die like rats is intolerable, but that he should give us an afterlife of total exclusion from those who have been the channel of his love would be to make a monster of God. When one has learned such love from a father, a mother, a husband, a wife, a child, or a dear and loyal friend, one cannot believe that, if God is love, as John says, he would exclude us forever from further encounter with such channels of his bounty.

Most of us have been introduced to concepts of God through parents or others who, while we were still toddling and lisping, tried to convey to us at least a glimpse of their own vision. I say "most of us" because of course there are many exceptions; but generally speaking whatever form our religious pilgrimage on this earth takes it has had its beginning in the building blocks provided by those who guided our footsteps in life. Needless to say, if we have any mental vitality at all we drastically rearrange these blocks, developing in some cases a much more complex understanding of God than that of which we could have been capable in infancy, although in other cases, instead of developing our childhood images, renouncing God-talk entirely.

John Baillie (1886–1960), a Scottish Presbyterian theologian much acclaimed in his day, writes of his childhood in a Highland village in Scotland: "As little can I reach a day when I was conscious of myself but not of God as I can reach a day when I was conscious of myself but not of other human beings. My earliest memories have a definitely religious atmosphere. They are already heavy with 'the numinous.' . . . I cannot remember a time when I did not already feel, in some dim way, that I was . . . claimed by a higher power which had authority over me." He goes on to write of his awareness, as early as he can remember, that his parents also "lived under the same kind of authority as that which, through them, was communicated to me."[1]

Early Recollections

I can empathize to some extent with Baillie's recollections of his childhood, for although my parents' attitude toward religion was not at all fanatical, we frequently had family worship in the evening. They were comparatively old to be my parents and I was an only child. My most impressive religious instruction, however, was from my maternal grandmother who was eighty-four when she began it and I a somewhat precocious two and a half. I have the most vivid recollection of it. I loved going to her home and being alone with her, where she would make me stand on a stool while she sat down and taught me to repeat verses, chiefly from the Lord's Prayer and the Twenty-third Psalm, sometimes in English, which she enunciated with great clarity and exceptional beauty of diction, and sometimes in her native Scottish Gaelic, which I did not understand, so the instruction (which came after these preliminaries were over and I had been rewarded for my performance with a glass of cream or the like) was in English. For this I was placed in a high chair opposite her so that she could see my face and I hers. Then followed a discourse beyond my capacity to understand fully in any language at my tender age. I could make out only a few recurring words such as *God* and *heaven*.

Yet I understood far more than words could have conveyed. For I watched her face, whose wrinkles seemed infinite in number and no less infinite in fascination, because somehow they communicated to me the mystery of what she was imparting. Her facial expression constantly changed. From that amazing picture book I received impressions that I pieced together with the few words that I did understand. With flashing smiles alternating with looks of infinite awe, she somehow succeeded in communicating to me something of her own sense of the awful Majesty and Glory of God, of how he could twirl the earth, the sun, the moon, and all the stars as easily as she or I could twirl marbles. Her vivacious old face, yellow as parchment, darkened with awe as she turned her violet-blue eyes upward in speaking of God. Her small white hands were extended in a magnificent gesture as she sought to convey to me the infinite power of him who could raise up mountains with a surer hand

186

than we could employ in spreading butter on bread. With a combination of words and facial expressions she conveyed to me the sense of a Being of such dazzling brightness and whiteness that if we could see him, which mercifully we could not, we should instantly fall down dead, like little moths before a bright light.

Then as I listened and watched, spellbound and enthralled, although no doubt a trifle scared, her whole countenance would change with dramatic suddenness. It was not merely that she was now smiling the smile that only mature wisdom can smile; her whole countenance seemed to be irradiated till every wrinkle seemed lighted up from behind and smiling. Her eyes, gently moist, looked at me with encompassing affection and her voice changed key as she told me that the most wonderful part was still to come. For he whose Presence was such as to strike terror in the strongest of men had a heart as infinitely stupendous as the rest of him. So it was, she whispered, that he had chosen to become a little child, smaller than even I then was, so that he might help us to become better and so go to heaven, a place very much more beautiful, she assured me, than earth.

My grandmama did not like her audience to be distracted while she spoke. Well do I remember how, on one such occasion, I was distracted by what seemed to be a mouse scratching from behind the baseboard.

"It's probably only a little mouse," she said. Then in her most magnificent manner she waxed eloquent in terms such as these:

"How would you like to turn yourself into a little mouse and crawl behind the wall into the dark hole that mice live in, so that you could help them grow into something more beautiful? You wouldn't. Neither would I. But the heart of our God who made us is greater than ours and that is what he did for us when he became Jesus, our Saviour. It was far more horrible for him to become one of us than it would be for you or me to become a mouse. For we are only a little better than mice, but he is good, he is holy, he is the Lord of all, the King of all."

Then she told me very simply of how cruel men had crucified Jesus and of how he, being God and Man, had risen in great glory and shown himself to his apostles. She told me of how Thomas had at first doubted. Thomas was my father's name, so perhaps I listened with a sort of proprietary interest at that point. At any rate, the general impression I had was of being in the presence of realities more vivid than those of ordinary life and certainly more interesting.

By the time I was three I think I understood the meaning of orthodox Christology as well as anyone not a theologian. Indeed, when I think of the chirpy twaddle and ponderous boilerplate sermons that I have since heard preached by priests and bishops who so obviously did not understand a word of what they themselves were saying whenever it was not about parish or diocesan finances or their pet political hobbyhorses, I find it hard to believe that God did not intervene so early in my life in these colloquies concerning his glory and his love. For all the religious doubts I have entertained from time to time (and I entertained them rather early in life), the revelations given me in my infancy through my grandmama's instrumentality have sustained me well, enabling me to issue comparatively unscathed from even the worst of sermons in the most sumptuous of pulpits.

Most such sermons, through the mercy of God, one forever forgets, but one homily does stand out bleak in my memory. It was a Christmas address to children, the main point of which was apparently to let us know that Jesus was *not* born on December twenty-fifth. Thanks to God and his instrument my grandmother, I knew enough to know that it could not have mattered if he had been born on February twenty-ninth in a non-leap year unless one held that the purpose of his coming was to enlist an army of Santa Clauses to tote around toys for kids. I was eleven by this time and my grandmother had died a few months earlier at the age of ninety-two, so that particular homiletic experience was memorably and poignantly bleak for me.

Reunion with Loved Ones

I have written at some length in so personal a vein in order to try to exhibit the rationale of the connection between a lively belief in God conceived in monotheistic terms and the hope of meeting loved ones in an afterlife. The latter is not a mere sentimental wishful dream but a hope inseparable from any hope of afterlife that belief in God implies. A typical case might be that of a partner to a Christian marriage in which, through all the turmoils, all the joys and sorrows of perhaps fifty years or more, the love that began as sexual attraction deepened into a bond so intimate and so profound that parting by death of the one is for the other like the loss of half of oneself. Such a loss cannot be treated as one treats the loss of even one's house or livelihood. The question, however, is this: With what image of afterlife is the hope of reunion at some point reconcilable?

Kingsley and the Romantic Movement Charles Kingsley (1819–1875), an Anglican priest and perhaps the most famous of Victorian Anglicans in the

Broad Church party, privately entertained a vision of afterlife that, had it been published in his lifetime, would have shocked beyond measure even the most broad-minded of the Broad Church party of his day. Kingsley, according to one of his biographers, envisioned in his love letters and other private documents the state of heavenly bliss as the ecstasy of an everlasting sexual embrace with one's marriage partner—an image of the afterlife that his wife Fanny seemed to endorse.[2] One must remember that even in "secular" circles the concept of romantic love (that is, sexual love with a deeply spiritual ingredient) was somewhat aberrant in the Middle Ages and even down to the early nineteenth century when it began to bloom under the influence of the Romantic movement in literature, art, and social culture.

What is especially noteworthy in Kingsley, whose public utterances on his view of afterlife were essentially the same although couched in more discreet language, is his virtual departure from what most theologians in the monotheistic tradition would have regarded as crucial: the focus on God as central to any image of heavenly bliss. It is one thing to recognize a happy marriage in all its aspects as a uniquely spiritualizing force in human life that must be in some way reflected in any adequate image of the hereafter. It is another to talk of heaven as consisting of an everlasting sexual embrace.

When we read Blake and look at his endearing engraving of the meeting of a family in heaven, and when Kingsley and others talk of the afterlife as one endless sexual embrace, we cannot avoid the conclusion that such visions deify human relationships. The deification of human love was a popular theme in the nineteenth century, expressing as it so well did the quintessence of the Romantic spirit. Romantic love becomes the supreme value, being in effect God. Where the *sāmkhya* school of Indian thought perceived God somewhat as a company of saintly souls, these nineteenth-century visionaries saw the divine as a collection of romantic love-relationships. The German Romantics (including Goethe in the Romantic aspect of his genius) especially divinized human love. The notion, however, permeated the great literatures of Europe and the English-speaking world, was echoed in many pulpits, and deeply affected the outlook of educated men and women. It was not merely a romanticized Christianity; it often became, in some Victorian circles, more a new religion than an interpretation of an old one. Many women writers eagerly engaged in the apostolate of this new religion. Some churchgoers, when hearing conventional doctrine from the pulpit, privately reinterpreted it in conformity with the widely fashionable and sometimes schmaltzy images of afterlife.

Not all Victorian writers, however, when they wrote poignantly of the

Fig. 17. A couple, among the redeemed awaiting entry to paradise, holding hands. *From sculpture on the west front of Notre Dame de Paris. Photograph by Jean Delaume, reproduced by his permission. Grateful acknowledgement also to André Michel.*

encounter of a dying person with a loved one on the other side of the veil, lost sight of the traditional theocentric focus. Some used it to distance the schmaltz in the Romantic element in such a way as to give greater credibility and cohesion to the whole. Florence Montgomery, for instance, in her *Misunderstood*, a beautiful and very Victorian little novel first published in 1869, which went into many editions and reprintings into Edwardian times, does this very skillfully in the final scene.

The story, superficially a simple one, is about the two little sons of Sir Everard Duncombe, a member of Parliament who had been widowed and whose work kept him so much in London that only too seldom could he visit his children, who were left in the hands of an efficient but *nerveuse* French governess, in the family's country home in Sussex. Miles, the younger of the two boys, has been such an infant when his mother, after her long illness, had been taken from him, that he did not remember her at all; but Humphrey, the older boy, remembers her vividly and misses her acutely, often secretly bursting into tears from his sense of loss. To his father and others he seems thoughtless and reckless, even heartless, and is always getting into scrapes of one sort of another through his impetuosity. Miles, by contrast, is an endearing child, three years younger than his brother, and enchants his widowed father by his babyish ways, while Humphrey seems to be always getting into mischief that is often the occasion of excited adverse reports by Virginie, the governess, during the father's visits home, so aggravating the father's predilection for Miles and his misunderstanding of Humphrey. Eventually, Humphrey does get into serious trouble by enticing Miles to climb a tree and crawl out on a rotten branch. Miles falls into a pond below and so escapes with only a wetting, but Humphrey, alas, sustains injuries to head and spine so severe that the doctors prognosticate that he will never walk again.

Finally, Humphrey is in delirium on his deathbed. To a boy who had been so full of zest for life and so restless that he had never seemed to be still for an instant from morning to night and who now would never walk again, death seemed merciful. In his confused brain he hears the sound of rushing and the singing of hymns in church. Then "Everything seems to be turning and whirling; and, as if to save himself, he opens his eyes. On what a sight did they fall! There, close before him, bathed in light and a glory round her brow, stands the figure of his mother, looking down upon him with a smile. And with a glad smile of welcome he stretched out his arms and cried, 'Has God sent you to fetch me at last, mother? Oh, mother, I'll come! I'll come!' "

The story, in its Victorian way, is exquisitely unfolded. The author, in her preface, begins by telling her readers that it is not a children's story. It is intended, she insists, for "those who are interested in children" and are "willing to stoop to view life as it appears to a child." Whatever the audience she intended, the story expresses an outlook on afterlife that succeeds in combining the traditional monotheistic focus with a sense of the eternal value of the human love through which that focus is achieved in life, whether the life be long or, as in little Humphrey's case, tragically foreshortened.

The Monotheistic Focus The hope of reunion with those who in one way or another have played a crucial part in our spiritual awakening and development is a hope that seems not only legitimate but essential as well. Nevertheless, in trying to reconstruct as far as possible an image of afterlife that can stand as a corollary of what, let us say, the Bible and the classic creedal formulae of the Christian Church mean when they talk of God, we do have some difficulties that will become more apparent as we proceed.

For instance, the notion of recognizing and joyfully meeting again our loved ones is very easy to fit into the scenario that modern spiritualism provides and that I have tentatively interpreted as that in which the auras or astral bodies of people on the other side of the veil may continue to exist and from which they may sometimes communicate with us. But if we consider, as I think we must, the possibility of re-embodiment by the operation of the karmic principle, then it is much more difficult to see how, once respectively re-embodied, my wife and I, for example, should be able to recognize one another, since she might be reincarnated in a Chinese culture and I in, say, a Jewish one or even one on another planet. Yet it is not necessarily to be ruled out, for by the same karmic principle we might, on the contrary, again be "thrown together" in another life. The saying that certain marriages seem to have been "made in heaven" may be a way of expressing such a notion. Most of us have known such marriages and some of us have experienced such a marriage in which two seemingly most unlikely partners have attained an extraordinarily happy marriage relationship. We are almost all familiar with the experience of sensing, in particularly profound and felicitous friendship, a relationship so special that it seems to antedate our present lives.

Then again, if we prefer to take seriously the traditional understanding of the Christian doctrine of the resurrection of the body, we might expect to recognize those we have loved in this life, in the glorified bodies that each would have received on the Day of Resurrection, but that might be so many thousand or even million years away that such a hope would be too remote to afford consolation or provoke joy. Accustomed as we are to a lifespan in which even a hundred years is still accounted unusual, we can hardly be expected to think realistically about joyful reunions promised to us at an undeterminable date that might be a million years away or more.

Notes

1 John Baillie, *Our Knowledge of God* (New York: Scribner, 1959), pp. 4f.
2 Susan Chitty, *The Beast and the Monk: A Life of Charles Kingsley* (London: Hodder and Stoughton, 1975), p. 17.

CHAPTER XIV

General Review of Images of Afterlife

Being a Sufi is to put away what is in your head (imagined truth, preconceptions, conditioning) and to face what may happen to you.

—Abu Said

The soul . . . if immortal, existed before our birth, and if the former existence noways concerns us, neither will the latter. . . . The Metempsychosis is, therefore, the only system of this kind that philosophy can hearken to.

—David Hume, *Essay on the Immortality of the Soul*

In reviewing the images of afterlife that have appeared in the history of human thought and have been expressed in literature and in the visual arts from antiquity onward, what strikes one most forcibly is the fact that, while the imagery is very confused, the concept of afterlife is extraordinarily persistent and belief in one form of it or another is almost universal. If what I have postulated at the outset is true (that belief in this or that form of afterlife is a corollary of this or that kind of belief in God), the confusion is not particularly surprising, since much the same might well be said of belief in

God: its persistence on the one hand and, on the other, the conceptual confusions attending it.

Where a religion is organized under the banner of a revelation and bound by a set of dogmatic tenets, one might expect the case to be different from that in which afterlife beliefs grow up "wild," without any such creedal restraints. To some extent we do find something to justify such expectations, but as we have seen in the case of Christianity and other monotheistic religions, confusions nevertheless abound.

The Graeco-Roman world, cradle of the great civilizations of Europe, was certainly bound by no common creed. People were generally, as elsewhere, mostly concerned with the present life, as of course, one ought to be, whether one believes in an afterlife or not. Despite their preoccupation with the affairs of everyday life, however, some sort of belief in afterlife was very general. As in the Orient, the dead were conceived as not only worthy of special reverence but capable, at least according to some views on the subject, of affecting the lives of the living as well. The tomb or urn was venerated as the special focus of the spirits of the dead. The belief, however, in a subterranean abode that housed the dead and in which they continued a conscious, if dreamlike, existence was widespread and found classic expression in Homer, notably in the eleventh book of the *Odyssey*. With this development comes a tendency to pay little or no attention to the dead on the ground that there is nothing we can do for them or they for us; nor is there much, if any, concept of judgment or of punishment or reward.

This tendency to indifference toward the dead, shared with many societies in antiquity, including that of the classic biblical writers, represents a distinct stage in the development of afterlife images. Compared with the earlier notions that had warranted such practices as providing the dead with food and coins and other objects on the supposition that they might need these for whatever "journey" they were to embark upon, this was a new attitude and, in a way, may be perceived as a more enlightened one. The older ideas nevertheless persisted among the people. After all, it would have been indeed astonishing had they not persisted since, as we have seen, the practices expressing such beliefs went far back into the mists of prehistory, as archeological findings show.

Alongside Homer's acceptance of the widespread concept of Hades, the underworld of the dead (Sheol in classical biblical imagery), he recognized, however, another and very different destiny for some of those who pass beyond this present life: certain great ones, heroes, who escape death and are transported to Elysium, the Isles of the Blest, situated somewhere at the "ends" of the earth. Homer mentions this notion in the fourth book of the *Odyssey* and Hesiod follows him in recognizing such a notion. This is of some significance, for Hesiod was probably the first of the Greek poets to pass beyond myth and legend and introduce ethical concerns into his poetry. This concept of a paradise for heroes introduces some notion of judgment, some idea of reward for what is acclaimed as admirable moral behavior. The locale of Elysium was changed later to the underworld, but that seems to have been merely an attempt to conform to the traditional Homeric focus for all who had passed through death and so might seem no less appropriate for those who, by their heroism, had circumvented it. Such ideas of a paradise for the highly favored can be found, as we have seen, in other and often notably different societies—not only in ancient Egypt but, much later, in Pure Land Buddhism and elsewhere in the Orient.

Increased Ethical Awareness

Increased ethical awareness injected among the people generally a fear of punishment after death. Reassurance, however, came from the development of an ethically grounded doctrine of transmigration or reincarnation, according to which such punishments as the afterlife might bring had a happy ending.

Both the Pythagoreans and the Orphics taught some form of such a doctrine of rebirth through a cycle of lives in the course of which the soul, gradually purified of its blemishes, would reach perfection and the bliss attending it. Many have been the attempts to find some direct historical linkage between this Pythagorean and Orphic teaching and that of the Upanishads that has so strikingly permeated Indian thought, but while there are striking resemblances between Occidental and Oriental developments at this point, direct influence from one side or the other has not been established and may very well be (perhaps indeed probably is) unwarranted. More likely is the view that the two developments of this theme, one in the Orient, one in the Occident, arose out of separate recognitions by thoughtful minds on each side that within the mixture of legend and lore, speculation and fantasy, thought and reflection that had been handed down from the past lay a great and everlasting truth: that the universe is not at the mercy of whim or chance but is in some way guided if not governed by a moral principle.

The Hebrew prophets came to see this in their own very different way and proclaimed it. Before the time of Amos in the eighth century B.C.E. some may have already adumbrated this message in their prophesyings, but if so they have not been recorded, for before the time of Amos prophecy had been oral. Amos was an obscure man who had interrupted the worship at a royal sanctuary of Jeroboam II of Israel and had been consequently rebuked by the resident priest and driven from the sanctuary. He was the first of a series of Hebrew prophets who were to proclaim an ethical and cosmic dimension to the faith of their fathers and whose proclamations were recorded and incorporated in Scripture.

We may say that before Plato (427–347 B.C.E.) speculations about afterlife, at least in the West, were based largely on a perception of the implicates of religious beliefs. Plato's belief in the immortality of the soul, which he wisely never defined with precision, was no doubt also rooted in his religious outlook. An Athenian by birth and of a noble family, Plato had been destined for a political career but because of his profound admiration for Socrates and his love of that kind of wisdom that is reached through reasoned argument he devoted his life to philosophy. He may be said to have been the first in the West to supply reasoned argument to support his moral and religious convictions. His argument for the immortality of the soul, as developed in the *Phaedo*, immensely influenced the philosophical as well as the religious outlook of the West. The nobility of his character, the grandeur of his perceptions, and the incisiveness of his intellect profoundly affected not only the Greek thinkers who immediately succeeded him but also in time incalculably enriched and enlivened, notably in Alexandria, both Jewish and early Christian thought. Moreover, despite the well-known and potent influence of Aristotle both in the Arab world and, after his rediscovery by the twelfth century in the Latin West, Plato's influence still pervaded, unconsciously or otherwise, the outlook of Christian thinkers there too. It is not too much to say that Thomas Aquinas himself was a Platonist at heart, paradoxical though it may seem to those who see his thought as a sort of baptized Aristotelianism. The Neoplatonic tradition had been bequeathed to Latin Christianity through the mold of the thought of its greatest Father, Augustine (354–430), who before his conversion had already so molded his own mind.

All this must be recognized in spite of the fact that Aristotle (384–322 B.C.E.) did not see any reason to believe in an afterlife for anything but the intellectual part of the tripartite human soul and despite, moreover, the indubitable fact that generally speaking the thinkers of the Hellenistic age who adorned the Academy that Plato had founded were, to say the least, disinclined to recognize any afterlife at all. At a more popular level, however, belief in afterlife of one sort or another played a very large part in the religious outlook of the Greeks, notably in the many cults that prospered at that level. Moreover, by the first century B.C.E. a revival of interest in the notion of afterlife, including the concept of transmigration to which Plato had acceded, provided one of the many alternative ways of thinking of the path of the life everlasting that was to be an entailment of the Christian apostolic proclamation.

The concept of transmigration, however, was never built into the institutional structure of the West as it was in India. It functioned in early Christian thought among the learned, especially in the Alexandrian school, as one way of thinking of the intermediate state, a way of purifying the souls of the redeemed to fit them for their blessed destiny. In India not only had it become ingrained into the outlook of the entire people, from the most learned to the most simple; it was exported as a matter of course through Buddhist and other channels, becoming an integral part of the conceptual furnishings wherever people gave any thought to afterlife at all. Confucianism, on which the societal structure of China so much and for so long depended, has never focused on afterlife, but such is the syncretism of religious ideas in the Orient that where Confucius seems silent other voices can be clearly heard by those who seek to hear them. Wherever these voices (Buddhist, Taoist, or whatever they may be) speak of afterlife, the model they follow is a reincarnational one.

Immortality and Judgment

We have seen from the first the universality of afterlife expectation, whether as hope or as fear. To anyone giving even casual thought about the brevity of human life and the enormity of the panorama of ideals, duties, and concerns with which this life confronts us, an interest in what happens after death is unsurprising. Except for those who claim to see no meaning in human life beyond the daily round of little pleasures and chores, trivial hopes and fears, and therefore can entertain no concept of God or cosmic moral principle at work in the universe, some expectation of survival in one form or another is inescapable. The only question is what kind of afterlife is really conceivable (that is, not self-contradictory or otherwise unthinkable) and what (whether we accept it as adequate or not) would at least seem to fit the case.

Any form of belief that the human soul is *intrinsically* immortal depends on a presupposition that all human beings, by virtue of their humanity, are so essentially one with God that they can no more be separated from God than can a ray of light be separated from whatever light is. In other words, we are intrinsically immortal in the sense that the physical universe is intrinsically governed by the law of gravity. God need not have anything to do with it. This seems to me sheer arrogance on our part, not least in face of what we now know of our human limitations and the immensity and grandeur of the universe.

The alternative view is that we are immortal because God has so willed us to be, irrespective of our conduct, and since God is also just, such immortality entails the horrific doctrine of everlasting misery in hell, for, being immortal yet unfit to company with God we must survive death and yet be forever excluded from God's presence. Such a fate, whether it includes the horrors of hell as traditionally and popularly depicted or is simply the pain of losing forever the spring of life and happiness is hell enough. It is to be forever damned. This scenario is surely incompatible with what believers hold about the superlatively benevolent nature of God.

The image of judgment, which is almost universal in all developed religions, is both intelligible and, if one believes in any kind of moral governance of the universe, inevitable. It is one image that is inseparable from any world view that recognizes individual responsibility. This does not mean that the judgment must take the form of a cosmic court of justice or that depicted in Michelangelo's famous but fearsome painting. Judgment may take place without so much as an angelic whisper, let alone an oracular or judicial sentence. It might come simply as a moral consequence of one's moral conduct, as a stone hits a tree in consequence of my throwing it. In some form or other, judgment is built into any image of afterlife that is dependent on a benevolent Creator or any cosmic moral law. With no such concept it seems difficult, if not impossible, to see any reason why one should survive death at all.

Ghostly Survival and Re-embodiment

The notion that the dead survive as ghosts may be mere primitive superstition in the form in which it predominantly appears in the history of religion. I die, yet some shadow of me remains. But why should it? In its pre-ethical form such a belief seems unwarranted. It would appear to have arisen merely because people see the departed in their dreams and for merely psychological reasons feel their presence in certain circumstances, as when reminded of them by a scene or a place or a tune. Both love and fear are notoriously powerful emotions, capable of evoking vivid imagery.

Yet if there were some good reason for believing in the ontological reality of departed spirits, such belief might well be warranted. That is to say, the possibility of some shadow of myself temporarily surviving my death need not then be entirely ruled out. But in what form? A disembodied spirit? That, I have maintained, is inconceivable. What, however, is commonly thought of as disembodied may not be disembodied at all; indeed, even in primitive ghost stories ghosts seem to have some sort of embodiment. Some of them, as they pass by us or through us are cold and clammy; that they can float through solid oak doors does not exclude their being seen or heard as having some *kind* of form. Even so, to what purpose? Merely to scare us or perhaps in some instances to provide us with fleeting consolation for our bereavement?

Surely more is needed in the context of any belief in cosmic justice, to say nothing of evolutionary moral and spiritual development. The "resurrection body" envisioned by Paul and in one form or another elsewhere in the monotheistic tradition meets the case in the sense that it provides me with what might be called an improved edition of my present embodiment, not an attenuated one. If only a shadow of me were to survive, then I could not truly either enjoy the rewards or suffer the punishment due to me. Neither justice could be done nor mercy fully accorded. If, by reason of my life (including the grace and mercy that God so freely bestows upon me) I deserve bliss or have it bestowed on me, it must be a bliss of which the whole "me" is capable of enjoying. There would be no use in giving me a ticket for the heavenly concert if with my attenuated embodiment I lacked the capacity to hear it. Even as matters stand with me I can catch only fragmented murmurs of that music. What I need is a richer endowment of embodiment, not an impoverished one. Resurrection as traditionally depicted in mainstream Christian thought fits the requirement, for it is resurrection to new and richer life: a life that encompasses the kind of embodiment I now enjoy.

Even in Christian thought it has been sometimes understood, as we have seen, as a literal re-assembling of the particles or atoms that constitute my present body! Absurd and obscurantist as such a notion is, at least it did bring out the invaluable notion of continuity: it is *I* who am to be resurrected; it is *I* who am to be reborn. So far, so good. On closer examination, however, we can see that not only was the primitive notion of the reassemblage of the particles of my body absurd; hardly less unsatisfactory is the notion of a resurrected body that, however grandly fashioned and finely organized, will endure everlastingly. Even if we grant that I might eventually achieve, by the grace of God and my own appropriation thereof, so great a destiny, the idea that I could walk out of my present lamentably limited human condition (with Death leering and pointing his finger at me throughout my entire life) directly into a state of everlasting bliss is inconceivable except by downgrading the quality of that everlasting bliss. To say the least, it would be as if a caterpillar were to turn "overnight" not into a butterfly but into a Leonardo or a Kant.

The concept of rebirth can be adapted to the Christian hope as celebrated in Easter. It is a re-embodiment. It is indeed new life. It can be understood as the disclosure of God's loving purpose: the fulfillment of his promise to restore, to redeem, to save his people. Since, however, it is susceptible to a variety of interpretations, we must both consider problems of interpretation and clarify what we are to understand by rebirth.

The concept of reincarnation or transmigration, widespread though it be in the history of religion, cannot be said to have been the standard or dominant interpretation of afterlife in the mainstream of Christian faith and practice. To many Christians, indeed, it seems alien, even repugnant. Since it is such a widespread image, however, those of us who seriously adhere to the Christian Way ought surely to ask ourselves whether the concept of rebirth is really as alien from the Christian Way as we may have supposed. As we now review images of the hereafter in this final chapter of our inquiry, we must address ourselves not only to this immensely influential image in the history of religious thought in general but to its incidence in Christianity and especially to its compatibility or incompatibility with the fundamentals of Christian faith. Christianity is numerically the dominant religion of the West, so while reviewing the forms of imagery of afterlife that have affected religious thought generally, we ought to give some consideration to why the Christian Church has been so inhospitable to so generally influential an afterlife image.

The fact that the image of rebirth is so widespread in the history of religious ideas from their most primitive to their most developed forms does not by any means in itself warrant our finding a place for it in our much-needed reconstruction of an intelligible and comprehensive vision of the meaning and truth of afterlife. Many ideas related to afterlife must be, I submit, discarded in any such reconstruction. I do not believe that many intelligent, educated, and spiritually sensitive people today would find possible the acceptance of anything like the traditional images of heaven and hell. What, then, should we take seriously in the reconstruction of an intelligible image of afterlife?

A Personal View

In my view, the most penetrating insight in the history of religious ideas is that expressed in the great monotheistic religions: the uniqueness and otherness of God as the creative source of being. This insight yields another that goes in tandem with it: God, as the creative source of existence so loves his creatures that sacrificial love may be ascribed to him as his special attribute. As his creatures we are utterly dependent on him, but the dependence, far from being a servile constriction, is the basis of the greatest joy of human life: the recognition that, because of the nature of him to whom we owe our existence, our experience of God here and now warrants our expectation of a meaningful life in the hereafter. This interpretation of the meaning of human life and the nature of God's creative love is dramatically expressed in the creedal documents of Christian orthodoxy, but it is also the motif that runs through the Bible and the literature of all the monotheistic religions.

To understand the significance of all this we must discover what it excludes, for to have any meaning at all it must not only include something but exclude something. What it excludes is, for instance, the notion that existence is another name for God: that God and existence are to be identified in such a way that as I say "I exist" I can say also "I am part of the stream of existence, which is God; therefore I am God." Indeed, on this view that I propose to exclude, to say that I take joy in God *means* that I take joy in existing. I must discover, however, what existence is, and such discovery may be called my self-realization: the realization that despite the obstacles that obscure this self-realization, I am part of divine Being. All is one and therefore I am part of that oneness. Such is the view that I would exclude.

The difference between the view for which I am contending and the view it excludes usually does not seem at first sight so important as to warrant the radical distinction on which I am insisting, but it does warrant it. The respective implications of the two views are to be perceived most forcefully in the afterlife corollaries that they entail. In the case of the view that I am excluding, afterlife, if there is one, must consist in further opportunities to do the self-realization job that I have not so far been able to finish. (This means that eventually I shall so realize my oneness with the One—with existence itself—that I shall no longer be out of harmony with it.) By contrast, in the view on which I am insisting, the afterlife entailment is one in which what I am to realize more and more is my creatureliness and the delight of serving my Creator, whom to serve (as the ancient prayer so succinctly puts it) is perfect freedom. The difference is somewhat like the difference between, on the one hand, an orphan's discovery of the parents and family that he assumed to be dead and finds to be alive and loving and, on the other, his discovery of the constitution and by-laws of the orphanage to which he has always belonged and always will, so long as he lives. If you are in any doubt about the importance of the difference, ask any orphan.

What is consonant with the fundamental monotheistic vision? For example, the notion of survival for a time in an "astral" or "subtle" or "luminous" body, lacking both the impediment of our flesh-and-bones body and its instrumentality seems to be not only intrinsically unobjectionable but to accord with much of the traditional Christian metaphorical vocabulary used of those recently departed. They are "at rest" or "asleep" or "waiting," pending resurrection. In Catholic practice one may pray publicly or privately *for* them and probably even, at least privately, *to* them for their help and guidance as we pray both publicly and privately to the "official" saints of the Church for their intercession. We are, in short, "in communion" with them, not in some abstract way but recognizing them by name and as we hold them in our memories: George or Mary or Bessie. For being "at rest" or "sleeping" does not necessarily mean that they are comatose; it means only that they are not engaged in the kind of activities that we think of as such. They do not go to parties to sing and dance, for instance, as sometimes we may; but that does not preclude their having work to do. To a blue-collar worker, white-collar work may seem to be "just sitting in a chair" but it can be just as exhausting as any blue-collar work; so work in the realm of "astral" embodiments may seem like floating around in air when in fact it may be very much more than that. It is presumably, however, very different from the kind of work we do, whatever the hue of our collars. So we may say with propriety that those who "die in the Lord" rest from "their earthly labors." They also presumably see things from a different perspective. The notion that they, unseen by us, can accompany us to church, for instance, is eminently compatible with a monotheistic stance. Many Christians no doubt feel an awareness that their deceased loved ones are with them as they kneel to pray.

In the concept of rebirth or reincarnation I see also one of the great religious insights in the history of religious ideas. Job, as we noted in the last chapter, saw hope for a tree, because when felled it can continue to sprout shoots and so be reborn, but man dies "and lifeless he remains." True, man does not, at death, behave as does a tree. Man cannot (at least in the present state of medical knowledge), grow even a new arm or leg when he loses one, as can happen at lower levels of evolution. Nevertheless, he might be reborn, reincarnated in some other and indeed more interesting way, involving his interior evolution: the domain in which he is so pre-eminent among all other forms of life at present empirically known to us. At any rate, in view both of the long and widespread history of the image of afterlife in terms of rebirth or reincarnation and the extraordinary interest in it that has developed in recent years in the West, I do not think that anyone should dismiss it cavalierly as alien to Western thought in general and to the monotheistic outlook in particular.

Unfortunately, many people in the West still associate the image of rebirth so much with Oriental religions and culture that they set it aside as alien to the Western mind and specifically incompatible with Christian faith, lacking, as they suppose, the concept of salvation by grace that is at the heart of Christian theology.

While I find such misgivings understandable, I am also quite convinced that they are unwarranted. Moreover, I think the compatibility is clearly demonstrable and propose now to conduct such a demonstration. First, however, let us make sure that we know exactly what we are to understand by karma and reincarnation before we attempt any such investigation. We must also dispel the error that it is alien to Western thought.

Karma The karmic principle is a principle of moral balance in the universe. As such it is expressible, for example, in terms of Kant's categorical imperative or of the Torah or Law of Moses, which Jesus said he came not to destroy but to complete. "Do not imagine," he is reported to have said, "that I have come to abolish the Law or the Prophets. I have come not to abolish but to complete them." (Matthew 5:17). Moreover, karma is anything other than a fatalistic notion; on the contrary, it is pre-eminently a free-will principle. As we saw it interpreted by the Jains, for instance, we might be warranted in criticizing it for its being too exclusively a free-will principle. It can be so understood, but it need not be. Yes, as a principle it is as inexorable in the spiritual realm as are the "laws" of physics and chemistry in the empirical domain. That does not mean, however, that we are necessarily imprisoned by it. On the contrary, we create our individual karma by our own acts. Karma is *jeté là, comme ça,* to use Sartre's phrase: it is "thrown down to us" as our circumstance. Everyone is born into this circumstance or that and *circumstance* means, etymologically, "that which stands around" us including, for instance, our biological heredity, which is also part of our circumstance. Nobody is infinitely free. I cannot change the date or the place of my birth. Many facts I have to face are given to me and I can do nothing about them; but if I take seriously the karmic principle and its implicates I can change my karmic heritage in such a way as to provide me with a more favorable one in my next life. So to that very considerable extent I make my own destiny.

As the spiritual principle of the universe, the law of karma entails the spiritual evolution of the individual. This evolution is an ongoing process. It cannot be confined to one lifespan or even a few; it needs a span large enough to provide time for the individual to move from humble beginnings to the realization of his full potential. Hence the rebirth principle: reincarnation, transmigration, metempsychosis, or whatever name one may choose to give it. The length of this process is not determinable, but if one reflects on the enormous time it has taken to achieve the biological development represented by our present human condition, one would certainly expect the process of spiritual development to take even longer, perhaps indeed an indefinitely long time. The embodiments are whatever may be required by the karmic law that governs the process. The popular notion that a man or woman might be reincarnated as a dog or a pig is, however, so far-fetched as to merit no serious consideration. It belongs to a very primitive mental outlook. In any case, what is important for an understanding of the reincarnational principle is that it works in tandem with the law of karma, the instrument by which we are being constantly judged and continually educated. It is to be regarded (as evolutionary process ought to be regarded at every level) as "God's way of doing things." It is the instrument of the creative love of God.

The fact that karma sounds to many people too automatic, even perhaps too mercantile, to fit God's freedom and God's grace need not disconcert us. A school prospectus often sounds lifeless and even dismal when read "cold." Only in light of the life of the school do we begin to understand the function of the structure, which is merely a way of controlling and ministering to the school spirit that gives the school its vitality and its worth. The infrastructure provided by karma and rebirth can be seen as ministering to God's creative love and the action of the Holy Spirit.

A reincarnational view, if accepted and made one's own, provides an explanation of the most difficult of all problems that confront thoughtful people as they reflect on the problem of evil in a universe that the monotheistic religions all claim to be the creation of an infinitely loving and compassionate Creator. Why do the wicked prosper and the righteous suffer? Why does life seem to be, as the nihilistic philosophers have called it, meaningless and absurd? It is because we are looking at only a tiny slice of a vast and continually moving panorama. For the life of each individual stretches incalculably far back into history and no less incalculably is it projecting far forward into the future. What you are looking at is at best but one scene of one act of an enormously long evolutionary drama that, if we could but see the whole of it, would explain itself. Not only is death not the end of a human life; birth is likewise not the beginning of it.

But in the view that I am proposing, what becomes of prayer, which is regarded in Judaism, Christianity, and Islam, as basic to the practice of one's faith? It is true that many who have learned to accept a karmic and therefore a reincarnational scenario see little or no point in prayer, at any rate not as commonly understood in any of the great religions. Meditation, yes, but not prayer in the sense of intercession or petition or thanksgiving. For, they suppose, since bad karma can be eliminated only by the acquisition of good karma and this change can be wrought only by action, prayer is of little if any value. Deeds, not words, are what are needed.

Now of course there is plausibility to such a view, but it represents only a certain stage in the understanding of the karmic principle. Although each one of us must work out his or her own salvation, we can all profit from help and guidance. I suppose I could learn Russian all by myself with nothing but a grammar, a dictionary, and perhaps a few audio tapes; but I should be very foolish to dispense with a teacher, for obviously that would immensely facilitate my undertaking. All the monotheistic religions revere the role of the teacher, and Christians, emphasizing the great ancient insight that in certain fundamental respects we have "no power of ourselves to help ourselves," recognize the infinite value of Jesus Christ as Saviour.

Accepting Christ as Saviour most certainly does not mean that one is to sit back and rejoice that one has nothing more to do than praise God for having taken care of the entire process of one's salvation. The work of Christ consists, rather, of providing me with the *conditions* that make it possible for me to work out my salvation. That is enough to be cause for my everlasting gratitude. If a physician restores your broken bones to the point where you can use your limbs again and gradually, by exercise, bring the muscles of your limbs into full working order, you do not complain. He has made your recovery possible; that is surely ample cause for your undying gratitude. In traditional Christian theological language, Christ "saves" me by putting me into a condition of "righteousness," so that it remains to me only to work out the "sanctification" that he has made possible.

Both reincarnation and resurrection are forms of re-embodiment. Resurrection, however, as traditionally understood, implies the revivification of my body sometime (possibly if not probably a very long time, such as a thousand or even a million years) after my death. The revivified body that I am to receive, on this view, is a permanent one. It is to be not merely better or more durable as are our "second" teeth to our "baby" ones; it is to be everlasting. It is also said to be more "glorious," more "luminous," than my present embodiment. But whatever spiritually improves my condition improves in some way or other the "luminosity" of my embodiment. Some of my friends are much more "luminous" even in their present embodiments than are others, and that is surely a proper expectation and a warranted hope in the mind of anyone who trusts in the God of love. The view I am proposing conforms to the hope of such "glory" in two ways: after death the self, whatever it is, is relieved of the encumbrance of its present "heavy" embodiment and can shine emancipated therefrom; then after some time it is drawn to further embodiment. In the lyrical words of John Masefield, British poet laureate in his day and a firm believer in some form of reincarnation.

> With sturdier limbs and brighter brain
> The old soul takes the road again.

In our chapter on Jain and other Oriental religions we saw that a reincarnational view is perfectly compatible with what is in effect a thoroughgoing atheism such as prevails in Jain teaching. It is no less thoroughly compatible with a monotheistic stance. As an image of afterlife in the latter case, however, the karmic rebirth scenario must be shown to encompass concepts such as divine intervention, grace, and the loving and redemptive action of God.

The concept of rebirth pervades, in one way or another, the heart of all religion. It expresses whatever it is that happens when a person "sees the light" and so is "born again" or becomes "a new man." There are other ways, however, of conceiving of a sort of immortality. Much used in memorial services is the well-known passage in Ecclesiasticus (44:1–14) which assures us that the *names* of certain people shall not perish: "their bodies are buried in peace; but their *name* liveth for evermore." That may console a relative or admirer or friend, but it has little if anything to do with the persistence of a conscious self. Nor has what we may call, for shorthand, genetic reincarnation, such as we may see in the descendant of a person when we say "It's uncanny—she *is* Aunt Bessie." Not even does the belief that seems to satisfy some at least nominally religious people, that one is to "live on" in the ongoing Church or other community-focused model such as "Abraham and his seed for ever," provide for the *kind* of rebirth that an authentic deep love for and gratitude to God seems to me to demand. Is not even an attenuated life in Sheol to be preferred over a mere commemoration in stone or brass in a corner of even Westminster Abbey?

What is presupposed in the ancient philosophical and religious traditions about reincarnation as it is presented in terms of the karmic principle is the persistence of an entity (self, soul, spirit) that in some way transcends the empirically observable "me." Whatever be this hypothetical self, it is not reducible to anything that can be observed by any of the methods by which the human sciences proceed. It is a metaphysical or religious concept, dependent, as we stipulated at the outset, on a prior belief in God of which belief it is a corollary.

Opposition to Reincarnational Beliefs Why then is not reincarnation a universal tenet of all religions? Why are many religious thinkers content to view immortality or any sort of survival in terms of participation in the ongoing community, such as the Church, the people, the remnant of the redeemed, "Abraham and his seed for ever," or other community-focused model? Why, more especially, has it tended to appear in the monotheistic religions only as an underground movement or esoteric interpretation of the official teachings of Church or Synagogue or Mosque? Why does it appear so abundantly in the humane literature associated with such religions while their official utterances are content to conceptualize in terms such as *Israel*, the *New Israel*, and *Abraham and his seed for ever*?

Why indeed should great intellects such as Pythagoras and Plato so readily accept and teach a reincarnational view implying the existence of some ongoing entity such as a "soul" or "self" entirely apart from the great tradition of the Hebrew prophets and centuries before the emergence of the Christian Way? Why, in the great Renaissance of European culture and thought should the *umanisti* (the often profoundly religious thinkers who, in the West, presented a revitalized understanding of the Christian Way) have entertained views favorable to the reincarnationist tradition in classical European thought? No vision of afterlife was more sustained by the men of the

Renaissance than that of the rebirth of an enduring individual self. The Church, however, while not explicitly denouncing such opinions, definitely discouraged them. Why?

No special sociological training is needed to arrive at the answer. The Church and its counterparts in other religions are pre-eminently organizations. Organizations are naturally suspicious of any view or attitude or teaching that is potentially capable of undermining their societal and political power. The concept of an individual self with capacity for independence from the institution or organization is instinctively suspect. A reincarnational image of afterlife falls into this category. That does not by any means imply that those who believe in a reincarnational schema are generally or even frequently inclined to ignore or set aside the Church as unnecessary or otiose. On the contrary, they may and very often do find institutional religion immensely helpful. Nevertheless, the Church admittedly cannot have the same hold on them that an organization by its very nature prefers to have over its members. Such fears on the part of the ecclesiastical hierarchy may be in fact unwarranted. Nevertheless, they are psychologically understandable, for it is true that those who subscribe to the kind of rebirth outlook that focuses on the individual rather than the group are inclined to feel capable, *in the last resort*, of dispensing with the institution and finding their own way to salvation. As we saw in the last chapter, this need not mean that they do so in reliance solely on themselves and their deeds or works. They may cast themselves fervently upon the grace of God in one way or another, as Christians do in recognizing the saving power of Christ. To separate themselves from the Church or whatever counterpart has captured and sustained them is obviously the source of intense anguish. Yet it *can* be done. The Church or other established religious institution naturally suspects and dislikes this outlook as it suspects and dislikes what it regards as cults: new and often lively movements on the fringe of the Church or beyond its frontiers.

We must expect, then, that institutional religion, even in its most benign forms, should prefer to ally itself with ideas that do not seem to endanger its structure and to reserve its blessing for those images of afterlife that reflect corporate rather than individual preoccupations. Adversity, runs the old adage, makes for strange bedfellows. So the Church, while talking of the salvation of the individual, feels comfortable with images such as a Day of Judgment, when all are assembled together, faithful sheep to the right, faithless goats to the left. Righteousness triumphs and is rewarded; unrighteousness is punished; everything is done *en bloc*, once and for all and forever. Immortality can be interpreted alongside such a model as the immortality of the Church, the congregation of the faithful, the People of God, the Household of Faith, which has an ongoing life. The institution may talk of individual hope, but the hope is not geared to the notion of individual survival but to survival of the group *qua* group. As an individual I am emptied into the group and the life everlasting becomes the ongoing life of the New Israel, the life of the Church into which I am emptied, as the pitcher is emptied into the river that carries it on. Rebirth, resurrection, yes; but the focus is on the community. It is, after all, the group onto which the individual has been ingrafted in the first place, through baptism or the like.

Rebirth Rebirth, however, in one form or another, is the most persistent image of afterlife in the history of religion. If we take death seriously (and only by sheer fantasy can its macabre reality be sidestepped), how else can we provide a model consonant with the believer's moral awareness of duty to God and of the divine purpose of God in the believer's life? My survival in my biological descendants is not enough, for the duties that I owe to God cannot be made over to and imposed upon them like encumbrances on an estate. Only I can fulfill these duties. Not even the Church, the People of God, can assume them for me. God would not impose them on me personally as he does without giving me the possibility of fulfilling them. True, as we have seen, the inexorable character of the karmic principle, known in biblical terms to Jews and Christians as the Law or Torah, can be surmounted by the grace and mercy of God. That is the foundation of the Catholic prayer (one of the central prayers of the Mass): *Agnus Dei, qui tollis peccata mundi, miserere nobis . . . dona nobis pacem* (Lamb of God, who takes away the sins of the world, have mercy upon us . . . grant us thy peace).

As I pray this most beautiful prayer at Mass I am pleading with Christ to grant *me*, along with the rest of the faithful, the benefits of the redemption he has so dearly purchased for us. Yet even as I humbly accept his gracious bounty I know that as an individual focus of consciousness the duties imposed upon me by God remain for me to try to fulfill. I desire to fulfill them. I could not be able with honesty to accept Christ's gracious gift of love to me personally were I to feel able to shelve these duties, throwing them into a genetic river or encumbering the Household of Faith with them. They are *my* duties: certainly no less my duties by reason of the gracious gift of Christ; surely rather, indeed, more than ever my duties because of the fuller understanding of the love that I owe to God in the fulfillment of them.

Salvation Christianity is not alone in proclaiming that human salvation depends fundamentally on God, not on the good deeds that human beings may do. The notion is very strong, for example, in some forms of Mahayana Buddhism, notably in the Pure Land school. Amitabha, known to the Chinese as O-mi-to, is one of the greatest of the gods of Asia. As a monk many eons ago he took the vow to become a bodhisattva in order to help humanity in its spiritual development. He has now risen so high that, having called into existence a Land of Bliss, a Buddha-field called Sukhavati, he presides over this paradise and freely admits to it any who call upon him in faith. As the bodhisattvas serve to sustain humankind in its struggles here on earth, so Amitabha assures future happiness to those who invoke his name in faith. So spiritually powerful is Amitabha that one can eventually in some sense transcend the karmic principle and at the hour of death depart this present level or plane of existence and be reborn, by the grace and power of Amitabha, in the Buddha-domain, the Pure Land, the land of eternal bliss. The masses think of this as a sort of short cut to heaven.

In the apostolic proclamation of the nature of the Christian Way, as reported in the New Testament and other early Christian literature, we find a similarly strong emphasis on the notion that my individual salvation is assured to me through my individual faith in and reliance upon Jesus the Christ. He is neither merely my teacher nor merely my guide; he is my Saviour. I am said to be saved through his shedding of his blood for me and for many others (*peri pollōn*) in sacrificial love (Matthew 26:28).

Although the concept of my being saved through the Blood of the Lamb is one that appears with more vigorous (not to say more strident) emphasis in the Evangelical Protestant tradition than in the Catholic one, it unquestionably pertains to the very roots of Christian faith. It is through Christ that my salvation is accomplished. It is he who makes possible the redemption of the world. *Ave crux, spes unica*: Hail, O Cross, our only hope. But how can such an insistence on the grace of God as our only hope be squared with such a "free will" doctrine as the karmic law? If salvation is through grace and faith, what need is there for a karmic principle?

Karma and Grace The karmic law stands to grace much as the Torah (expressed for instance in the Ten Commandments) stands to the Gospel, the "Good News." Jesus declared that he had not come to abolish the Law but to complete it (Matthew 5:17). The moral law is ultimately the law of the spiritual dimension of existence as, say, the law of gravity is the law of the physical universe. Neither can be set aside or nullified, but both can be overcome or transformed. The moral law, whether expressed as Torah or karmic principle, is as inescapable as is the law of gravity in the physical world. Yet classic Hebrew thought recognized that to love God is the essence of the Law (see Deuteronomy 6:4–9).

According to Luke's account of the Gospel, Jesus, having been asked by a lawyer what one must do to inherit everlasting life, drew from him a reference to this deuteronomic teaching, which Jesus applauded. One must love God with all one's heart and soul and strength and mind and one's neighbor as oneself. The lawyer, however, persisted: "Who is my neighbor?" In response Jesus recounted perhaps the best-known of all his parables: that of the Good Samaritan. To try to observe the Law in literalistic style is commendable, but it is impossible to attain perfection that way. The only way to attain perfection is to go right to the heart of the Law, which can be done only through love (Luke 10:25–37). Luke follows this up with the account of Martha and Mary (Luke 10:38–42). Martha, in her effort to do the right thing, busied herself with all the chores needed to serve Jesus, her guest, in the best possible way. Annoyed that Mary leaves her to do all this serving by herself, while she, Mary, sits at Jesus' feet listening to him intently, Martha asks Jesus to tell Mary to help her. Jesus, however, while recognizing that Martha was doing well, said that Mary was doing even better in attending to the one thing needful: listening in love. Luke, in recounting this story here, is really continuing the same theme. Love is the essence of the "good works" that constitute the observance of the Law.

By no means is Jesus offering a "short cut" to salvation. Love is anything other than a short cut. Authentic love entails unlimited sacrifice. For Jesus it entailed rejection and, in the end, the agony and ignominy of crucifixion. It is the distillation of the essence of observance of the Law. Only in that sense can it be said to override the Law.

There is a parallel to this concept in Hinduism in which, while *karma-yoga* is a recognized way of trying to attain salvation through good works, *bhakti-yoga*, a way of attaining salvation through personal devotion and love, is another avenue to the same end. The parallel is not exact, but it points in a similar direction. Sacrificial love *is* the observance of the law in the most concentrated form that such observance can take.

Christian theology has always emphasized the theme that only through God's grace (*charisma*) is salvation possible. Nowhere has this basic doctrine been questioned. Indeed, apart from it the other pillars of Christian teaching would crumble. What has been controversial in the history of Christian thought is the relation of faith to works, expressed in technical terms in disputes over "justification" and "sanctification." *Justification* in theological usage means the action of making the individual "right with God," while *sanctification* means actualization of that "rightness" in the moral and spiritual fruits that the individual bears. At the risk of oversimplification, one might propose an analogy. Finding myself in financial bankruptcy I am in a hopeless case, facing, if not debtors' prison, at least a bleak economic future. To my surprise and joy, however, you come along and provide me with an interest-free loan (in effect a gift) of a large capital sum that releases me from my economic bondage and enables me to make a fresh start. Your backing me not only frees me from my financial burden; it floods me with gratitude and confidence and provokes in me a passionate desire to use your gift in the best possible way. Without your gift I could not have moved. As expressed in the popular hymn "Amazing Grace," I was lost and now am found, was blind and now see.

In attempting to measure the value of your gift in relation to the excellent use that I (let us suppose) make of it, there can be no possible doubt of the indispensability of your gift and therefore of its basic value in the redemptive process. Nevertheless, while it has provided me with the conditions for success, I do play an important part in the hard work I put into the business of making use of your gift. Such is human ingratitude and thoughtlessness that I might have squandered your gift, perhaps not deliberately but at least through carelessness or other human frailty or weakness. How then do you rate my role in the process in contradistinction to yours?

Your gift, since without it I could have done nothing, is plainly all-important for my economic salvation. God's grace, therefore, is rightly celebrated with joy as the cornerstone of the structure of the Christian life. Without it the karmic principle (call it what you will) could not even begin to work for me. My spiritual evolution would be not merely hindered; it would be radically impeded in such a way as to enslave me. Theoretically I should be able to break the bonds that have immobilized me; practically I am no more able to do so than a man sinking fast into a bog can extricate himself by himself. The more he struggles the deeper he sinks. When, however, someone throws him a rope that enables him to get a footing and so make his struggle productive, he has been saved from a horrible death. Of course his rescuer's act is of supreme and unique importance to him. Such is the importance of the grace of God in the process of salvation.

In the structure of the Christian drama divine grace in no way abrogates the force of the karmic law, which therefore cannot be deemed (as many Christians suppose) at odds with the central Christian concept of reliance upon the grace of God. The karmic principle, they think, leaves no room for self-sacrificial love. On the contrary, all orthodox Christian teaching insists that the salvation that is accomplished through Christ is purchased at enormous cost. Christ is represented as taking the sins of humankind and their terrible consequences upon himself in a supremely self-sacrificial act: the agony of his passion and death, indeed the entire act of his self-humbling. God does not save the world by a magical act, the waving of a divine wand. On the contrary, he bends down in humility and self-sacrifice to take upon himself the sins of the world and all the burdens they entail. Far from canceling out the karmic law, he conforms to it while at the same time taking away its fatal consequences.

It is precisely because, according to Scripture and Christian tradition, God chose to redeem the world by such an act of self-abnegation, self-emptying (*kenosis*) that the karmic principle remains compatible with grace. If God had chosen to ignore the karmic principle and act independently of it, Christian theologians might have been indeed warranted in seeing an incompatibility between karma and grace. The pellucid testimony of Scripture and tradition, however, is that he chose *not* arbitrarily to override the Torah, the karmic law. The astounding claim of Christian faith is that he chose to submit to it by assuming the pain that obedience to this spiritual law entails.

In the language and thought of old-fashioned theological expositions of the Atonement, Christ assumed the debt, paying the ransom the Devil demanded. Modern theologians do not like that "ransom" concept, which is of course indeed a crude one; yet for all its crudity it recognized a central fact about the Atonement: the awesomeness of its cost. Such was the price tag that God not only suffers in and with his creation, as I have maintained in my *He Who Lets Us Be*; he undertook at a specific point in history and locale to be incarnate in human flesh, to be rejected, reviled, misunderstood and spat upon. He chose to submit to all the agony that the karmic law demanded as the cost of human redemption, so revealing to humanity the boundlessness of the sacrificial love he extends to even the least lovable of his human creatures. To take away this element in the Christian account of the drama of human redemption would be not merely to emasculate it; it would be to destroy its very heart. For this is indeed the heart of the Christian proclamation and its most distinctive feature.

So Christ's sacrificial act, far from cushioning me or saving my skin, provides a goad. "Love so amazing, so divine," writes Isaac Watts in his famous hymn, "demands my soul, my life, my all." Those whose understanding of the Christian drama is superficial tend to suppose that grace somehow destroys the operation of the laws of nature. That is to make God into a cosmic conjuror. Grace, as Thomas Aquinas says, does not destroy nature but perfects it (*gratia non tollit naturam sed perficit*). Grace is not a substitute for human goodness. It is, rather, according to all orthodox Christian doctrine, both in the Catholic tradition and in the Reformation heritage, the condition of its realization. Grace is to free will (so strikingly an implicate of the karmic principle) as is capital to labor. It is the condition that makes the karmic law work in my favor.

Those who see the concept of grace as fundamentally at odds with the karmic principle cannot but have forgotten the immensity of the cost of Christ's redemptive act. Whatever objections may legitimately be raised against the concept of reincarnation that goes hand in hand with the concept of karma, its incompatibility with Christian orthodoxy cannot be deemed one of them. But we may well ask why the karmic principle should be supposed to imply rebirth as it is generally presented in reincarnational literature. This is a convenient place to discuss such a concern.

The Problem of Evil The problem of evil arises, in one form or another, in all religions. What precisely is at the heart of it? It is not expressed in its full poignancy in the age-old question. Why do the wicked prosper and the righteous suffer? So long as pain and suffering may be seen to be in some way educative, one need not complain, for such is the nature of all evolutionary progress, biological and spiritual. Everything that we learn well is learned "the hard way." "No cross, no crown" is no mere pious saying but a description of the very nature of growth. The pain of childbearing ends in the joy of motherhood and new life. No tragedy in that. If one can look back on the unfolding of one's life and see in it poverty or disease or other severe adversity gradually overcome, one cannot complain. Indeed, one may see in it the very hand of God benevolently guiding one's way. It is when one sees the unfolding of the meaningfulness of life suddenly interrupted and the meaning apparently destroyed, not to say mocked, that we find ourselves confronted by tragedy and the "problem of evil" in all its starkness. The child who has brought so much joy to his or her parents prospers well, going from strength to strength; then when all seems set for a life of glorious promise a crippling accident or disease makes a mockery of all such hopes.

True, not all lives are stricken with such tragedy. There is, however, one tragedy that intrudes upon every human life, disguise it as we may: Death. As Horace writes with alliterative force: *Pallida Mors aequo pulsat pede pauperum tabernas regumque turres*: "Pale Death with impartial step knocks at the doors of the hovels of the poor and the palaces of kings." Nor is the impartiality of Death its most fearsome aspect. It is, rather, that it waits for no man. It comes at awkward moments, for example, when a cure for one's malady is just on the horizon but is not yet medically available, or just as one is nearing the completion of the most important project in one's life. Such tragedies are tragic not merely because they forestall the fulfillment of our hopes but also because they impede us even from accomplishing what we believe to be our duty. The assurance, Christian or otherwise, that death is not the end does not in itself eliminate the sense of tragedy. Least of all does it soften the sense of injustice. Is it really enough to be assured that after death there is a bright future for all who trust in the saving power of Christ? Or that your cross and mine are each to be exchanged for a crown in heaven? Such blanket assurances do nothing to explain why your cross should be so much more terrible than mine.

The vision of an ongoing purgatorial process of development and growth makes infinitely greater sense and is in fact developed (albeit sometimes, caricatured) in traditional Catholic theology. It can be well wedded to the Christian doctrine of prevenient grace. Indeed, a doctrine of purgatory is in fact so wedded in traditional Catholic thought, as "justification" is wedded to "sanctification" in one way or another in all Christian theology. Why not, then, express the process of an ongoing purgatorial development in terms of rebirth? Everything else is subject in one way or another to some form of rebirth. Why should "official" Christian thought be inclined to resist this solution to an otherwise intractable problem in any vision of afterlife?

The instinct to be silent if not resistant to any detailed expression of the nature of afterlife is understandable. One may well argue that Christian thinkers and visionaries might have done better with more rather than less reluctance to speak of its nature. After all, they have not done very well with their popularizing images of the pearly gates and crystal rivers of heaven or the fiery furnaces and diabolical tortures of hell. So indeed there is something to be said for silence about the details of the Christian hope. But since theologians have said so much on the subject already, a relapse into silence after so much eloquence on the subject could be in itself more eloquent than speech. No doubt one should exercise reticence in committing Christianity to a particular understanding of *how* rebirth works in the context of Christian eschatology. Yet it seems to me that when so much is whispered about it behind the scenes and when so many who courageously follow the Christian Way in life privately yet wholeheartedly accept it as the best expression they can find of their afterlife hope, it needs to be at least discussed seriously by trained Christian theologians. The urgency of this need is aggravated by the fact that so much nonsense is talked about reincarnation by those whose minds are untrained in dealing with philosophical and theological questions.

Rebirth, as indubitably one of the most widespread and most important of all images of afterlife, may be envisioned in many ways. The model handed down to us in Indian thought is fascinating and provocative, yet it entails presuppositions that are by no means indisputable. To say the least, they run counter to much that is important and valuable in Western thought. The notion of a series of layers that are to be stripped off, one after the other, like the leaves of an artichoke, to reveal the innermost and "real" self, is indeed not only picturesque but meaningful to those who understand the reality of planes of consciousness and psychic depths. What such imagery expresses, however, is so expressed in terms of a particular mode of conceptualizing. It may illumine for some the truth it expresses while obscuring it for others. One need not and probably should not seek to commit the Christian faithful to any such particular symbolic form.

I suggest, then, that we must concur with David Hume, not the least skeptical of philosophers in the history of Western thought, in asserting that if we are to believe in any form of afterlife at all, then metempsychosis (reincarnation, rebirth) may be the only one worthy of our attention. It is, as we have abundantly seen, capable of functioning as an interpretation of the doctrine of purgatory and the counterparts of this doctrine that are to be found in the Orient and elsewhere in the great religions of humankind. It is geared (as models such as heaven and hell are not) to the finitude of our capacity and the limitations of our human nature.

We have obviously no experience and therefore no direct knowledge of afterlife. Many of us may be content to conclude that there is none, invoking therefore the final injunction in Wittgenstein's *Tractatus* (7) : *Wovon man nicht sprechen kann, darüber muss man schweigen* ("What we cannot speak about we must consign to silence"). Yet, although we of course have no direct experience of afterlife, are we really without any knowledge of it at all? Those of us who find it a satisfactory conclusion in terms of our own experience of life cannot be expected to discard it merely because others reach a different conclusion. Our conclusion is to say the least not a disreputable hypothesis. Those of us who reach this conclusion about human destiny do so despite the appalling injustice that we, in common with everybody else, see in the world (even indeed an apparent *dys*teleology in it), for there remains in our experience such a deep sense of purpose in our lives that we cannot interpret it as other than an aspect of a cosmic purpose beyond our personal concerns. For us who are so minded the hypothesis of afterlife is an eminently plausible and respectable one not only because it has been upheld by so many of the greatest minds in human history, in all the greatest of the world's civilizations, but because it has its spring in our own most profound and lively experience.

We are rightly untroubled by the charge that such a belief is explicable in terms of wishful thinking, for it might just as warrantably be accused of having its roots in groundless fear. In any developed form of afterlife belief is an ethical element that entails belief in human responsibility for our thoughts, words, and actions, and this responsibility in turn entails reckoning of one sort or another, expressed in the notion of judgment, which we have seen to be such a universal expectation in all the great religions of the world, whatever beliefs they may respectively entertain about afterlife. It may be that some people, after a lifetime of selfish unconcern and of talk of nothing but the stock market and football scores and sex and favorite restaurants and the latest fashion in drapes, have nothing in them capable of surviving death. Who dares say? For the rest of us, the only question about afterlife that remains is the form that it may take. The author's hope is that this book may assist readers to judge that for themselves.

Bibliography

Addison, J. T. *Life Beyond Death in the Beliefs of Mankind* (1932).

Alvarez, Octavio. *The Celestial Brides* (1978).

An extensive study of the various kinds and images of paradise in the Mediterranean world, with their origins in India, Egypt, and elsewhere. Copiously illustrated.

Andrews, Carol. *Egyptian Mummies* (1984).

Appleby, L. "Near Death Experience: Analogous to Other Stress Induced Psychological Phenomena," *British Medical J.* 298 (1989):976–77.

An important paper written from a medical standpoint on the nature of experiences reported as connected with near-death and their occurrence in non-near-death circumstances.

Armstrong, A. Hilary. *Expectations of Immortality in Late Antiquity* (1987).

Bailey, Lloyd R. "Gehenna: The Topography of Hell," *Biblical Archaeologist* 49, 3 (September 1986):187–189.

Baillie, John. *And the Life Everlasting* (1933).

Benson, Elizabeth P. (ed.). *Death and the Afterlife in Pre-Columbian America* (1975).

Papers arising out of a conference at Dumbarton Oaks, Washington, D.C., October 1973. Two papers are of special interest for their discussion of afterlife: J. Wilbert, "Eschatology in a Participatory Universe," and Michael D. Coe, "Death and Afterlife in Pre-Columbian America."

Berdyaev, Nicolas. *The Destiny of Man* (1937). See especially pp. 249–265.

Berndt, Ronald M. *Australian Aboriginal Religion* (1974).

Illustrations and bibliography.

Brune, François. *Les Morts nous parlent* (1988).

Bibliography

Budge, Ernest A. T. W. *Egyptian Ideas of the Future Life* (1899, 1976).

Camporesi, Piero. *The Fear of Hell* (1991).
> A scholarly exposition, written with literary style and sensitivity, of the grotesque depictions of punishments in hell used in the sixteenth and seventeenth centuries and influential thereafter in striking terror in the popular imagination.

Chittick, Wm. C. "Eschatology," in Seyyed Hossein Nasr, *Islamic Spirituality* (1987).
> A scholarly study of the subject with details of the various kinds of resurrection envisioned in Islam and other topics.

Cohn, Samuel K., Jr. *Death and Property in Siena, 1205–1800: Strategies for the Afterlife* (1988).
> This study, although a specialized historical one, contains some very interesting materials relating to social and religious attitudes toward afterlife.

Cranston, S., and C. Williams. *Reincarnation: A New Horizon in Science, Religion, and Society* (1984).
> A highly informed treatment of reincarnation by two authors who have conducted profound inquiries into the history of the subject.

Curry, Patrick (ed.). *Astrology, Science and Society: Historical Essays* (1987).
> Illustrated.

Davis, T. (ed.). *Death and Afterlife* (1989).
> A collection of essays from opposing viewpoints, including contributions by John Hick, Kai Nielsen, and Paul Badham.

Dearmer, Percy. *The Legend of Hell* (1929).
> A repudiation of the traditional Christian images of hell by an Anglican divine, a much respected theologian in his time.

Dermenghem, Émile. *Muhammad* (trans. from the French by Jean M. Watt) (1958).
> Contains (pp. 114–116) a Muslim account of the journey to heaven.

Dinzelbach, Peter. "The Way to the Other World in Medieval Literature and Art," *Folklore* 97, 1 (1986):70–87.

Dobbs, Betty Jo Teeter. *Alchemical Death and Resurrection* (1990).
> An interpretation of alchemical symbolism based on studies of Newton.

Ducasse, C. J. A. *A Critical Examination of the Belief in a Life After Death* (1961).
> A work by a trained philosopher skeptical of the concept of afterlife.

Eklund, R. *Between Death and Resurrection According to Islam* (1941).

Eliade, Mircea. *From Primitives to Zen* (1967).
> See especially Chapter IV, pp. 321–419: "Death, Afterlife, Eschatology."

El-Saleh, Soubhi. *La Vie future selon le Coran* (1971).
> An examination of the Muslim concept of afterlife as expounded in the Qur'ān.

Farrer, Austin. *The End of Man* (1972).

A collection of characteristically scintillating essays by Farrer; the first three are especially relevant to afterlife questions.

Feest, Christian F. *Indians of North Eastern North America* (1986).
Bibliography. Illustrations include grave boards, and an Indian in a Christian hell.

Gardiner, Eileen (ed.). *Visions of Heaven and Hell Before Dante* (1989).

Geertz, Armin W. *Hopi Indian Altar Iconography* (1987).
Illustrations and bibliography.

Gill, Sam. D. *Songs of Life: an Introduction to Navajo Religious Culture* (1979).
Illustrations and bibliography.

Goodrich, Anne. S. *Chinese Hells: The Peking Temple of Eighteen Hells and Chinese Conceptions of Hell* (1981, 1989).
Interesting and profusely illustrated.

Grazia, Sebastian de. *Machiavelli in Hell* (1989).

Grof, Stanislav and Christina. *Beyond Death* (1980).
Copiously illustrated; brief bibliography.

Harris, J. E., and Wente, E. (eds.). *An X-Ray Atlas of the Royal Mummies* (1980).

Heim, A. "Notizen über den Tod durch Absturz," *Jahrbuch des Schweizer Alpenklub* 27, 327 (1892) (Trans. by R. Noyes and R. Kletti, "The Experience of Dying from Falls," *Omega* 3, 45 [1972].)
A rare late-nineteenth-century account.

Hick, John. *Death and Eternal Life* (1976, 1987).
A philosophical study of the problems connected with ideas of afterlife by an eminent contemporary philosopher and Christian theologian.

Hiltebeitel, Alf (ed.). *Criminal Gods and Demon Devotees: Essays on the Guardians of Popular Hinduism* (1989).

Himmelfarb, Martha. *An Apocalyptic Form in Jewish and Christian Literature* (1983).

Hügel, F. von. *Eternal Life* (1912).
A study by a distinguished Roman Catholic layman and theologian.

Hughes, Robert. *Heaven and Hell in Western Art* (1968).

Jaspers, Karl. *Death to Life* (1968).

Johnson, J. S., and Marsha McGee (eds.). *Encounters with Eternity* (1986).
Views on afterlife in a variety of religious traditions.

Kampen, M. E. *The Religion of the Maya* (1981).
Illustrations and bibliography.

Kant, Immanuel. *Critique of Practical Reason*, Book II, Chapter 4.
A great classic passage on the argument for afterlife.

Lamm, Maurice. "Survival Beliefs and Practices: Judaism," in Robert and Beatrice Kastenbaum (eds.). *Encyclopedia of Death* (1989).

Le Goff, Jacques. *The Birth of Purgatory* (1984).
Translated from the French, *La Naissance du Purgatoire*.

Lewis, H. D. *The Self and Immortality* (1973).

> The author, an English philosopher, contends that an interactionist mind/body theory does better justice to human experience than do mind/brain identity theories. There is a chapter on reincarnation.

Lowe, Michael. *Chinese Ideas of Life and Death: Faith, Myth, and Reason in the Han Period* (202 B.C.E.–220 C.E.) (1982).

> Shows that allusions to afterlife abound in Chinese mythology although arguments in support of an afterlife are lacking.[1]

MacGregor, Geddes. *Reincarnation in Christianity* (1978).

———. *Reincarnation as a Christian Hope* (1982).

———. *The Christening of Karma* (1984).

———. (ed.). *Immortality and Human Destiny: A Variety of Views* (1985).

McDannell, Colleen, and Bernhard Lang. *Heaven: A History* (1988).

> Contains a wide variety of concepts of heaven, including an important chapter specifically on the idea of progress in the hereafter.

McTaggart, John Ellis. *Some Dogmas of Religion* (1930).

> The author affirms belief in immortality but does not affirm belief in God in anything such as the Judeo-Christian concept.

Morris, L. "Eternal Punishment," in E. F. Harrison, G. W. Bromiley, and C. F. H. Henry (eds.). *Baker's Dictionary of Theology* (1967): 196–197.

Motlagh, H. *Unto Him Shall We Return* (1985).

> Selections from Baha'i writings on the immortality of the soul and the nature of the afterlife.

Moody, Raymond. *Life After Life* (1975).

> A popular book on near-death phenomena and other topics relating to questions of afterlife.

Moss, Thelma. *The Probability of the Impossible: Scientific Discoveries and Explorations in the Psychic World.* (1974).

> Contains an extensive chapter on Kirlian photography, with illustrations; also a section on making "electrical" photos.

Myers, Frederic W. H. *Human Personality and Its Survival of Bodily Death* (1961).

> This book, the original form of which was published in 1903, is a celebrated classic of the now-extensive literature on psychical research.

Nickelsburg, G. W. E. *Resurrection, Immortality, and Eternal Life in Intertestamental Judaism* (1972).

Oppenheim, Janet. *The Other World: Spiritualism and Psychical Research in England, 1850–1914* (1985).

> Illustrated; extensive scholarly notes.

O'Shaunessy, T. *Muhammad's Thoughts on Death: A Thematic Study of the Qur'anic Data* (1969).

Ostrander, Sheila, and Lynn Schroeder. *Psychic Discoveries Behind the Iron Curtain* (1970).

A remarkable and highly informative account of the lively interest in psychic research within the Soviet Union at a time when it was to a great extent culturally closed to the rest of the world.

Owen, D. R. R. *The Vision of Hell: Infernal Journeys in Medieval French Literature* (1971).

Owens, J. E., E. W. Cook, and I. Stevenson. "Features of Near-Death Experience in Relation to Whether or Not Patients Were Near Death," *The Lancet* 336 (1990): 1175–1177.

A highly important paper in one of the leading medical journals in the world reporting the investigation of the phenomena associated with "near death" and showing, from a comparison between the phenomena as they occur in patients actually near death and in patients not at all in that circumstance, that these phenomena, although they do apparently occur frequently among patients approaching death, also occur fairly often in other situations.

Palacios, Miguel Asin. *Islam and the* Divine Comedy (1968).

Phillips, D. Z. *Death and Immortality* (1970).

A short discussion in terms of the kind of work being done in the late 1960s in the English-speaking world on the subject of afterlife, with the author's personal outlook on it.

Plato. *Phaedo.*

A classic on the subject of the immortality of the soul.

Prieur, Jean. *L'Aura et le corps immortel* (1983).

Pringle-Pattison, Andrew Seth. *The Idea of Immortality* (1922).

The author, a much respected philosopher in his time, was notably influenced by Hegel, an influence markedly reflected in his Gifford lectures, *The Idea of God* (1920) and *The Idea of Immortality.*

Sorenson, Hendrik Hjort. *The Iconography of Korean Buddhist Painting* (1989). Illustrations and bibliography.

Stevenson, Ian. *Twenty Cases Suggestive of Reincarnation* (1974). "Some Questions Related to Cases of the Reincarnation Type," *The Journal of the American Society for Psychical Research* 68 (1974): 396–416.

The author is well known for his scientific investigation of claimed remembrances of past lives.

Sullivan, Lawrence E. (ed.) *Death, Afterlife, and the Soul* (1987, 1989).

A collection of entries on afterlife from Mircea Eliade (ed.), and *The Encyclopedia of Religion.*

Swedenborg, E. *Heaven and Hell.* The first English translation in the United States (as *Heaven and Its Wonders and Hell*) was published in 1852 and there were numerous subsequent printings.

A Swedenborgian classic. Detailed descriptions of the Hereafter, which in Swedenborg's thought is in many respects contiguous with the Here.

Bibliography

Taylor, A. E. *The Christian Hope of Immortality* (1938).
> The author was a leading British philosopher and religious thinker in his time.

Taylor, J. B. "Some Aspects of Islamic Eschatalogy," *Religious Studies* 4 (1968): 57–76.

Teiser, Stephen F. "Having Once Died and Returned to Life," *Harvard J. of Asiatic Studies* 48, 2 (December 1988): 433–464.
> Representations of Hell in medieval China.

Toynbee, Arnold, Arthur Koestler, et al. *Life After Death* (1976).

Van Oort, H. A. *The Iconography of Chinese Buddhism in Traditional China* (1986).
> Illustrations and bibliography.

Wittgenstein, Ludwig. *Tractatus Logico-Philosophicus* (1961). See 6.431–6.432.

Wright, Barton. *Pueblo Cultures* (1986).
> Illustrated; bibliography.

Yü, Ying-Shih. "O Soul, Come Back: A Study in the Changing Conceptions of the Soul and Afterlife in Pre-Buddhist China," *Harvard J. of Asiatic Studies* 47, 2 (December 1987): 363–395.
> The author inquires into the nature of indigenous Chinese conceptions of afterlife before the advent of Buddhism to China. After reconstructing the ritual of *fu*, he considers the origin and development of the ideas of *hun* and *p'o*, both still pivotal for an understanding of Chinese notions about afterlife and the soul. He then examines the roots of the ideas of heaven and hell that came to China by way of Buddhism.

Zaleski, Carol G. *Otherworld Journeys: Accounts of Near-Death Experiences in Medieval and Modern Times* (1987).
> An open-minded and readable study.

Index

Index

Index

Index

Meir, Golda, 127
Mencken, H. L., 122
Menhirs, 55
Meno, 158
Mental events, 11
Mesmer, Franz Anton, 22ff
Metamorphosis, 62
Metempsychosis, 42
Methodist Catechism, English, 171
Michael, Archangel, 152
Michelangelo, 53, 198
Michel, André, 190
Millennium of reign with Christ, 164f
Milton, John, 50, 163, 164
"Mind" and the "I," 11ff
Mind/Body problem, 9ff
Ming dynasty, 104
Misery, Human, 98n.
Mississippi, 14
Mīzān, 112
Moksha, 84, 119, 120
Monism, Meaning of, 80f
Monism and monotheism, 80ff
Monotheism, Meaning of, 54f, 81f
Monotheistic solution, Resistance to, 66ff
Montgomery, Florence, 190f
Moody, Raymond, 32, 33, 36
Mormon, Book of, 135
Mormon concept of afterlife, 134f
Moroni, 135
Morse, Melvin, 34, 38n.
"Mortal" sins kill immortal soul, 125, 160
Moscow Parapsychology Conference (1968), 25
Moses, 31, 67, 68
Muhammad
 leads faithful across bridge spanning fires of
  hell, 117
 mocked when he spoke of resurrection of the
  body, 153. *See also* Paul
 on the eschaton, 112
 on resurrection, 97
Muhammad's ascent into Paradise, 114
Mummification, 59
Muslim vision of Paradise, 115
Myers, Frederic W. H., 23, 27ff, 31

Natura naturans, 46
Natura naturata, 46
Naturwissenschaften, 8
Neanderthals, 55
Nefesh, 67
Nefs, 67
Negativity in Hindu, Jain, and other
 interpretations of karma and rebirth, 93
Neolithic Age, 55f
Neoplatonism, 133, 196

Nephthys, 101
"New Age" groups, 46
Newcomb, Simon, 21
Newton, Isaac, 6, 37
Newtonian physics, 6f
Nirvāna, 91
Noble Eightfold Path, 91
Noble Truths, Four, 91
Notre Dame de Paris, 190
Nudism, 88

Oblations for the dead, 138
Observation of the invisible and the intangible,
 6ff
Oceanus, 72
Odyssey, 194
Olam ha-Ba, 132
Oliphant, Carolina (Baroness Nairne), 184
Olympus, 157
O-mi-to, 210
Omnia vincit amor, 144
Origen, 125, 159f, 161
 on the "intermediate state," 138
Orphism, 63, 73, 195
Osiris, 59, 60, 101
Ostrander, Sheila, 10, 24, 25
Otherness of God, 46, 66
Owens, J. E., 38n.
Oxford Movement, 141

Palladian architecture, 68
Pallida mors, 214f
Pantheism, 45ff
Pao-p'i, 173
Parallelism, 13
Parsees, 102
Parousia, 110
Participation in divine immortality, 128f
Paul, 97
 on conditional immortality, 43
 mocked by Athenians when he talked of
  resurrection, 125. *See also* Muhammad
 on "putting on" immortality, 123
 on reaping what one sows, 63
Paul's belief in afterlife, 152, 154f
Paul VI, Pope, 29
Persephone, 72
Personal identity in afterlife, 14
Peter at day of Pentecost, 95
Petronius, 56
Phaedo, 73, 196
Pharisees, 42, 62, 94f, 138, 164, 170
Philo, 170
Plato, 13, 42, 43, 53, 63, 68, 73, 74, 124,
 129, 147, 149, 150, 158, 169, 196, 207
Plato's *Republic*, 64, 73, 77f

Index

Plotinus, 53
Plutōn, 72
Pneuma, 157
Pneumatikos, 155, 156
Poena damni, 126, 129
Prayer, Karmic law does not eliminate value of,
 205
Prayers for the dead, 138
Primus in orbe deos fecit timor, 56
Prison motif, 65
Pre-Columbian America, afterlife beliefs in, 58
Prehistoric beginnings of afterlife belief,
 52ff
Price, H. H., 167
Prieur, Jean, 30, 31n.
Priscilla, 148
Proud in Dante's *Purgatorio*, The, 139, 146
Psychē, 157
Psychical Research, Societies for, 20
Psychotronics, 25
"Pure Land" Buddhism, 92, 195, 210
Purgatory, 56, 138ff
 as penal, 132
 interpreted reincarnationally, 146ff
Pyramid Texts, 101
Pythagoras, 63, 73, 147, 207
Pythagoreans, 195
 Felicitous hypotheses of the, 9

Qiyāma (Resurrection), Muhammad on, 97, 111
Qur'an, 97, 100, 111, 113, 117, 136
Qutayba, Ibn, 97

Raudive, Constantine, 29, 30, 31
Ravenna, 57
Rebirth adaptable to Easter hope, 200
Rebirth, Persistence of image of, 209
Reid, Thomas, 3
Reims, 57
Reincarnation, 42. *See also* Rebirth,
 Metempsychosis
Renaissance art, Images of Heaven in, 174
Requiescant in pace, 56, 116
Responsibility for consequences of what we
 cannot recall, 149
Resurrection, 42m, 152ff
 as form of reembodiment, 156
 as ambiguous term in Old Testament, 164
 Centrality of, in Christian *kerygma*,
 93, 154
 Christian hope of, 96, 199
 Immortality and, 123f
 Possible influence of Zoroastrianism on Jewish
 and Christian concepts of, 62
Reunion with loved ones in afterlife, 191f
Rig Veda, 83

Ring, Kenneth, 32
Rochester, New York, 18
Ruysbroeck, Jan van, 33

Saadia, 133
Sabom, Michael, 32
Sadducees, 42, 62, 94, 123
Saint Peter's, Rome, 29
Salvation, Work of Christ provides conditions
 for, 205f
Salvation Army, 172
Salve Regina, 98f
Samaritans, 94, 189
Samos, 63
Samsāra, 65, 66, 91f, 148
Santa Maria Maggiore, 57
Santayana, George, 163
Sanctification, 212
Sartre, Jean-Paul, 203
Sarx and *Sōma*, 156
Sat and *Asat*, 83
Satan, 125, 160
Schelling, Friedrich Joseph, 183
Schroeder, Lynn, 10, 24, 25
Scientific objections to belief in an afterlife, 3ff
Sebastian de Grazia, 136, 137n.
Seidel, Franz, 30
Sekhert-Aaru (Field of Reeds), 61
Self, Continuity of the, 45
Self in Hindu thought, as core of a series of
 "sheaths," The, 86
Self in Theravada Buddhism, 99
Self-Judgment, 102f, 118ff
Self-realization, 85
Seneca, Lucius Annaeus, 4
Shakespeare, William, 41
Shaman, 17
Shaw, George Bernard, 4
Shekinah, 132f
Sheol, 158, 167, 168, 207
Sheol and Hades, 13, 26, 57f, 71ff, 93f, 194
Shi'a branch of Islam, 117
Shudras, 64
Sidgwick, Henry, 27ff
Signorelli, Luca, 76
Silva, Lynn A. de, 99n.
Sirāt bridge, 117. *See* Chivat
Skia (shadow), 42
Smith, Jane I., 112, 121n.
Smith, Joseph, 135
Smith, Sir William, 109
Socrates, 43, 63, 124, 196
Solomon, 68
Soul, 9f
Soviet Union, Parapsychology in the, 24
Spencer, Herbert, 5

Index